Asian Socioeconomic Development

Asian Socioeconomic Development

A National Accounts Approach

Edited by
Kazushi Ohkawa and Bernard Key

 **THE UNIVERSITY PRESS OF HAWAII**
Honolulu

Published by University of Tokyo Press and
The University Press of Hawaii

ISBN 0-8248-0743-X

Contents

Preface

The papers collected in this volume were first presented at the Second Asian Regional Conference of the International Association for Research in Income and Wealth (IARIW), held April 3–7, 1977, in Manila. The conference was co-sponsored by the School of Economics, University of the Philippines, and the International Development Center of Japan (IDCJ).

The First Asian Regional Conference of the IARIW was held in Hong Kong in 1960. Selected papers from the Conference were published in 1965 as *Asian Studies in Income and Wealth,* edited by V.K.R.V. Rao and K. Ohkawa. Regrettably, a second conference could not be held in the region as soon as had been hoped. In response to the increasing need felt by some IARIW members, a meeting to establish an organizing committee was held on 29 November 1976 at the School of Economics, University of the Philippines. At that time a six-member Organizing Committee was selected: the four session organizers (listed below) together with M. Mangahas and K. Ohkawa, as Chairman. Preparation was begun for the conference, and it was unanimously agreed that the subjects chosen for investigation should have close relevance to contemporary development problems of Asia and the Pacific region. Accordingly, plans were made for the Conference to consist of the following four sessions: National Accounts Framework for Developing Countries (organized by M. Kurabayashi); Measurement of Social Development (organized by M. Mukherjee); Income Distribution (organized by J. Encarnación); and Problems in Uses of National Accounts for Planning (organized by H. T. Oshima).

The Organizing Committee took the responsibility of selecting the papers for publication, relying upon the initial recommendation made by each session organizer. Selection not only was made on the basis of quality, but also took into account other factors such as the representativeness of the problem and its significance for future studies in the Asian context. The Committee requested Ohkawa to undertake the task of editing these papers in collaboration with Dr. Bernard Key.

The contents of this volume essentially follow the order of presentation at the Conference. No written papers were requested for the fourth session, on the uses of national accounts for planning. The discussion which took place at that session is summarized in the Introduction, and Oshima's remarks on national accounts and planning appear as one of the Additional Remarks at the end of the volume.

Two additions to the basic conference papers have been made for this for this volume. One is the description by Shimizu of the national accounts system and its evolution, which has been added as an Appendix to Part I; the other is a comment by Ohkawa on the importance of households to national accounts, which appears as one of the Additional Remarks at the end of the volume.

We owe a great deal to Encarnación and to Oshima and Mangahas who, with the help of their younger colleagues, made such careful preparation and administered the Conference in such a well-organized fashion. We also wish to acknowledge the various contributions made by Mr. Yutaka Shimizu at the preparatory stage with his work for the Organizing Committee, during the Conference in his role as Executive Secretary, and after the Conference in assisting with the editing. Finally, we would like to express our appreciation to Ms. Tamiko Sakatani for her invaluable secretarial assistance.

Generous support for the Conference has been provided by the Ford Foundation and the Japan World Exposition Commemorative Fund. The Asia Foundation kindly furnished support for the Organizing Committee. The publication of this volume was supported by the International Development Center of Japan. Neither the Conference nor the publication of this voume would have been possible without this assistance, for which we are deeply grateful.

Kazushi Ohkawa
Bernard Key

Asian Socioeconomic Development

Introduction

In Asia, the most populous part of the world, a number of "developing countries" have inaugurated modern economic growth in tandem with their struggle to attain political independence in the decades since World War II. Most of them have achieved the initial growth acceleration needed to get their economies moving towards further development through economic modernization. In the postwar quarter-century, the pace of their economic development has been fast, despite the unprecedentedly strong pressure of population growth—faster, in fact, than the earlier development of the present industrialized countries. However, development has not been without serious problems. Among them, two are particularly relevant to the subject of this book: a widening range of growth rate differentials among industrial sectors, particularly between the modern and the traditional sectors, and the lagging of social development behind economic growth. In recognition of the fact that these two phenomena are not unrelated, "socioeconomic development" rather than "economic development" has recently become the right term in which to present the problem. Our purpose is to contribute to better performance in socioeconomic development through making progress in the national accounts approach.

National accounts, taken as a whole, comprise a conceptual system, consistent and articulate, with which macro-sectoral economic performance can quantitatively be described. The system has a long prewar history of application to the developed countries. It began, however, to be applied much more widely to contemporary developing countries in the postwar period. This process of "diffusion" has both extended the coverage and estimates of national accounts and improved their statistical reliability. They have contributed greatly to the formation of

3

development plans and policies of governments as well as to augmenting systematic knowledge about the development process.

Nevertheless, economists and statisticians specializing in this field have faced a number of problems in responding to the rising expectations of what can be achieved during the development process in the course of applying the refinements made in the national accounts themselves. The internationally standardized system of national accounts is quite new (for a detailed explanation, see the Appendix to Part I which begins on p. 107) and has raised a number of problems to be solved during the transition from an old to a new system. The social aspect of the accounting system has lagged behind the economic aspect, both conceptually and statistically; greater efforts are needed to attempt to come to grips with the real nature of social development.

These challenges, one may say, are not specific to the developing countries, but are rather of a general nature, requiring the attention of developed countries as well. However, it is our view that for most of the developing countries in Asia these challenges have different and more serious implications. These countries face, so to speak, a trinity of challenges in implementing the system of national accounts: the requirement for improving estimates at the conventional level; the larger inputs required by the new system of the national accounts; and the greater efforts needed for introducing and systematizing the social development approach. The situation of course is not uniform but rather differs widely among the Asian countries, even apart from the somehow exceptional case of Japan. On the one hand, a number of countries still have serious problems in improving the statistical reliability of such basic data as that on consumption, investment, and even output. Even for the countries which can collect reliable data, conceptual and statistical problems are still serious, especially in estimating activities of the traditional sectors. On the other hand, a few countries have already started to construct an integrated system of accounts. These differences in level are one of the major reasons why the exchange of information among countries is beneficial.

The contributors to this volume have concentrated their attention on four aspects of national accounts: their applicability in general to developing economies; the measurement of social development; the analysis of income distribution; and the use of national accounts for planning in the developing countries.*

---

* Our summary descriptions of the papers in this volume are taken largely from session summaries prepared for the Second Asian Regional Conference on Income and Wealth by Y. Kurabayashi and K. Sato (Part I), M. Mukherjee and A. K. Ray (Part II), and B. Barros (Part III and the discussion on planning).

National Accounts Framework for Developing Countries

In the construction of national accounts and in the collection of data for that purpose, the developing countries face particular problems. The uniform System of National Accounts published and utilized by the United Nations establishes a basic framework which must be adhered to in order to maintain the usefulness of the accounts in cross-national comparison of economic data; however, a number of structural features of the developing economies differ from those of the "standard" economy which inspired the SNA system and which is most easily adapted to it. Moreover, in the developing countries perhaps the most important application of national accounts data is to planning for economic development; thus there is often a need for kinds of data which are not integral parts of the SNA system.

With these special requirements in mind, much of the work in national accounts theory which has been done in Asia during the past five years has been focused on the construction of a national accounts system for developing economies—one which is compatible with the SNA but tailored to the special requirements of rural and developing economies. In this section, four authors present their recent work and thinking on this line of research.

Uma Datta Roy Choudhury discusses some of the problems and advantages in using a system of accounts suited to the special characteristics of developing economics which she and her colleagues have designed. The proposed system departs from the SNA in the following instances: a systematic distinction is made between goods and non-material services; a uniform set of transactors is employed for all accounts, classified into three mainly institutional groups (distinguishing, for example, between modern and traditional forms of production, between wage payments in cash, in kind, and self-employed income; between market transactions, barter, and own consumption); own capital production appears both in investment and saving. The proposed accounts are simpler than those of the SNA in that "commodities" and "industries" are not separated and that the sector classification is based on establishment units.

Choudury points out that these new accounts should be suitably adjusted in response to the special characteristics of individual developing countries, but that considerable flexibility must be allowed in order to make intercountry comparisons possible. Special features of developing countries that need to be highlighted in a generalized system of accounts include the following characteristics: (i) unincorporated enterprises are important; they form the "informal" sector within the household sector (without industrial classification); (ii) a few key commodities or industries that dominate economic activities in developing countries should be shown in separate accounts, probably as sub-sectors within broad sectors; (iii) particular types of organizations (*e.g.* multinational corporations) might be shown in separate accounts within individual sectors or within the economy as a whole; (iv) enterprises may be classified by ownership within each sector as it is useful for public and private sectors to be distinguished by industry to the extent possible; (v) the self-employed should be set up as a separate category and their income should be listed as mixed income; (vi) the distinction between goods and non-material services should be eliminated. The new accounts are a sub-system of the SNA and embody all its basic features; they are, however, flexible enough to allow modifications by individual countries.

The peasant economy differs from the urban economy in that production, consumption, and investment decisions are made by a single economic unit, the peasant. Theories of the peasant economy that emphasize this difference are, however, not supported by the systematic collection of data. The Hayami paper reports an experiment conducted by a team he headed at the International Rice Research Institute to collect such data continuously over one year in a Philippine village.

The sample consisted of 12 households (4 large farmers, 4 small farmers, and 4 landless workers) out of the total 95 households in the village. The households prepared daily records of work and transactions under the weekly supervision of a full-time investigator. Six accounts are constructed from these records in the fashion of the SNA; they treat (1) agricultural production (rice and non-rice), (2) non-agricultural production, (3) income-expenditure, (4) capital production, (5) saving-investment, and (6) outside-of-household activities.

The important features of the accounts include the following: (i) income and saving are gross; (ii) the capital production account reports the amount of one's own work; (iii) imputations are made to farm labor and rice. For consistency checks, monthly cash and rice balances reported by respondents were examined. When significant discrepancies were discovered, re-interviews were conducted to eliminate from the records as many inconsistencies as possible.

The tables given in the paper present major findings concerning the value-added ratio, factor shares, the propensity to consume and the like. They reveal that the results are plausible. This survey represents a type of research which is essential for improving the quality of national income statistics in developing countries.

V. V. Divatia summarizes flow-of-funds studies of the Indian economy carried out by the Reserve Bank of India since 1956. The studies divide the economy into six sectors: two financial (banks, other financial institutions) and four non-financial or real (corporate business, government, government enterprise, households). Intrasector flows (*e.g.* the borrowings of households, including unincorporated businesses, from moneylenders) are netted out. Flow-of-funds data reveal increasing monetization in the economy over the past two decades, which in turn reflects the creation of financial institutions to assist in economic development. An increase in the FIR (Financial Inter-relations Ratio) also indicates the growing complexity of the financial system.

Flow-of-funds tables can be applied in a number of ways. For instance, a cross-country regression on the relationship between the FIR and per-capita income was made to ascertain India's position with some international perspective. A flow-of-funds table can be employed like an input-output table in determining how savings are distributed over the four real sectors for a given set of investments undertaken by the same sectors. The exercise also reveals individual cells in the table. It can be applied to estimate sectoral composition of investment for a given set of savings. However, the flow-of-funds table is less stable than the input-output table.

Finally, Divatia notes the effect of data limitations. For instance, differences in valuation between lenders and borrowers (*e.g.* equity issues) make the two sides inconsistent. Individual sectors are not as homogeneous as is desirable. Because the household sector not only comprises activities of unorganized industries, small businesses, and moneylending operations but also includes those of non-profit-making institutions, it is extremely difficult to maintain functional and institutional homogeneity.

Kazuo Sato is concerned with theoretical issues in measuring real national product from the production side. Some economists point out that the double-deflation method can pervert real value added. Sato contends that this potential perversity does make invalid the concept of real value added, showing that the derived real value added becomes immune when measured on a Divisia index. The minimum requirement justifying the Divisia index is the equality of the marginal products of intermediate inputs and their relative prices. The Divisia index is also uniquely determined if the underlying production function satisfies a certain separability condition.

Analogous to the concept of real value added, real quasi-rents are also a possibility. In this case, real quasi-rent is measured as gross output less the contributions of intermediate and labor inputs to production;

this also can be expressed in the form of a Divisia index. It is shown that the Divisia index of real quasi-rents is unique if and only if in the underlying production function constant returns to scale are maintained with respect to capital inputs and capital inputs are separable from other inputs. Real quasi-rents are free from the measurement problems of capital inputs and represent the limit to which one can go without knowing capital inputs.

The measurement of total factor productivity depends upon many more assumptions about the production function and market pricing. The difficulty is with the quantification of capital inputs because they are not malleable, and heterogeneous items can no longer be summed up in an index which is invariant. In the final part of this paper, it is shown that the assumption required for the measurement of real value added and real quasi-rents is that the underlying macro production function remains "invariant". The invariance requirement is satisfied if and only if the efficiency distribution of firms in the industry is invariant in its relative form. The macro production function that provides the basis for the analysis in this paper is an ex-post function which has both advantages and disadvantages; these will become clearer as work continues on the development of a comprehensive national accounts theory.

Measurement of Social Development

As economic development is measured and studied with increasing precision, its close relationship with social development has become more and more evident. The importance of social change as an integral component and not just a by-product of economic development has been widely recognized. Thus, paralleling the development of a national accounts system, work has begun on developing a framework within which the components of social life and well-being can be quantified, evaluated, and compared. This work is most commonly known as social indicators research.

In the three papers which follow, the problem of integrating social and economic data into a coherent system is approached from several angles.

Yoshimasa Kurabayashi's detailed paper aims at proposing a synthetic approach for measurement of economic and social performance of an industrially developed society like Japan and, to this end, examines the UN proposal for a System of Social and Demographic Statistics (SSDS) as well as the details of the National Bureau of Economic

Research (NBER) project where emphasis is placed on relating social indicators and social statistics directly with the national accounts.

Subsequently, the author takes a consolidated approach which is a synthesis between the SSDS and the NBER approach and is a mutually interlocking framework for the measurement of economic and social performance. He argues that it is possible to present the details under this system if data can be collected under the auspices of projects similar to the Basic Survey of Social and Community Life initiated by the Bureau of Statistics, Office of the Prime Minister, Government of Japan. This survey provides considerable information for the construction of time budgets, which is an essential part of the SSDS.

The system devised by Kurabayashi indicates the approach to be taken in the study of social welfare. Given the present state of data systems in developing countries, however, such detailed studies on the subject can immediately be carried out in great detail (in terms of the individual's way of living and utilization of leisure) only in countries like Japan. For developing countries these can serve as a guide, but it will be quite some time before such detailed surveys can be undertaken and the individual's welfare and life style analyzed.

M. Mukherjee and A. K. Ray focus more closely on the problem of choosing indicators and constructing an index for the measurement of socioeconomic development. They suggest a method of constructing a composite indicator of the standard of living in which the chosen variables are weighted statistically in an attempt to avoid subjective judgment.

Mahar Mangahas describes the social indicators project which he was instrumental in designing for the Philippines, outlining in detail the work done on the subject and the survey undertaken to study the living conditions of the people. The variables used in the Philippine analysis include not only health, education, income, and so on, but also political freedom and justice. Mangahas makes a strong case for the usefulness of social indicators data to those in policy-making positions, and states that commitment to the quantitative measurement of progress in an area of social concern should be used as a yardstick by which to measure seriousness of government purpose in tackling social problems.

It is clear that much work remains to be done in the measurement of social development; there is still ample room for disagreement on the types of variables which should be used in constructing indices, for example. However, the integration of social change with economic development is clearly an important and useful step in the analysis of national and cross-national economic data.

Income Distribution

The papers in Part III focus on the problem of income distribution, analyzing past trends in income inequality in five Asian countries within the framework of income growth and structural change.

V. V. Bhanoji Rao and M. K. Ramakrishnan argue that for Singapore there was no discernible relationship between reduction in income inequality and economic growth for the period 1966 to 1975. The authors advance the proposition that structural change, defined to include changes in the characteristics of income recipients as well as the composition of income, is the basic cause of changes in income inequality and that "...depending on the direction in which all other factors change, one may or may not find a reduction in income inequality over a period of GDP growth." In this case, the most important of these "other factors" were the increase in the female labor force participation rate and the changes in the employment structure by sector (from tertiary to secondary) and by occupational status.

An interesting aspect of the paper is the attempt to deflate the size distribution of income in order to arrive at trends in inequality in real terms. By computing a consumption class-specific price index from consumption patterns obtained in a household expenditure survey, Rao and Ramakrishnan find that real income Gini ratios exhibited similar but smaller declines. The desirability of such analysis, for over-time and cross-country comparisons, cannot be overemphasized, although many difficult questions arise. For example, when price indices are defined in terms of consumption groups and when no allowance is made for over-time household mobility between nominal income classes which make for modifications of the consumer basket in any income class, then such indices may describe consumption patterns remarkably well but may not be particularly demonstrative of price variations.

L. C. Chau's paper is a progress report on his study of the effects of industrialization on Hong Kong's income distribution from 1961 to 1971. From his examination of the relevant statistics he concludes that changes in occupational status and in the distribution of education among workers, in addition to narrowing inter-sectoral income differences, all promoted greater income equality. It also seems that growth has favored industries wherein income concentration has been lower.

Chau's conclusions are perhaps least debatable when applied to the distribution of wages. As he himself points out, there is no conclusive evidence on the trend of overall income distribution (especially between 1966 and 1971) since the income question in the surveys conducted has been voluntary. Labor absorption and industrialization, on the other hand, almost certainly affected the dispersion of wages, especially after full employment was reached in the early 1960s. A closely related concern is the extent to which proprietors' incomes, which could account for a significant portion of income, might alter the income distribution picture. Although there has been a decline in the proportion of proprietors in each sector, there is scant information on their earnings. Of course the problem of misreported or unreported proprietors' dividend and interest income is not restricted to Hong Kong; it arises in connection with any sample survey.

Using national income accounts data on labor and capital, Han-yu Chang analyzes the Taiwan experience from the years prior to 1964, when the first large sample household survey was conducted, to 1975. The Taiwan case, he notes, closely resembles that of Japan: decreasing disparities in income after around 1968 were associated with a shift from a labor surplus to a labor shortage economy.

Fei, Ranis, and Kuo[1] arrived at similar conclusions about the affinity between the onset of a tight labor market and Taiwan's declining inequality of income by using only income and expenditure surveys which date back to 1964. Chang's approach differs from theirs, however, insofar as he employs national accounts data to infer that from 1952 on, "all the factors for the period before 1968 contributed to the larger inequality of the nationwide distribution of Taiwan's family income." He thus broadens his analysis to include a period of over twenty years. Nevertheless, in the absence of firsthand information about the years before 1964 from income and expenditures surveys, some doubts have been expressed about whether the sudden decline in inequality after 1968 was just a statistical artifact or was an indication of a "turning point" in the growth and equality pattern. Small sample surveys carried out in 1953, 1959, and 1961 show narrowing income disparities for these years and tend to intensify these doubts.[2]

Mizoguchi, Takayama and Terasaki attempt to provide insights into the likely causes of observed over-time change in the size distribution of household income in Japan from the late 1950s to the early 1970s.

---

[1] J. Fei, G. Ranis, and W. Y. Kuo, "Growth and the Family Distribution of Income by Labor Components," *Discussion Paper No. 223*, Economic Growth Center, Yale University, March 1975.

[2] K. Chang: "An Estimate of Taiwan Personal Income Distribution in 1953," *Journal of Social Science*, August 1956; "Report on Pilot Study of Personal Income and Consumption in Taiwan," cited in S. Kuo, "Income Distribution by Size in Taiwan Area- Changes and Causes," *Income Distribution and Employment in East and Southeast Asia Vol. I*, Japan Economic Research Center and Council for Aisan Manpower Studies, July 1975.

These changes have been largely associated with the process of industrialization and growth. In particular, the noticeable decline in income inequality during the 1960s was characterized by changes in the distribution of employee compensation due to a labor scarcity, by the expanding importance of non-agricultural income in traditionally agricultural households, and by narrowing income gaps between employee, agricultural, and non-agricultural households.

Although her paper does not deal directly with the size distribution of income, Oey Astra Meesook examines the process of income formation in Thai households by using detailed data from a 1968–69 socioeconomic survey. If total household income is viewed as the sum of income earned by all the household members, then household and personal characteristics are important in determining labor force participation rates and employment profiles, which in turn explain different aspects of the size distribution of income. The author attempts to estimate labor force participation equations for family members other than the household head in terms of age, sex, educational attainment, adequacy of the household head's income, presence of children, number of adults in the family, sector of the household head, and area of residence. She also attempts to estimate the probabilities of being an unpaid family worker, choosing a given economic sector, and receiving certain types of income (wages, salaries, self-employment, rent, interest, and transfer income).

Among other things, Meesook finds that the relationship between education and labor force particpation is not straightforward, that the effect of the presence of children under seven is not weaker in the rural areas, and that economic necessity (measured as the adequacy of the income of the household head) is an important factor affecting the labor force participation rate. As expected, "holding other characteristics constant, increasing age is associated with higher income, except for a falling off of wages and self-employment income for those 60 and over in the non-agricultural sector"; more education, urban residence, and male sex go with higher incomes.

The approach adopted is useful in considering direct and indirect distributional effects of demographic changes that accompany economic development. Meesook's investigation of the concept of a threshold income in labor force participation behavior is of particular interest. However, there are some difficulties. Whenever labor force participation is measured for a certain cell of the population (persons in a given age group, with a given educational attainment, with a certain location of residence, etc.), within-cell variation cannot be identified. The allocation of income to any one family member, particularly non-money income in agricultural households, is a problem. A similar problem is posed by unpaid family workers, as it is difficult to assign earned income to them.

The picture presented here of changes in income distribution patterns in five Asian countries is of special interest in view of the desire in most nations to reduce inequality of income while attaining high levels of economic growth. That the two often go hand in hand is apparent from these studies. An interesting question, particularly raised by the data from Japan and Taiwan, is whether a "turning point" from a labor surplus to a labor shortage economy is a prerequisite for lower levels of income concentration.

National Accounts and Planning: A Discussion

The fourth session of the conference brought planners and statisticians together to discuss what progress has been made in the area of data collection *vis à vis* planning requirements as well as in what directions statistical agencies should move in view of many new policy objectives.

The experience of Thailand's Economic and Social Planning Division was summed up by Phisit Pakkasem. Thai planners of late have made scant use of national accounts data. To explain this, Phisit enumerated several shortcomings of statistical output which, in his opinion, have prevented more extensive use of figures for planning. Most serious, in his view, is the absence of both analytical and predictive value in the accounts. Income and production data have tended to be all too descriptive and are often untimely as a result of numerous revision, with a lag phase of one or two years.

Phisit also noted the growing gap between statisticians and planners inasmuch as the former have failed to keep statistical design and approach in tune with shifts in the nature and scope of planning. In particular, these shifts have been from an orientation towards a high growth rate to one which is more concerned with the pattern and distribution of growth, and from a macro, project-allocative approach to one which is subnational or regional and issue (*e.g.* employment, rural development, natural resources)-oriented. Futhermore, more emphasis is now being placed on social stabilization and reinforcement of political stability.

Philippine planner Filologo Pante, of the National Economic Development Authority, reflected quite a different image of the relationship between planner and statistician in the Philippines. All in all, there has been extensive use of national accounts to link the macro model to virtually all submodels of the plan as well as in evaluation of economic performance and projection. Reliability of data has been generally good and is probably most questionable in the semestral estimates. Noticeable improvements have been made in the areas of methodology and the data base. Notwithstanding, recommendations of planners and of government and academic researchers have been sought in an attempt to add to and improve statistics on social indicators, value added, savings, the disaggregation of investment, and regional income and product. But Pante also noted that there is a need for reorientation and re-direction in the light of changing demands.

Tito Mijares of the Philippine Bureau of Census and Statistics, National Census and Statistics Office, stressed the need to supplement national income accounts, especially when proxies for unavailable data (for example, fixed proportion of production for value added computed from censuses) do not conform to the planners' experience and when GNP is estimated from a sectoral basis. He suggests, consequently, greater emphasis on sectoral based surveys, particularly those that include the unorganized sector, alongside the sharpening of the concepts and definitions of subsectors and the extension and widening of the coverage and period of response of such sectoral and household surveys.

Saw Swee Hock indicates that, although Singapore has no national economic development plan as such, national account estimates are used fairly widely to monitor the general economic situation and to a lesser extent in the planning for the growth of certain sectors. Towards these ends, a number of statistical projects were launched in the first half of the 1970s, including a new series of labor force and household budget surveys. Saw seems to agree with Mijares in suggesting closer examination of and improvements in these surveys so that they yield information not only on employment, income, and expenditure, but also on output per worker and the like.

The Indian situation is another in which planning and data collection are relatively well coordinated. This is due to the fact that the statistics office is an arm of the planning commission. Uma Datta Roy Choudhury of the Central Statistics Office reported that there has also been reliance on periodic surveys and sectoral data such as the National Sample Survey of Household Activities and the economic surveys of unincorporated enterprises to supplement and provide checks of value added, consumption, and production statistics. Mukherjee and Choudhury pointed out that, although the collection and response problem are relatively insignificant, the surveys have not been conducted regularly; when they have been, the time involved in processing and tabulation has been noticeably long. Divatia added that orientation towards household surveys in sampling design has resulted in inadequate coverage of unregistered enterprises.

Ghafoor Khan, the Pakistani representative from the Bureau of Statistics, informed the session that acute lack of staff support and financial resources at the statistics office are the principal constraints on the construction of a sufficient data base that will permit an extension of Pakistan's regional planning effort. Plans to streamline the collection of national accounts figures and other parts of the statistical framework, again, seem to rely a great deal on special household (urban and rural) sectors and subsistence unit surveys.

Khan did not delve into some of the problems that statisticians may meet in the actual conduct of field surveys in Pakistan such as the high rate of illiteracy and misresponse in Bangladesh, a problem that has been, according to A. Ghafur, a major one faced by Bengali enumerators.

Koichi Emi provided a historical sketch of data availability and collection in Japan over time, at different levels of economic development and under varying social conditions. He traced how the gathering of statistics proceeded first from the primary, then to the secondary and finally to the tertiary sector; from large-scale business to small-scale family enterprises; from the sectoral and regional levels to the national economy; from economic to social indicators; and from an elementary to an advanced methodology.

The session was notable for the recognition that development planning was in the process of transition to meet the challenges of new goals and policies. The consensus was that, in addition to better national accounts data, other types of data must be generated if planning is to be successful.

PART I

National Accounts Framework for Developing Countries

Further Thoughts on Economic Accounts for Developing Countries*

Uma Datta Roy Choudhury

The present United Nations System of National Accounts (SNA) does not bring out clearly the special features of developing countries which are pertinent to policy formulation and to meaningful measurement of factors of growth.** The use of a different system of national accounts, the Material Product System (MPS), by the socialist countries suggests that a separate system of economic accounts for developing countries may not be entirely out of line. To serve this purpose, a system of Economic Accounts for Developing Countries (EADC) has been developed as a subsidiary system within the framework of the SNA (Mukherjee, Choudhury, and Rao, 1975). The modifications have been made in a manner which would bring forward the special characteristics of the developing countries. The main features of the SNA have however been retained insofar as possible.

In the Economic Accounts for Developing Countries (EADC) the first important point of departure from the SNA is a systematic distinction between goods (including material services) and non-material services. The EADC also proposes a uniform set of transactors for all the accounts and further classifies them into three broad groups which are mainly institutional in character. This classification makes a distinction between modern and traditional forms of production. However, the transactions appearing under these categories are not always uniform. Thus, for example, in the unincorporated household sector, compensation of employees has been subclassified into payment

* The views expressed are those of the author and not necessarily of the Central Statistical Organisation to which the author belongs.
** (Editors' note: for a detailed explanation of the System of National Accounts and a discussion of the problems it has raised, see the Appendix to Part I.)

in cash and payment in kind. Similarly, gross product has been classified as sold in the market, bartered, or used for the producer's own consumption; and private final consumption expenditure has been classified as purchased and/or self-produced. Such classifications are particularly important for studying the structural and organizational shifts over time in developing economies.

Another important transaction appearing under *value added* and *forms of income* is "income of self-employed". For enterprises which are under individual ownership and are operated mainly by the proprietors with or without the aid of unpaid family workers and/or wage labor, income cannot always be divided between the factors of production and the aggregate of labor; capital income is classified under "income of self-employed". This would comprise total income-generated *net* wage payment (in cash or in kind) and other factor payments like interest and would include the imputed labor income of proprietors and family workers as well as the operating surplus generated.

In the Capital Formation Account, similarly, gross domestic fixed capital formation is shown to include asset formation out of "own production". Asset formation in the traditional sector can be either through the market economy or from "own production". In the former case, asset formation is a result of the purchase of either capital goods or material inputs and services from the market for production of goods of a capital nature, including newly constructed residential houses. Such additions to capital assets are classified as "purchased". In the traditional sector, however, capital formation can also occur as a result of use of one's own labor and materials which either are produced by the enterprises or are of no economic value and hence available freely. Examples of such asset formation are land improvement, minor irrigation projects, and rural houses constructed by the use of materials like mud, straw, grass, etc. The value of capital formation in this case would consist of the imputed value of one's own labor together with the imputed values of such materials as bamboo which have recognized economic value. Such additions to capital stock would obviously involve no market transactions and hence no corresponding financial measure. For a complete accounting, therefore, it is essential that such asset formation is also included as a part of the savings of the unincorporated household sector. In the present sub-classification, therefore, saving is defined to occur in the form of increases in "financial assets" and "physical assets". The sub-categorizations under *saving,* however, are expected to be mutually exclusive and within well-defined boundaries.

Though substantially simplified and generalized, the EADC is built around the usual matrix form and can be used for ultimate integration with the SNA. Thus in the EADC, as in the SNA, no separate accounts are envisaged for "commodities" and "industries"; classification by type of establishment (according to economic activity as the primary unit of classification) is used. For most of the developing countries this is not likely to give rise to problems because in these countries multi-unit establishments are not likely to be too numerous, and unit-wise breakdown is obtainable without much difficulty. It is also presumed that it will not be necessary to have a large number of industrial groups for the EADC. Minimum branch classification would suffice, and, broadly, could be (i) agriculture and allied activities; (ii) mining and quarrying; (iii) modern manufacturing (including electricity, gas, etc.); (iv) traditional manufacturing; (v) construction; (vi) transportation and communications; (vii) distributive trade and storage; (viii) finance and insurance; (ix) real estate and ownership of dwellings; (x) general government; (xi) health, education, and other social services; and (xii) personal services.

The transactions have been coded in a standard form similar to the one proposed in the SNA. This is necessary and desirable not only for the identification of the transactions but also for the compilation of the data bank. In the present context, systematic storage of information in the data bank is the first step in formulating any reasonable hypothesis regarding the patterns of growth and structural change in the developing countries. Any economic analysis based on the details in these accounts would, therefore, require their storage over a period of time, necessitating subsequent retrieval and analysis as well as identification in the context of the total system. Any system of accounts which does not lend itself to such systematization is ultimately of very little practical use and would stand in the way of standardization of the system. Like the SNA, in the EADC the coding has been done on the basis of the transactors' account, class and category of transaction, and sector to which the transaction refers; the codings can be easily matched.

Though the developing countries form a group of nations which possess features distinguishing them from the advanced countries, the characteristics are not always equally distributed within the group.[1] The EADC formulated by the author mainly takes into account the special features of countries in Asia, and particularly those in South East Asia. For a generalized system for all developing countries, it would be

[1] This aspect was brought to light during the discussion at the UN International Seminar on the Revised System of National Accounts (held at Caracas 8 – 19 December 1975) which was specially organized for the developing countries of the world and which the author attended.

essential to incorporate the special features of countries in Africa, Latin America, and Western Asia, which are often different and need special consideration. Even if it is not possible to accommodate all such features in the system, it should be possible to adjust the EADC suitably to allow for information on such special characteristics. It should also leave enough room for individual countries to partially modify the system when necessary in order to highlight certain aspects of their economy, and at the same time to allow generalization at the overall level to facilitate inter-country comparison within the group. Before such modifications are suggested to make the EADC more adaptable to all developing countries, it might be worthwhile to review the special characteristics which need to be highlighted in such a generalized system.

First and foremost, the incorporated unit as defined in the SNA is hard to find in most developing countries. Thus, for agriculture in most countries, available statistics will not provide regular data to prepare the accounts of "quasi-corporate agricultural enterprises", though such enterprises are "important and large". One would therefore be forced to adopt a definition of corporate and quasi-corporate sectors which is more restrictive than that proposed in the SNA and to provide for a household sector which would include production units whose business is "important and large". For developing countries such enterprises would normally be termed private unincorporated enterprises. The household sector thus defined would correspond to the sector often referred to as "informal" or "traditional" and be distinguished from the organized corporate sector whose business structure is very similar to corresponding units in developed countries. The informal sector, of course, would not be limited to agriculture alone but would cover all small-scale, labor-intensive activities, and thus would include the small workshops of artisans such as tailors and furniture makers as well as small-scale operators in mining, construction, transport, distribution, and medical and educational services. This informal sector obviously will need to be highlighted in any set of accounts for the developing countries, and the EADC proposes to present them separately under the household sector.

Many developing countries are heavily dependent on either a few cash crops or minerals or on a dominant export sector which provides much of the foreign exchange: oil in the oil-exporting countries, cocoa in the case of Ghana, or sugarcane in the case of Mauritius. In such cases it will be essential to have a separate account for such a sector, with detailed statistics on production of, internal requirements for, and exportable surpluses of such commodities and world market trends with particular reference to such commodities. Often such enterprises are largely foreign-owned, and in such cases it will be necessary to have the proper definition of a foreign sector including financial and non-financial enterprises, corporate and quasi-corporate enterprises, and, if necessary, even private non-corporate enterprises which fall within the informal sector. The detailed accounts for such sectors can perhaps be most conveniently provided by sub-classifying within the relevant sector, *e.g.* sugarcane within agriculture and oil within mining. Such sub-classifications can very conveniently be provided within the EADC.

For the study of policy issues and the formulation of development strategies, it might often be necessary to prepare summary accounts for particular types of organizations. This, for example, is particularly true for the multinational corporations, which might either be sub-classified within the relevant sectors or be grouped into a multinational category. Such separate accounts will help in bringing out the details of a nation's total foreign exchange outlays and their contributions to domestic income, capital formation, and saving, all of which is extremely important information for the country concerned.

The institutional setup of the enterprises and their ownership is another important aspect which needs to be highlighted in developing countries for policy purposes. This is important because in these countries, quite often, it is impossible for the government to influence effectively the activities of enterprises outside the public sector. These details are also important for analyzing the shifts in the country's structural setup. In India, for example, detailed analysis is undertaken of the public sector enterprises; not only are data on all the main macro-aggregates available according to ownership of the institutions, but separate accounts are prepared for public financial and non-financial institutions. It is, therefore, useful to incorporate in the system detailed data on the public and the private sectors of the economy, separately by industries insofar as possible. This sub-classification within each of the sectors can be introduced in the EADC without difficulty. The countries can make a choice and use any or all of the classifications: public–private, national–domestically owned, modern–traditional, and the like.

In most of the developing countries there exists a large subsistence or non-monetary sector which qualifies for special consideration. The non-monetary sector is important not only for its contribution to total output, but also for its role in current consumption and capital formation. The EADC provides for presentation of such details within the system. Also, the mixed income of the self-employed needs to be recognized as a distinct category for the developing countries. The SNA treats the entire income of self-employed workers as operating surplus, with no allocation for labor income. This classification is artificial to the extent that the income of the self-employed covers both labor income and operating surplus. For developing countries, therefore, it is important to show this as a distinct category under forms of income.

Lastly, the EADC suggests the distinction between goods (including material services) and non-material services as the two main branches of economic activity within the three main sectors of public, private corporate, and household non-corporate enterprises. This distinction is not equally important for all of the developing countries, though for the planning of balanced, simultaneous development of goods and services a distinction between the two categories may be extremely useful. For a generalized system for developing countries it might be desirable to eliminate this sub-classification, which quite often might lead to additional estimational problems (*e.g.* bifurcation between material and non-material services).

The suggested row/column classification for the consolidated matrix presentation of the Economic Accounts for the developing countries is shown in Table 1 in the form of a list of items. The list takes into account all the special features of the developing countries, generalizing

Table 1. Economic Accounts for Developing Countries: Classification for Consolidated Matrix Presentation

Production		Public	Industries	1
		Private corporate	Industries	2
		Multinational	Industries	3
		Household non-corporate	Total	4
			Sold in the market	5
			Bartered	6
			Used for own consumption	7
Consumption	Expenditure	Population	Total	8
			Purchased	9
			Own production	10
		Government administration	Total	11
			Purchased	12
			Own production	13
	Income and Quality	Value added	Compensation of employees — Total	14
			Compensation of employees — Cash	15
			Compensation of employees — Kind	16
			Income of self-employed	17
			Operating surplus	18
			Consumption of fixed capital	19
			Indirect taxes, net	20

Consumption	Income and Quality	Forms of income		Wages and salaries	Total	21
					Cash	22
					Kind	23
				Employers' contribution		24
				Income of self-employed		25
				Operating surplus		26
				Property income		27
				Direct taxes on income		28
				Social security contributions		29
				Current transfers by enterprises		30
				Social security benefits		31
				Social assistance grants		32
				Other current transfers by governments		33
				Current transfers by population		34
				Current transfers by rest of the world		35
		Sectors of receipts		Industries		36
				Government administration		37
				Population		38
Accumulation	Increase in Stocks	Industries		Public		39
				Private corporate		40
				Multinational		41
				Household non-corporate		42
	Fixed capital formation	Industries	Purchased	Public		43
				Private corporate		44
				Multinational		45
				Household non-corporate		46
			Own production	Household non-corporate		47
	Capital Finance	Industrial capital formation		Construction		48
				Machinery and equipment		49
				Increase in stock		50
		Capital transfers		All categories		51
		Financial assets		Currency and deposits		52
				Securities		53
				Other financial claims		54
		Sectors		Industries		55
				Government administration		56
				Population		57
Rest of the world				Current transactions		58
				Capital transactions		59

Note: To highlight transactions of particular industries or sectors, industries can be divided into three categories: public, private corporate, and multinational.

as far as possible so as to be widely adaptable. Using the codes and notations suggested in the EADC, the complete matrix of the system can be presented. This is not attempted in this paper as the basic structure is already available in the complete publication of the EADC (Mukherjee, Choudhury, and Rao, 1975). The complete list of accounts given in Table 2 also has the same format as in the EADC.

Table 2. Complete List of Economic Accounts for Developing Countries

    I. Consolidated Accounts of the Nation
        Gross domestic product and expenditure
        National disposable income and its appropriation
        Capital finance
        External transactions
   II. Supply and Disposition of Goods and Services
  III. Domestic Production
        Branches in public sector
        Branches in private corporate sector
        Branches in household non-corporate sector
  IV. Consumption Expenditure
        General government
        Population
   V. Income, Outlay, and Capital Finance
        Branches in public sector
        Branches in private corporate sector
        Branches in household non-corporate sector
        General government
        Population

Note: The accounts presented here, as well as their cross-indexing with the SNA account, were suggested by the author in (Choudhury, 1972). However, separate classification of goods (including material services) and non-material services will be dispensed with.

In conclusion, it may be mentioned that the classification suggested in the present paper simplifies the system to the extent desirable but does not, in the process, lose sight of the essential details which need to appear in the EADC if it is to prove useful to the developing countries. It also needs to be emphasized that the accounts have been formulated as a sub-system of the SNA and embody in them all the basic features of the SNA. The system at the same time is flexible enough to allow modifications by individual countries to highlight special features and make for greater relevance for policy purposes. With these modifications, it can be hoped that the EADC will be found useful for adoption by the developing countries in the not too distant future.

References

Choudhury, U.D.R. "A Simplified Integrated Form of SNA and MPS," *Review of Income and Wealth*, September 1972.

Choudhury, U.D.R. "Use of National Accounts for Development Planning in India." OECD, 1972.

Mukherjee, M. and Rao, D.S.P. "On an Economic Accounting Framework for India and other Developing Countries." Indian Association for Research in National Income and Wealth, 1971.

Mukherjee, M., Choudhury, U.D.R. and Rao, D.S.P. "Economic Accounts for Developing Countries," *Review of Income and Wealth*, December 1975.

The Economic Accounts of Households in a Philippine Village*

Yujiro Hayami, Piedad F. Moya, Luisa Maligalig, and Masao Kikuchi

The "peasant", the basic unit of the rural economy in developing countries, is a complex of economic activities including production, consumption, and capital formation. These peasant characteristics present a sharp contrast to the urban sector in which there prevails a clear division of economic functions between firms and households.

Theories of modern economics, such as "the theory of the firm" and "the theory of consumer behavior", assume the typical urban functional divisions between different economic agents. The conventional approach to the analysis of the peasant economy has been to abstract "producer", "consumer", and "investor" from the peasant complex to which the theories of modern economics are applied separately. Although such an approach is useful as a first approximation, its effectiveness in dealing with the single peasant complex is limited to the extent that the approach is based on the unrealistic abstraction of different economic functions.

Since the classic work by Chayanov (1966), there have been a number of attempts to develop the "theory of peasant economy", including those by Hymer-Resnick (1966) and Nakajima (1969). However, such theoretical efforts have not been paralleled by the systematic collection of data which are amenable to the analysis of the peasant complex. A large body of statistics on the peasant economy has been collected from farm management and production cost surveys as well as household

* The major field work and the preliminary analysis on which this study was based were conducted at the International Rice Research Institute. Further analysis was, in part, supported by a grant from the Seimeikai Foundation and a grant from the Economic Planning Agency of Japan to the International Development Center of Japan.

29

income-consumption surveys. However, little effort has been made to collect statistics for the analysis of the peasant complex in its entirety. As a result, the recent boost in "integrated rural development programs" suffers from the lack of an appropriate statistical basis.[1]

In order to fill this gap, we attempt in this study to document the complex of economic activities in rural households in the Philippines in terms of a set of double-entry accounts that summarize the flows of goods and services. The data on which this study was based were generated from the integrated household record-keeping project conducted in a rice-cultivating village in the Philippines. Supplementary data to complete the system of accounts, such as information on inventory changes, were collected from the assets surveys conducted at the beginning and at the end of the record-keeping period. Finally, as a subsidiary checking device, an output survey was conducted to identify how much rice was produced in any given month. Thus, we will be dealing here with three sources of information: the integrated household records, the asset survey, and the output survey.

Data Collection and Estimation Procedures

Study site

As shown in Figure 1, the Municipality of Pila is located about 25 kilometers east of Los Baños, or about 90 kilometers southeast of Manila. Tubuan is one of 13 *barrios* (villages) of Pila. It is connected to the Poblacion (urban district) of Pila by a narrow unpaved road of about 12 kilometers. Common means of transportation are tractors and tricycles.

Tubuan is a relatively small *barrio* consisting of 95 houses according to the benchmark survey conducted for this project in November 1974. A map of the *barrio* is presented in Figure 2. The houses of Tubuan are hidden in the coconut grove which looks like an island in the midst of an ocean of paddy fields, a landscape typical of rice-producing areas in Southern Luzon. The northwestern side of the *barrio* is demarcated by the Laguna de Bay. There is little difference in height between the paddy fields and the lake water.

The coconut grove under which most houses are located is slightly elevated from the paddy fields. Villagers reside under the coconut

---

[1] For insight into the integrated rural development programs of the aid agencies, typically the World Bank, see (Yudelman, 1976). A skeptical view was expressed in (Ruttan, 1975).

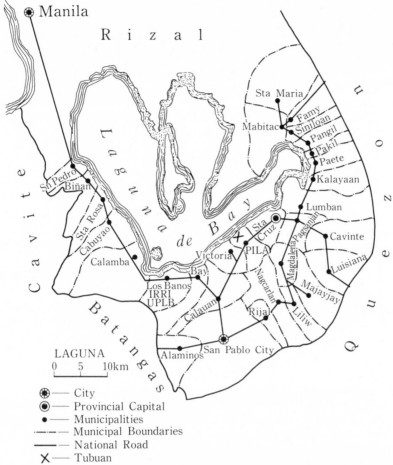

Figure 1.   Map of Laguna

trees with the implicit consent of the coconut owners who live outside
the *barrio*. By custom they are allowed to utilize the space below the
trees by planting fruits and vegetables or raising livestock and poultry.
In return they serve as caretakers by performing such tasks as clearing
undergrowth from the grove.

Absentee landlordism is pervasive in this area. Due to the extension
of the national irrigation network, double-cropping of rice is commonly practiced with the use of modern semi-dwarf varieties. Rice
farming is by far the most dominant enterprise. Coconuts are a relatively minor source of income for the villagers. Duck raising is a
common side enterprise using shellfish from the Laguna de Bay as

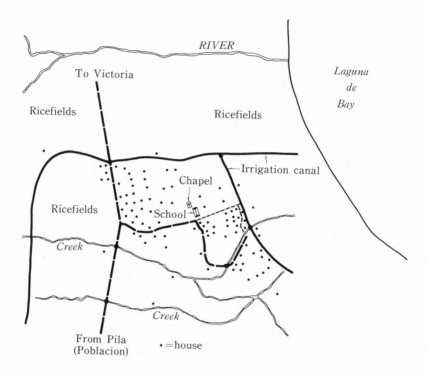

Figure 2.   Map of *Barrio* Tubuan

feed. Fishing is practiced on a very minor scale, primarily for home and village consumption.

Sample households

From the total of 95 households in the village, twelve participants were selected for the record-keeping project. Details concerning the selected households are presented here in Table 1. The selection of the participants was not random, but based on our judgment of their ability and willingness to cooperate in the project. Included in the sample were the households of four large farmers (cultivating more than 2 hectares), four small farmers (cultivating less than 2 hectares), and four landless workers. However, we found the quality of the records of one of the small farmers to be considerably lower than the others and omitted his records from our analysis of sample averages.

During the course of the project, two participants who belonged to

Table 1. Family and Farm Characteristics of Sample Households, June 1, 1975

			Family size (number)				Farming status	
		Total		Male		Female	Farming	Tenure
		Total	Active[a]	Total	Active[a]	Total	Active[a]	area	type[c]
Large farmer									
	A	5	4	1	1	4	3	3.5	L (1.5 ha.)
									S (2.0 ha.)
	B	11	5	6	2	5	3	3.3	L
	C	8	7	3	3	5	4	3.0	L
	D	6(7)[b]	2	3(4)	1	3	1	3.0	L
Small farmer									
	E	6	2	3	1	3	1	1.0	L
	F	3	2	1	1	2	1	2.0	S
	G	7	3	5	1	2	2	1.0	S
Landless worker									
	H	9	5	4	2	5	3	0	—
	I	4	4	1	1	3	3	0	—
	J	4	2	1	1	3	1	0	—
	K	2	2	1	1	1	1	0	—
Special									
	Z[d]	5(6)	2	1	1	4(5)	1	2.0	L (0.5 ha.)
									S (1.5 ha.)

[a]Economically active members (13 to 65 years old).
[b]Includes children born during the project period.
[c]L: leasehold tenancy, S: share tenancy.
[d]The records of this household were excluded from the analysis.

the landless class subleased small parcels of paddy field (0.25 hectare each) from other tenant farmers. Henceforth, their records included information on rice farming.

Record-keeping procedures

Daily records of economic activities were kept by the participants in the record books that we distributed. The record-keeping period extended for one year from 1 June 1975 to 31 May 1976, using the two preceding months (April and May 1975) as a test period.

The record book consists of (a) labor sheets and (b) transaction sheets. The labor sheets were designed to record the use of all labor (in terms of hours worked) including that of family members and hired or exchange workers. Only income-generating (in the conventional sense) work was recorded; housekeeping work, such as cooking and child care, was not recorded. The transaction sheets were designed to record all transactions in cash and kind, including exchanges and grants. Also recorded in the transaction sheets was home consumption of agricultural products as well as its use for seeds or feed. Records were regularly checked twice a week (Tuesday and Friday), and the record books were distributed and collected every Friday.

Accounting framework

The accounting system that we designed to summarize the economic activities of the village households consists of six accounts: (1) the current agricultural production account, (2) the current non-agricultural production account, (3) the income-expenditure account, (4) the fixed capital production account, (5) the saving-investment account, and (6) the outside-of-household account. Considering the critical importance of rice in the economy concerned, the current agricultural production account is divided into a rice production account and a non-rice agricultural production account. Therefore, our system consists of seven accounts which are "completely articulated" as shown in Appendix Tables I–VI.[2] The system is largely consistent with the framework of the recent UN *System of National Accounts* (UN, 1968).

The current rice production account (Appendix Table I–R) establishes the identity between the total value of rice output and the total cost paid (and/or imputed) to the inputs applied to the rice production process. The non-rice agricultural production account (Appendix Table I–N) establishes the same identity with respect to other products such as livestock and poultry. It should be noted that the rice production account was prepared not only for farmers, but also for landless workers who did not produce rice. This was because landless workers received rice (paddy) as wages in kind and consumed it at home or sold it outside. Also, the non-rice agricultural production account was prepared for landless workers because some of them were engaged in raising pigs and ducks.

The village households not only engage in farming, but also run a wide spectrum of non-agricultural enterprises including commerce, transportation, and manufacturing. The current non-agricultural production account (Appendix Table II) establishes the revenue-expenditure identity with respect to non-farm production activities.

Values produced by the factors owned by the rural households, together with earnings of wages from outside employment, represent the major sources of household income. The household income-expenditure account (Appendix Table III) records how the income thus generated was disposed of for consumption and savings.

[2] Appendix Table I includes both the rice production account (Table I-R) and the non-rice agricultural production account (Table I-N).

In addition to current production activities, the village households engage in the production of capital goods by building houses and digging irrigation ditches. The fixed capital production account (Appendix Table IV) shows how much of the increase in the value of fixed capital is attributable to family-owned factors and how much of it is contributed from outside. The saving-investment account (Appendix Table V) identifies the sources of funds for financing investments, including fixed capital formation and investments in inventories and financial assets. Finally, the outside-of-household account (Appendix Table VI) puts together all the transactions of the households with the outside.

Imputation

The major problem in accounting for the economic activities of the village household is the imputation of the values of goods and services which do not go through market transactions. Two major items whose non-market transaction proportions were especially high were rice and family labor.

Not only was a major portion of the rice produced in the village consumed directly by the producers' households, but rice was extensively used as a medium of exchange and as payments for hired labor and land rent. In this study we adopted the standard rates (*i.e.,* the typical market prices during the period of study) for imputing the value of rice: 1 peso per kilogram of paddy (rough rice) and 2.05 pesos per kilogram of milled rice. The cost of rice milling for home consumption, usually paid to millers as a portion of the rice (or bran) milled, is assumed to be 5 percent of the value of the milled rice. The values of other agricultural products which were consumed directly by producers or used for exchange were imputed according to the valuation of the record keepers themselves.

The imputation of family labor costs was based on the standard market wage rates (by tasks) which prevailed during the period of record keeping (Appendix Table VII). Those standard wage rates were also used for separating labor costs from capital costs in the payments to tractor job contractors. Since these payments include both the operator's wage and the capital rental for the tractor, we assumed the difference between the total payment and the imputed wage cost as the capital rental.

Because our farmer participants were all tenants and actually paid rents to landlords, we did not make any imputation of land rents. However, the tenancy title commands a value in this village (Hayami and Maligalig, 1976). This means that the tenants are receiving a part of the functional income share of land. Therefore, our rent data may be underestimating functional land rent.

Cash and rice balance

Besides the basic accounting tables, we prepared balance sheets for cash and rice as a check on the accuracy of data. This information is presented here in Appendix Tables III and IV, respectively. The cash balance establishes the identity between the total amount of cash received by the household from various transactions, such as the sale of agricultural products and wage earnings from outside employment, and the total amount of cash paid by the household for various purposes, such as the purchase of consumer goods and services. The rice balance establishes a similar identity between the total receipt and the total disposition of rice. Those two balance sheets were prepared every month.

The amount of cash on hand at the beginning of every month was entered in the assets survey. Another estimate for cash on hand at the beginning of the month was compiled using the data (also taken from the assets survey) relating to the cash on hand at the beginning of the previous month and the increase in cash on hand during the month. During the record-keeping project, those two estimates of cash on hand were compared; the discrepancies were minimized by reexamining the data and reinterviewing the cooperators. A similar check was made with respect to the rice balance. The difference between total rice receipt and dispostition gives an estimate of rice output. Another direct estimate was obtained from a rice production survey conducted independently of the record-keeping. The comparison of those two estimates served as an effective data check.

Major Findings

The accounts of village households are presented in Appendix Tables I–VI as the averages of all sample households as well as separate averages for large farmers, small farmers, and landless workers. The major findings are as follows.

Costs and returns of rice production

Costs and returns of rice production are summarized in Table 2. On the average, the value of total rice output per farm household was ₱15,492

Table 2. Costs and Returns of Rice Production: Averages per Household per Year*

Code	All farmers	Large farmers	Small farmers
		₱	
1.1 Payment to external inputs	9,566	10,994	7,663
1.1.1. Wage	2,896	3,635	1,912
1.1.2 Rent	3,981	3,663	4,404
1.1.3 Interest and rental	523	738	236
1.1.4 Current inputs	2,166	2,958	1,111
1.2 Seed use of rice	342	484	153
1.3 Imputed income of family factors	5,584	7,869	2,538
1.3.1 Family labor wage	1,936	2,697	921
1.3.2 Owned land rent	0	0	0
1.3.3 Farm profit (residual)	3,648	5,172	1,617
A. Total output	15,492	19,347	10,354
Av. per ha.	6,455	6,046	7,965
B. Total value added (A-1.1.4– 1.2)	12,984	15,905	9,090
Av. per ha.	5,410	4,970	6,992
		%	
Value added ratio (B/A)	83.8	82.2	87.8
Family income ratio (1.3/A)	36.0	40.7	24.5
(1.3/B)	43.0	49.5	27.9
Factor shares:			
Labor (1.1.1 + 1.3.1)/B	37.2	39.8	31.2
Land (1.1.2 + 1.3.2)/B	30.7	23.0	48.4
Capital (1.1.3 + 1.3.3)/B	32.1	37.2	20.4

* Data from integrated household records.
ᵃ ₱: Pesos.

($2,213).[3] The average per household for large farmers was ₱19,347 ($2,764), slightly less than double that of the small farmer. However, the average per hectare was slightly smaller for large farmers than for small farmers: ₱6,046 ($864) vs. ₱7,965 ($1,138). The value added from rice farming calculated by subtracting current intermediate inputs (including rice seeds) was about 84 percent of total output value.

The average family income for all farmers, the sum of imputed incomes of family factors, was 36 percent of total output and 43 percent of value added. About one-third of family income originated from return to family labor and two-thirds from the residual profit which is supposed to represent the return to family-owned capital. Comparing the large and small farmer, we should note that the ratio of family income to total value added for large farmers was substantially larger

[3] All calculations were made on the basis of 7 pesos (₱) to 1 U.S. dollar, the exchange rate which prevailed during the period of the record-keeping project.

than that for small farmers. The major reason for the low family income ratio for small farmers was the large payment of rent. The average rent payment of large farmers (₱3,663) was smaller than that of small farmers (₱4,404), despite the fact that the average farm size of large farmers was 3.2 hectares whereas that of small farmers was only 1.3 hectares.

The difference in the rate of land rent (₱1,145 per hectare for large farmers vs. ₱3,388 per hectare for small farmers) seems to be primarily due to differences in tenure arrangements. Whereas two out of three small farmers were under share tenancy, three out of four large farmers were under leasehold tenancy.[4] This suggests the possibility that large farmers were capturing a part of the functional income share of land in the form of residual farm profit.

Costs and returns of non-rice agricultural production

Table 3 summarizes the costs and returns of non-rice agricultural production. Major non-rice agricultural enterprises in this village were duck and hog raising. For those enterprises, the purchase of current inputs, especially feeds, comprised the major item of external payment. A part of the rice output was also used for feeding ducks. Since the intermediate inputs were of major importance in duck and hog raising, the value added ratios in non-rice agricultural production were relatively small. The family income ratios with respect to total output were also small, but the ratios with respect to value added were as high as 100 percent.

As duck and hog raising were backyard enterprises and did not use any farmland, the share of land in value added was zero. According to our estimates, about 30 percent of income share went to labor and 70 percent to capital (or residual profit). However, it must be emphasized that, because duck and hog raising is a sideline enterprise requiring only a few minutes each day, the recording of labor use is much less accurate than for rice farming. Also, the wage rate used for imputation may not reflect the contribution of family labor for such enterprises. Thus, the estimates of factor shares for non-rice agricultural production should be taken with great reservations.

Costs and returns of non-agricultural production

Table 4 summarizes the costs and returns of non-agricultural enter-

----

[4] The other one cultivates part of his land under leasehold tenancy and part under share tenancy.

Table 3. Costs and Returns of Non-rice Agricultural Production: Averages per Household per Year*

Code		All households	Large farmers	Small farmers	Landless workers
				$\mathbb{P}$	
1.1	Payment to external inputs	684	1,382	581	63
	1.1.1 Wage	2	1	5	1
	1.1.2 Rent	0	0	0	0
	1.1.3 Interest and rental	0	0	0	0
	1.1.4 Current inputs	682	1,381	576	62
1.2	Seed use of rice	376	573	615	0
1.3	Imputed income of family factors	1,114	1,359	1,656	463
	1.3.1 Family labor wage	318	390	497	111
	1.3.2 Owned land rent	0	0	0	0
	1.3.3 Farm profit (residual)	796	969	1,159	352
A.	Total output	2,174	3,314	2,852	526
B.	Total value added	1,116	1,360	1,661	464
	(A-1.1.4-1.2)				
				%	
	Value added ratio (B/A)	51.3	41.0	58.2	88.2
	Family income ratio (1.3/A)	51.2	41.0	58.1	88.0
	(1.3/B)	99.8	99.9	99.7	99.8
	Factor shares:				
	Labor (1.1.1 + 1.3.1)/B	28.7	28.8	30.2	24.1
	Land (1.1.2 + 1.3.2)/B	0	0	0	0
	Capital (1.1.3 + 1.3.3)/B	71.3	71.3	69.8	75.9

* Data from integrated household records.
ᵃ $\mathbb{P}$: Pesos.

prises. In fact, among our sample households, only one (which belonged to the category of large farmers) ran a motored tricycle cab as a non-agricultural enterprise. Therefore, the data in Table 4 represent the tricycle operation of this farmer. The largest cost item was the fuel for running the tricycle. The second largest was the cost of family labor. Residual profit was high, and capital's share was about 50 percent, so that the income share was almost equally divided between labor and capital.

Structure of household income and expenditure

Table 5 shows the incomes of village households by source. The average household income for all households was $\mathbb{P}8,153$ ($1,165). Large farmers' incomes were the highest and landless workers' incomes were the lowest in terms of both averages per household and averages per household member. Taking the average of all households, income from

Table 4. Costs and Returns of Non-agricultural Enterprises: Averages per Household per Year*

Code		All household	Large farmers	Small farmers	Landless workers
				₱	
2.1	Payments to external inputs	34	94	0	0
	2.1.1 Wage	4	12	0	0
	2.1.2 Interest and rental	0	0	0	0
	2.1.3 Current inputs	30	82	0	0
2.2	Imputed income of family factors	54	149	0	0
	2.2.1 Family labor wage	24	66	0	0
	2.2.2 Profit of non-agricultural enterprise (residual)	30	83	0	0
A.	Total non-agricultural output	88	243	0	0
B.	Total value added (A-2.1.3)	58	161	0	0
				%	
	Value added ratio (B/A)		65.9	0	0
	Family income ratio (2.2/A)		61.4	0	0
	(2.2/B)		93.1	0	0
	Factor shares:				
	Labor (2.1.1 + 2.2.1)/B		48.3	0	0
	Capital (2.1.2 + 2.2.2)/B		51.7	0	0

* Data from integrated household records.
ᵃ ₱: Pesos.

rice production was about 42 percent of total income. Family factor income accounted for 84 percent of total income. Labor income was about 40 percent of total income and 47 percent of family factor income. The highest value for both the rice income ratio and the family factor income ratio was set by the large farmers and the lowest by the landless workers. In contrast, the highest value for the labor income ratio was set by the landless workers and the lowest by the large farmers.

Table 6 shows household expenditure in terms of average expenditure per household member. The disposable income of an average household per year was ₱1,234 ($176), 90 percent of total household income. On the average, ₱977 ($140) or 79 percent of disposable income was spent for consumption. The ratios of consumption of home-produced agricultural product to total disposable income and to total food consumption were 27 and 40 percent, respectively. The Engel coefficient, defined as the ratio of food consumption to total consumption, was 66 percent.

The lowest value for the average propensity to consume was set by the large farmers and the highest by the landless workers. The lowest Engel coefficient value was also set by the large farmer. The value set

Table 5. Structure of Household Income: Averages per Household per Year*

Code		All households	Large farmers	Small farmers	Landless workers
				P	
1.3 R	Total income from rice	3,478	7,869	2,538	—208
1.3.1 R	Labor income from rice	1,307	2,697	921	206
1.3 N	Total income from non-rice crops	1,114	1,359	1,656	463
1.3.1 N	Labor income from non-rice crops	318	390	497	111
2.2	Total income from non-farm enterprise	54	149	0	0
2.2.1	Labor income from non-farm enterprise	24	66	0	0
3.9	Labor earnings from outside	1,591	1,058	685	2,805
3.10 & 3.11	Other factor incomes from outside	665	1,823	7	0
3.12 & 3.13	Non-factor incomes	1,251	1,022	1,267	1,469
A.	Total household income	8,153	13,280	6,153	4,526
	Average per household member	1,382	1,771	1,161	943
B.	Family factor income (A-3.12 & 3.13)	6,902	12,258	4,886	3,057
	Average per household member	1,170	1,634	912	637
C.	Labor income (1.3.1R + 1.3.1 N + 2.2.1 + 3.9)	3,240	4,211	2,103	3,119
	Average per working household member	1,543	1,684	1,618	1,418
				%	
	Rice income ratio (1.3 R/A)	42.7	59.3	41.2	—4.6
	Family factor income ratio (B/A)	84.7	92.3	79.4	67.5
	Labor income ratio (C/A)	39.7	31.7	34.2	68.9
	(C/B)	46.9	34.4	43.0	102.0

* Data from integrated household records.
ª P: Pesos.

by the landless workers was the second highest. These were reasonable results considering the differentials in income level. The ratios of home produce were about the same among the three household classes. It should be noted that the home produce of landless workers was primarily rice received as wages in kind.

Table 6. Structure of Household Expenditure: Averages per Household Member per Year*

Code		All house-holds	Large farmers	Small farmers	Landless workers
		₱			
3.1	Home consumption of agricul-tural products	262	300	269	195
3.2	Purchase of consumption goods and services	715	843	632	576
	3.2.1 Food	380	406	389	328
	3.2.2–6 Non-food	335	437	243	248
3.3	Interest payment on consumption loan	67	92	10	73
3.4	Grant	78	90	105	34
3.5	Tax and rate	3	4	6	0
3.6	Household surplus	257	442	139	65
A.	Total household income = expenditure	1,382	1,771	1,161	943
B.	Disposable income (3.1 + 3.2 + 3.6)	1,234	1,585	1,040	836
C.	Total consumption (3.1 + 3.2)	977	1,143	901	771
D.	Food consumption (3.1 + 3.2.1)	642	706	658	523
		%			
	Propensity to consume (C/B)	79.2	72.1	86.6	92.2
	Engel coefficient (D/C)	65.7	61.8	73.0	67.8
	Home produce ratio (3.1/C)	26.8	26.2	29.9	25.3
	(3.1/D)	40.8	42.5	40.9	37.3

* Data from integrated household records.
ᵃ ₱: Pesos

Capital formation

Data on the capital formation of village households are presented in Table 7. The average gross investment for all households was ₱1,591 ($227), of which ₱630 ($90) or 40 percent was in fixed capital. Investment in agricultural fixed capital was relatively small, only 19 percent of total gross investment and 48 percent of fixed capital investment. The total investment of large farmers was more than 4 times that of small farmers and 7 times that of landless workers. Large farmers' fixed capital investment was about 3 times as large as that of small farmers. However, the highest fixed capital investment ratio was achieved by the landless workers because of a relatively large investment in residential construction.

Table 8 shows the costs of producing fixed capital. On the average, total fixed capital formation was ₱630, of which ₱558 (or 88 percent) was

Table 7. Structure of Capital Formation by Investment Outlay: Averages per Household per Year*

Code	All house-holds	Large farmers	Small farmers	Landless workers
			₱	
4.3 Agricultural fixed capital formation	304	304	42	500
4.3.1 Land infrastructure	182	0	0	500
4.3.2 Machinery and implements	80	195	33	0
4.3.3 Livestock and perennial plants	42	109	9	0
5.2 (4.4) Non-agricultural fixed captial formation	224	447	223	0
5.3 (4.5) Residential construction	102	0	21	264
5.4 & 5.5 Inventory change	346	830	29	99
5.6 Acquisition of financial assets (residual)	615	1,786	426	412
A. Gross investment	1,591	3,367	741	451
B. Gross fixed capital investment (4.3 + 5.2 + 5.3)	630	751	286	764
			%	
Ratio of fixed capital investment (B/A)	39.6	22.3	38.6	169.4
Ratio of agricultural fixed capital investment:				
(4.3/A)	19.1	9.0	5.7	110.9
(4.3/B)	48.3	40.5	14.7	65.4

* Data from integrated household records.
ª ₱: Pesos.

Table 8. Costs of Producing Fixed Capital: Averages per Household per Year*

Code	All house-holds	Large farmers	Small farmers	Landles workers
			₱	
4.1 Payments to external inputs	558	698	281	624
4.2 Contribution of family factors	72	53	5	140
4.2.1 Family labor wage	60	0	4	161
4.2.2 Farm-supplied materials	0	0	0	0
4.2.3 Residual	12	53	1	−21
A. Gross fixed capital production = Gross expenditure	630	751	286	764
			%	
Ratio of family factor contribution (4.2/A)	11.4	7.1	1.7	18.3
Ratio of family labor contribution (4.2.1/A)	9.5	0	1.4	21.1

* Data from integrated household records.
ª ₱: Pesos.

paid to external inputs and only ₱72 (or 11 percent) was the contribution of family factors, primarily labor. The weights of contribution of family factors were very small for farmers, but relatively large for landless workers (18 percent of gross fixed capital formation). The relatively large weight of the family factor contribution for landless workers was due to the construction of their residences (simple nipa and bamboo houses) by their own labor.

Table 9 identifies the sources of financing investments. On the average ₱1,518 or 95 percent of total investment (₱1,591) was from the household surplus. There is a sharp contrast here between farmers and landless workers. Both large and small farmers depended almost 100 percent on the household surplus for investment financing. The household surplus of landless workers was relatively small, and the major source of financing for their capital formation was the use of their own labor.

The minor contribution of family factors to capital formation corresponds to a low rate of family labor utilization in the slack months of rice production.[5] This seems to suggest that a large potential exists to mobilize the underutilized family labor for the construction of productive capital in the rural sector by adequate technical and financial assistance.

Table 9. Sources of Investments: Averages per Household per Year*

		All house-holds	Large farmers	Small farmers	Landless workers
		₱			
5.7	Household surplus	1,519	3,314	736	311
5.8	Contribution of family factors	72	53	5	140
4.2.1	Contribution of family labor	60	0	4	161
A.	Gross investible fund (5.7 + 5.8 + 5.9)	1,591	3,367	741	451
		%			
	Household surplus ratio (5.7/A)	95.5	98.4	99.3	68.9
	Family factor ratio (5.8/A)	4.5	1.6	0.7	31.0
	Family labor ratio (4.2.1/A)	3.8	0	0.5	35.7

* Data from integrated household records.
ᵃ ₱: Pesos.

[5] During the year of record-keeping, a working family member of the sample households worked an average of 170 out of 365 days. The rates of labor utilization were especially low in the slack months, August-September and February-March. For a more detailed treatment see (Hayami, Flores, and Maligalig, 1976).

Transaction balances

Table 10 shows the transaction balances between total receipts and payments which imply changes in the financial claims of households. On the average a sample household received from the outside the sum of ₱13,244 ($1,892) during the project period, of which about 57 percent was used for the purchase of production inputs and about 30 percent for consumption of goods and services. A surplus was recorded in the balance of payments, about 5 percent of total receipts, which presumably took the form of acquisition of financial assets by the sample households.

Table 10. The Balances of Household Transactions with the Outside: Averages per Household per Year*

	All house- holds	Large farmers	Small farmers	Landless workers
		₱		
6.10 Payments to external inputs for agricultural production	6,949	12,376	8,244	551
6.11 Payments to external inputs for non-agricultural produc- tion	34	94	0	0
6.12 Payments to external inputs for capital production	558	698	281	624
6.13 Purchase of consumption goods and services	4,218	6,321	3,350	2,764
6.14–15–16 Transfer payments	870	1,398	640	515
6.17 Acquisition of financial assets	615	1,786	426	412
A. Total receipt from outside	13,244	22,673	12,941	4,042
		%		
Ratio of input purchase: for agriculture (6.10/A)	52.5	54.6	63.7	13.6
for total (6.10 + 6.11 + 6.12/A)	56.9	58.1	65.9	29.1
Ratio of consumption purchase (6.13/A)	31.8	27.9	25.9	68.4
Ratio of surplus balance of payment (6.17/A)	4.6	7.9	3.3	−10.2

* Data from integrated household records.
ᵃ ₱: Pesos.

There were substantial differences in the outside-household trans-actions among the three household classes in the village. The total receipts of large farmers were almost twice as large as those of small farmers and 5 times those of landless workers. The structure of payments was similar for large and small farmers: about 60 percent of total receipts was paid for input purchases and about 25 percent for consumption purchases. In contrast, the ratio of input purchase was very low for landless workers, primarily because there is no input requirement for rice farming, and their consumption purchase ratio was as high as 70 percent.

The surplus in the balance of payments was quite large for large farmers (7.9 percent of total receipts), whereas relatively minor surpluses were recorded for small farmers (3.3 percent) and for landless workers (−10.2 percent). Such rankings in the balance of payments surplus ratio among the three classes correspond well to those in the average propensity to save (one minus the average propensity to consume) estimated in Table 6.

Consistency Check

As explained previously, the data were checked for accuracy by com-

Table 11. Cash Balance Check: Averages of All Households*

	Cash on hand at the beginning of month (1)	Cash receipt during month (2)	Cash payment during month (3)	Expected cash on hand [a] (4)	Statistical discrepancy (4) − (1)
			₱		
June	781	740	1,478	—	—
July	65	481	515	43	−22
Aug	43	472	482	31	−12
Sept	32	442	456	33	1
Oct	21	823	796	18	−3
Nov	50	1,199	1,002	48	−2
Dec	258	1,059	1,220	247	−11
Jan	96	537	564	97	1
Feb	59	337	373	69	10
Mar	25	431	424	23	−2
Apr	31	1,106	611	32	1
May	539	1,232	1,440	526	−13
June	329	—	—	331	2

* Cash on hand (1) data from integrated household records; cash receipts (2) and cash payments (3) data from assets survey.
[a] Cash on hand at the beginning of a previous month is added to cash receipts minus cash payments for the current month.
₱: Pesos

paring two sets of data for cash on hand at the beginning of the month: one was obtained directly from the assets survey and the other was an "expected" cash on hand obtained by adding to the cash on hand at the beginning of the previous month the change in cash during the month. As shown in Table 11, the discrepancies between the two sets of estimates were relatively minor, although there is a general tendency for the "expected" cash on hand to be smaller than the cash on hand figure directly obtained from the assets survey.

Another check for consistency was made by comparing the rice output data obtained from the output survey and the "expected" output obtained by subtracting the non-output receipt of rice from the total disposition of rice. The comparisons are shown in Table 12. Contrary to the above-mentioned case of cash balances, there is a tendency here for the "expected" outputs to be larger than the output estimates from the output survey; the discrepancies, however, were not large.

As a final check, we compared in Table 13 the investment data of the saving-investment account with the "expected" investments calculated from the assets survey as the difference between the asset value at the initial date (June 1, 1975) and that at the terminal date (May 31, 1976). Statistical discrepancies between the two estimates of investments were quite large, suggesting observational errors in the data collection process.

Table 12. Rice Balance Check: Average of All Households*

| | Rice balance | | | Rice | Statistical |
| | Total disposition | Non-output receipt | Expected output | output | discrepancy |
	(1)	(2)	(3)=(1)−(2)	(4)	(3)−(4)
			kg		
June	28	5	23	0	23
July	74	54	20	0	20
Aug	54	52	2	0	2
Sept	586	180	406	396	10
Oct	4,226	307	3,919	3,874	45
Nov	724	152	572	548	24
Dec	73	63	10	0	10
Jan	22	26	−4	0	−4
Feb	36	25	11	0	11
Mar	297	199	98	44	54
Apr	3,616	351	3,265	3,271	−6
May	2,153	29	2,124	2,138	−14
Total	11,889	1,443	10,446	10,271	175

* Rice balance data from integrated household records; rice output data from the output survey.

Table 13. Investment Check: Averages of All Households*

	Assets survey[a]			Gross investment	Statistical discrepancy
	Initial asset	Terminal asset	Expected investment		
	(1)	(2)	(3)=(2)−(1)	(4)	(3)−(4)
			₱		
Fixed capital	22,141	21,957	−184	630	−814
Inventory	1,084	1,430	346	346	0
Financial assets	−2,621	−2,274	347	615	−268
Total	20,604	21,113	509	1,591	−1082

* Gross investment (excluding inventory) data from the integrated household records (see Appendix Table V); inventory and asset data from the assets survey.
[a] Asset value inclusive of depreciation.
₱: Pesos

Conclusion

In this study we have experimented with documenting the production, income-expenditure, capital formation, and transaction activities of rural village households in a developing economy in terms of a set of economic accounts in a completely articulated double-entry system. For this purpose a record-keeping project was conducted in a typical rice-producing village in southern Luzon on a pilot scale. Despite large observational errors inherent in the process of highly complicated data collection for such an accounting system, the results were fairly plausible, judging from the conventional "great ratios" such as the factor shares and the average propensity to consume.

It should be emphasized that, by nature, this study represents an experiment in data collection and documentation for the purpose of analyzing the complexities of the peasant economy. It was not intended, by itself, to produce policy implications directly useful for rural development. Since the study was based on a very small sample in one village in one year, any generalization from our data can be highly dangerous. However, the study clearly shows that data consistent with the macro national accounts framework can be systematically collected and documented at the village household level. Applying our approach to various locations over time, a solid data base could be built up to advance the theory of the peasant economy as well as to aid in formulating rural development policy. Needless to say, in the process the reliability of national income accounts in developing countries will be increased dramatically.

Appendix

Table I-R. Current Rice Production Account*   (Unit: Pesos)

Code		Large farmers	Small farmers	Landless workers	All households
1.1	Payments to external inputs for rice production (6.10)				
	1.1.1 Hired labor wage	3,635	1,192	133	1,891
	1.1.2 Rent	3,663	4,404	305	2,644
	1.1.3 Capital interest and rental	738	236	49	351
	1.1.4 Purchased current inputs	2,958	1,111	1	1,379
1.2	Seed use of rice (1.7)	484	153	0	218
1.3	Imputed income of farm factors in rice production (3.7)				
	1.3.1 Family labor wage	2,697	921	206	1,307
	1.3.2 Rent to owned land	0	0	0	0
	1.3.3 Farm profit (residual)	5,172	1,617	—414	2,171
	Total rice production expenditure	19,347	10,354	280	9,961
1.4	Payments in kind to external inputs (6.1)				
	1.4.1 Hired labor wage	2,311	1,529	152	1,312
	1.4.2 Rent	3,663	4,404	55	2,553
1.5	Sale of rice and rice products (6.2)				
	1.5.1 Sale in cash	8,998	2,681	1,206	4,442
	1.5.2 Exchange	102	136	41	89
	1.5.3 Grant in kind	45	178	32	77
	1.5.4 Credit, interest and fee payment in kind	1,192	365	402	679
1.6	Home consumption of rice (3.1)	1,649	1,070	891	1,215
1.7	Seed use of rice (1.2R)	484	153	0	218
1.8	Feed use of rice (1.2N)	573	615	0	376
1.9	Inventory change in rice products and inputs (5.5)	830	29	99	346
1.10	(Deduct) Non-output rice receipt (6.19)	500	806	2,598	1,346
	Total rice output	19,347	10,354	280	9,961

* Data from integrated household records.

Table I–N. Current Non-rice Agricultural Production Account*   (Unit: Pesos)

Code		Large farmers	Small farmers	Landless workers	All house-holds
1.1	Payments to external inputs for agricultural production (6.10)				
	1.1.1 Hired labor wage	1	5	1	2
	1.1.2 Rent	0	0	0	0
	1.1.3 Capital interest and rental	0	0	0	0
	1.1.4 Purchased current inputs	1,381	576	62	682
1.2	Feed use of rice (1.8R)	573	615	0	376
1.3	Imputed income of farm factors in agricultural production (3.7)				
	1.3.1 Family labor wage	390	497	111	318
	1.3.2 Rent to owned land	0	0	0	0
	1.3.3 Farm profit (residual)	969	1,159	352	796
Total agricultural production expenditure		3,314	2,852	526	2,174
1.4	Payments in kind to external inputs (6.1)				
	1.4.1 Hired labor wage	1	0	1	1
	1.4.2 Rent	0	0	0	0
1.5	Sale of agricultural products (6.2)				
	1.5.1 Sale in cash	2,509	2,283	460	1,702
	1.5.2 Exchange	4	4	9	6
	1.5.3 Grant in kind	202	208	11	134
	1.5.4 Credit, interest and fee payment in kind	0	0	0	0
1.6	Home consumption of agricultural products (3.1)	598	357	45	331
1.7	Inventory change in agricultural products and inputs (5.4)	0	0	0	0
Total agricultural output		3,314	2,852	526	2,174

* Data from integrated household records.

Table II. Current Non-agricultural Production Account*　　　(Unit: Pesos)

Code		Large farmers	Small farmers	Landless workers	All households
2.1	Payments to external inputs for non-agricultural production (6.11)				
	2.1.1 Hired labor wage	12	0	0	4
	2.1.2 Capital interest and rental	0	0	0	0
	2.1.3 Purchased current input	82	0	0	30
2.2	Imputed income of farm factors in non-agricultural production (3.8)				
	2.2.1 Family labor wage	66	0	0	24
	2.2.2 Profit of non-agricultural enterprises (residual)	83	0	0	30
	Total non-agricultural production expenditure	243	0	0	88
2.3	Revenue of non-agricultural enterprises (6.3)	243	0	0	88
2.4	Inventory change in non-agricultural products and inputs (5.5)	0	0	0	0
	Total non-agricultural output	243	0	0	88

* Data from integrated household records.

Table III. Household Income-expenditure Account*   (Unit: Pesos)

Code		Large farmers	Small farmers	Landless workers	All households
3.1	Home consumption of agricultural products				
	(1.6R + N)	2,247	1,427	936	1,546
3.2	Purchase of consumption goods (6.13)				
	3.2.1 Food	3,046	2,062	1,572	2,242
	3.2.2 Personal needs	798	348	246	474
	3.2.3 Household needs and equipment	493	225	173	304
	3.2.4 Transportation and other services	557	278	280	380
	3.2.5 Health needs and recreation	297	320	122	240
	3.2.6 Education	1,130	117	371	578
3.3	Interest payment on consumption loan (6.14)	694	53	351	394
3.4	Grant from the household (6.15)	677	554	164	457
3.5	Tax and rate (6.16)	27	33	0	19
3.6	Household surplus (residual) (5.7)	3,314	736	311	1,519
Total household expenditure		13,280	6,153	4,526	8,153
3.7	Imputed income of farm factors in agricultural production				
	(1.3R + N)	9,228	4,194	255	4,592
3.8	Imputed income of farm factors from non-agricultural enterprises (2.2)	149	0	0	54
3.9	Earnings from outside employment (6.4)	1,058	685	2,802	1,591
3.10	Receipt of rent (6.5)	0	0	0	0
3.11	Receipt of interest and rental (6.6)	1,823	7	0	665
3.12	Grant to the household (6.7)	1,022	1,267	1,469	1,251
3.13	Government subsidy (6.8)	0	0	0	0
Total household income		13,280	6,153	4,526	8,153

* Data from integrated household records.

Table IV. Fixed Capital Production Account*   (Unit: Pesos)

Code	Large farmers	Small farmers	Landless workers	All house-holds
4.1 Payment to external inputs for capital production (6.12)				
4.1.1 Purchase of land	0	0	500	182
4.1.2 Purchase of machinery	0	0	0	0
4.1.3 Purchase of materials	589	272	124	334
4.1.4 Purchase of livestock and plants	109	9	0	42
4.1.5 Hired labor wage for construction	0	0	0	0
4.2 Contribution of farm factors to fixed capital production (5.8)				
4.2.1 Family labor wage for construction	0	4	161	60
4.2.2 Farm-supplied materials	0	0	0	0
4.2.3 Residual	53	1	—21	12
Gross expenditure for fixed capital production	751	286	764	630
4.3 Agricultural fixed capital production (5.1)				
4.3.1 Land infrastructure	0	0	500	182
4.3.2 Machinery and implements	195	33	0	80
4.3.3 Livestock and perennial plants	109	9	0	42
4.4 Non-agricultural fixed capital production (5.2)				
4.4.1 Building and structure	110	198	0	94
4.4.2 Machinery and implements	337	25	0	130
4.5 Residential construction (5.3)	0	21	264	102
Gross fixed capital production	751	286	764	630

* Data from integrated household records.

Table V. Capital Finance Account*   (Unit: Pesos)

Code			Large farmers	Small farmers	Landless workers	All households
5.1	Agricultural fixed-capital production	(4.3)	304	42	500	304
5.2	Non-agricultural fixed capital production	(4.4)	447	223	0	224
5.3	Residential construction	(4.5)	0	21	264	102
5.4	Inventory change in agricultural products and inputs	(1.7N + 1.9R)	830	29	99	346
5.5	Inventory change in non-agricultural products and inputs	(2.4)	0	0	0	0
5.6	Acquisition of financial assets (residual)	(6.17)	1,786	426	—412	615
	Gross investment		3,367	741	451	1,591
5.7	Household surplus	(3.6)	3,314	736	311	1,519
5.8	Contribution of farm factors to fixed capital production	(4.2)	53	5	140	72
	Gross investible fund		3,367	741	451	1,591

* Data from integrated household records.

Table VI. Outside-of-household Account*   (Unit: Pesos)

Code		Large farmers	Small farmers	Landless workers	All households
6.1	Payments in kind to external inputs (1.4R + N)	5,975	5,933	208	3,866
6.2	Sale of agricultural products (1.5R + N)	13,052	5,855	2,161	7,129
6.3	Revenue of non-agricultural enterprises (2. 3)	243	0	0	88
6.4	Earnings from outside employment (3. 9)	1,058	685	2,802	1,591
6.5	Receipt of rent (3.10)	0	0	0	0
6.6	Receipt of interest and rental (3.11)	1,823	7	0	665
6.7	Grant to the household (3.12)	1,022	1,267	1,469	1,251
6.8	Government subsidy (3.13)	0	0	0	0
6.9	(Deduct) Non-output rice receipt (1.10)	500	806	2,598	1,346
	Total receipt from outside	22,673	12,941	4,042	13,244
6.10	Payments to external inputs for agricultural production (1.1R + N)	12,376	8,244	551	6,949
6.11	Payments to external inputs for non-agricultural production (2. 1)	94	0	0	34
6.12	Payments to external inputs for fixed capital production (4. 1)	698	281	624	558
6.13	Purchase of consumption goods (3. 2)	6,321	3,350	2,764	4,218
6.14	Interest payment on consumption loan (3. 3)	694	53	351	394
6.15	Grant from the household (3. 4)	677	554	164	457
6.16	Tax and rate (3. 5)	27	33	0	19
6.17	Acquisition of financial asset (residual) (5. 6)	1,786	426	—412	615
	Total payment to outside	22,673	12,941	4,042	13,244

* Data from integrated household records.

Table VII. Standard Rates Used for Imputing Family Labor Costs

Code	Pesos/day[a]
Rice work	
Plowing	12.00
Harrowing	12.00
Weeding	12.00
Clearing dikes	11.00
Repairing dikes	11.00
Fertilizer application	11.00
Spraying chemicals	11.00
Harvesting and threshing	11.00
Transplanting and replanting	8.30
Clearing rice straw	5.00
Seedbed preparation	5.00
Visiting ricefields	5.00
Irrigating and draining	5.00
Rice processing	5.00
Drying	5.00
Non-rice agricultural work	
Fishing	5.00
Gardening	5.00
Feeding pigs	5.00
Feeding ducks	5.00
Non-agricultural work	
Tricycle	10.00
Carpentry	12.00
Storekeeping	5.00
Marketing	5.00

[a] We assume an 8-hour work day.

Table VIII. Cash Balance*   (Unit: Pesos)

Code	Large farmers	Small farmers	Landless workers	All house-holds
Sale of agricultural products	11,055	5,184	1,800	6,088
Sale of fixed assets	163	0	0	59
Revenue of non-agric'l enterprises	106	0	0	38
Wage received	869	160	667	602
Interest received	0	7	0	2
Rental received	1,687	0	0	614
Borrowing	547	1,324	753	834
Loan repayment to the household	151	219	201	188
Grant to the household	151	334	790	433
Total cash receipt	14,729	7,228	4,211	8,858
Purchase of consumption goods	5,955	3,062	2,530	3,921
Purchase of current inputs	2,755	783	67	1,240
Purchase of capital goods	762	271	151	406
Grant from household	331	222	114	222
Wage paid	1,086	360	149	547
Interest paid	350	95	10	156
Rental paid	15	71	48	42
Lending	216	351	604	394
Loan repayment from the household	4,276	2,042	610	2,334
Insurance	204	0	0	74
Tax and rate	41	33	1	24
Change in cash on hand (residual)	—1,262	—62	—73	—502
Total cash payment	14,729	7,228	4,211	8,858

* Data from integrated household records.

Table IX. Rice Balance*   (Unit: kg paddy)

Code	Large farmers	Small farmers	Landless workers	All house-holds
Receipt in kind for factor contribution				
Wage	299	491	2,192	1,040
Rent	0	0	0	0
Grant in kind to household	35	53	10	30
Purchase for consumption	154	0	126	102
Output (residual)	20,414	10,692	294	10,446
Total receipt	21,068	11,499	3,003	11,889
Intermediate inputs (seeds and feeds)	1,057	769	0	594
Payments in kind to external inputs				
Wage	2,311	1,529	152	1,312
Rent	3,663	4,404	55	2,553
Total consumption	1,802	1,070	1,016	1,317
Sale				
Sale in cash and credit	8,998	2,681	1,206	4,442
Sale in exchange	102	136	41	89
Grant in kind	45	178	32	77
Credit, interest and fee payment in kind	1,192	365	402	679
Change in inventory	1,898	367	99	826
Total disposition	21,068	11,499	3,003	11,889
Output (based on the output survey)	20,058	10,520	297	10,271

* Data relating to total receipts and total disposition from the intergrated household survey; output data from the output survey.

Table X. Record of Daily Activities

Name: _____   Date: _____

Day	Activities	Operator (Hours)	Family		Hired				Wage		
			No.	Hrs.	No.	Hrs.	Rate	Food Exp.	No.	Hrs.	Food Exp.
Monday morning	Did the cutting of rice stalks	1	2	4							
	Prepared garden for vegetables	1									
	Bought feed for ducks		1	2							
	Fed the ducks		1	1							
	Did the plowing with the use of tractor				2	4	7.00	6.00			
	Did the plowing with the use of animal								1	4	3.00
	Was tricycle operator	2									
	Did groceries for Sari-Sari Store		1	3							
	Dried palay		1	1							
	Did carpentry work	4									
	As hired farm laborer did the planting		1	4							
	As hired farm laborer did weeding work		1	4							

Table X. Record of Daily Activities (continued)

Name: _____   Date: _____

Day	Activities	Operator (Hours)	Family		Hired				Wage		
			No.	Hrs.	No.	Hrs.	Rate	Food Exp.	No.	Hrs. Exp.	Food
	As hired tractor operator		1	4							
Afternoon	Prepared the seedbed	1									
	Did the measuring of rice	1	1	1							
	Did the plowing with the use of a tractor				2	4	7.00				
	Did carpentry work	4									
	As hired farm laborer did the planting		1	4							
	As hired farm laborer did weeding work		1	4							
	Worked as hired tractor operator		1	4							
	Worked as tricycle operator	2									

Table XI. Daily Record of Income and Household Expenses

Date: _____   Day: _____

Name of head: _____

Name of wife: _____

Description of activities	Items given	Income Qty.	Income Value	Home-produced items	Expenses Qty.	Expenses Value
Sold 10 cavans of rice		400 kgs	P 400.00			
Sold 1 pig		80 kgs	584,00			
Paid interest to bank						P 50.00
Haircut expense						1.50
Transportation						2.00
Bought: salt						1.00
dress material					1 pc.	20.00
fish					1 kg	7.00
gasoline					1 ltr.	1.75
Cooked rice (3x)				1 ganta		(4.50)
Eggs				2		(1.00)
Sweet potato tops				1 bundle		(0.10)
Paid 2 hired laborers				2 gantas		(9.00)
Coconut given	2		(0.30)			
Gave rice as gift				2 gantas		(9.00)
Grant from children			100.00			
Credit from Sari-Sari Store			2.00			
Oil					1 bottle	1.50
Bread						.50

References

Chayanov, A.V. In Thorner, D., *et al.*, eds., *The Theory of Peasant Economy.* Homewood, Ill.: Richard Irwin, 1966.

Hayami, Y., in association with Kikuchi, M., Moya, P. F., Bambo, L. M., and Marciano, E. B. *Anatomy of a Peasant Economy: A Rice Village in the Philippines.* Los Banos, Philippines: International Rice Research Institute, 1978.

Hymer, S., and Resnick, S. "A Model of an Agrarian Economy with Non-agricultural Activities." *American Economic Review*, Vol. 59 (September 1966), pp. 493-506.

Nakajima, C. "Subsistence and Commercial Family Farms: Some Theoretical Models of Subjective Equilibrium." In Wharton, C. R., ed. *Subsistance Agriculture and Economic Development*, Chicago: Aldine 1969.

Ruttan, V. W. "Integrated Rural Development Programs: A Skeptical Perspective," *International Development Review*, Vol. 17, No. 4, (1975/4), pp. 9-16.

United Nations. *A System of National Accounts*, Series F, No. 2, Rev. 3. New York, 1968.

Yudelman, M. "Agriculture in Integrated Rural Development: The Experience of the World Bank," *Food Policy*, Vol. 1, (November 1976), pp. 376-81.

Financial Flow-of-funds Accounts: The Indian Experience

V. V. Divatia

The work of developing suitable flow-of-funds accounts for the Indian economy was initiated in 1956 under the joint auspices of the Central Statistical Organization (CSO) and the Reserve Bank of India (RBI).* Later, in 1959, a model set of accounts which could be followed was suggested by a Working Group constituted for that purpose. This Group took due note of statistics then available and the work already done in the country, including the important study carried out by Professor H. W. Arndt of the Australian National University in 1959 in consultation with the CSO, the Ministry of Finance, and the RBI. The Group in its report gave sector-wise accounts for some of the years, particularly for 1957–59. Further developments in the RBI led to inter-sectoral two-way tables and to some exercises in financial planning which will be mentioned later in this paper.

In financial flow-of-funds accounting in India, to bring out two basic features mentioned below, special attention has been given to designing the sectors, to registering the flow of funds through the money market by catching the saving-investment gap in different producing sectors, and to the total which borrowing and lending operations needed to fill. These points are amplified in Statements I, II, and III. First, the

---

* Enhancing the scope and application of financial flow-of-funds accounts in the Indian economy has been constantly engaging the attention of the Reserve Bank of India ever since the first article on the subject was prepared and published in the March 1967 issue of the *RBI Bulletin*. The experience gained over the years has pinpointed the importance of sectoring the government and household sectors, particularly in a developing context, in such a way that the functional homogeneity conditions are not violated. The significance of an inter-sectoral flow of funds matrix as a tool for financial planning has also been demonstrated. These and related issues form the main theses of this paper. The views expressed in the paper are those of the author and not necessarily of the institution to which he belongs.

tables depict in detail the changes in the financial assets and liabilities by types of instrument and by sectors of the economy, *i.e.,* the changes in financial claims held as assets or issued as liabilities by each sector. Secondly, these tables show how the investment-savings deficits of different sectors are made up by the savings of surplus sectors over their own investments. The temporal and cross-sectional (*i.e.,* sectoral) comparisons provide insight into changing patterns of the degree of development of financial intermediation, the increasing distance between the saver and the investor, and the paths which the surplus savings take to reach the investing sectors. The Indian experience should be of particular interest to other less developed countries inasmuch as the emerging patterns bring to the fore the increasing dependence of the investing sectors on external finance, either on financial intermediaries or on markets which bring the savers and the investors in direct contact (*e.g.* stock exchanges). The role of the government in mopping up and directing surplus savings to desired channels for financing planned projects also becomes evident through these sets of tables. A set of financial indicators emerges, providing ways to perceive important developments on the financial side.

Sectoring

Sectoring of the Indian economy is based mainly on the following five criteria: (i) activity—financial or real, (ii) functional homogeneity, (iii) institutional homogeneity, (iv) data availability, and (v) cooperability to the extent possible with other national accounts. Activity-wise, an attempt is made to segregate the financial and the non-financial. Within financial activities, functional and institutional homogeneity are sought by considering two main sectors, banking and other financial institutions (OFI). Banking is mainly concerned with providing short-term or revolving finance whereas OFI provide long-term finance for creating real fixed assets. Each of these sectors is sub-divided in order to achieve further homogeneity. Thus, the RBI and commercial banks, cooperative banks, and credit societies could be sub-sectors of banking; long-term financial institutions, provident funds, and insurance could be sub-sectors of OFI .

Three other sectors belong to the "real" side: the private corporate sector, the government, and the households. In addition, the rest of the world (ROW) is needed to bring in loans and aid from abroad. With the massive investments in public sector undertakings and the need to borrow funds from financial institutions or government budgetary capital accounts, it is necessary to split the government sector into two main sectors: non-departmental commercial undertakings, and the government general administration, including departmental undertakings. This separation has now been made for the accounts of recent years, although in the accounts presented here these two components form sub-sectors of the government sector. An additional sector for multinationals is also often suggested, but so far this segregation has not been attempted.

The household sector, as the only surplus domestic sector having an excess of saving over its own sectoral investment, is the most important in terms of both the level of this surplus and the manner in which it is passed on to other investing sectors directly or through the financial institutions. The financial claims it holds and the response it evokes to interest rates on different types of issues are in themselves worth studying separately. One would wish that the household sector were more homogeneous, functionally and institutionally, but, with the present structure of the economy, its degree of development, and present data availability, this seems hardly feasible. It is one main characteristic of the Indian economy (and perhaps also of those of a large number of less developed countries) that some of the activities of production, distribution, financial lending, and borrowing are all so thoroughly mixed up that it is well-nigh impossible to segregate each of these activities in order to present the "pure household" as a separate sector. The result is that the household sector comprises all such activities as agriculture, small unregistered and unorganized industry, small trade, and money-lending activities, carried out on a household or unincorporated establishment basis. In addition, it also includes non-profit-making institutional activities since these are not accounted for elsewhere in any of the other sectors.

All these flows of funds among the various sub-sectors within the household sector have to be treated as intra-sectoral flows and are, therefore, not reflected in any of the tables presented here. For instance, what an agriculturist borrows from a money-lender, usually at very high interest rates, does not get reflected in the Indian flow-of-funds tables. Its dimensions are ascertained through surveys organized every ten years by the RBI. The latest such survey was conducted for the year 1971–72 by the RBI in collaboration with the National Sample Survey Organization. Similarly, the dimensions of financial lending by money-lenders to unorganized industries and small traders remain unrevealed in the flow-of-funds tables. In effect, sectors other than the household

Table 1. The Indian Economy: Sectors and Subsectors

Sector	Subsector
1. Banking	1. Reserve Bank of India
	2. Commercial banks
	3. Cooperative banks and credit societies
2. Other financial institutions	4. Financial corporations and companies
	5. Insurance companies
	6. Provident funds
3. Private corporate business	7. Private non-financial companies
	8. Cooperative non-credit societies
4. Government, including departmental undertakings	9. Central government
	10. State governments and union territories
	11. Local authorities
5. Non-departmental commercial undertakings of government	12. Non-departmental commercial undertakings of government
6. Households	13. Households
7. Rest of the world	14. Rest of the world

sector are those which are organized and for which the financial data are generally available on a fairly reliable basis. The sub-sectors for each of the main sectors are listed in Table 1.

Flow of Funds through Money Markets

Over the last twenty years and more, a number of financial institutions have been set up to assist economic development, and a wide variety of issues have appeared in the market. The important institutions requiring mention are the RBI, the commercial and cooperative banks, the statutory financial corporations (State Financial Corporations, Industrial Development Bank of India, the Industrial Finance Corporation of India, and others), the provident fund and insurance, small savings (postal) offices, the Unit Trust of India and non-banking financial institutions such as hire-purchase agencies, investment companies, chit funds/Kuris, and Nidhis.

Money supply and monetary resources, shown separately by their components (currency, demand deposits, and time deposits), increased rapidly during these years, particularly during 1951–52, 1961–62 and 1971–72. The overall tendency has been a shift away from the holding of currency or cash to deposits and within deposits from demand to time deposits.

The increase in sources and uses of the statutory financial institutions occurred mainly through the instruments of shares, debentures, loans, and advances. These institutions cater to the special needs of development, extending long-term loans, routing foreign exchange obtained from abroad to the private sector, assisting industrial and agricultural development, aiding development of backward areas, and generally regulating and channeling the savings of surplus sectors to bring about planned development. Their assets/liabilities increased by 116 times during the period 1950–51 to 1970–71. The provident fund had a more or less set pattern of investment because of governmental regulation, largely investing funds in government securities. Insurance funds also helped long-term activity, and, apart from industrial development, insurance particularly helped finance the building of middle- and low-income housing. Insurance funds were also lent to the banking sector in the call money markets.

An important feature of the development of a financial infrastructure is the inter-institution financing of various types of financial institutions before funds reach the investing sector, giving rise to much more rapid growth in financial assets than in tangible assets. This effect is best seen through the layering ratio, defined as the proportion of inter-institutional issues among financial institutions as compared to their issues to non-financial sectors. This ratio (based on stock data) had a value of 0.09 in 1950–51, 0.12 in 1955–56, 0.19 in the 1961–62 to 1965–66 period, and 0.24 in the 1969–70 to 1972–73 period. The development of the financial infrastructure and its increasingly important role in investment activity can be seen through the set of financial indicators shown in Table 2, which are based on "flow" data.

Table 2. Indicators of Financial Development in India

Indicator	1951–52 to 1955–56	1961–62 to 1965–66	1969–70 to 1971–72
1. Financial inter-relations ratio (FIR) (Total issues ÷ Investment)	0.63	0.98	1.06
2. Proportion of investment financed by financial institutions	0.17	0.31	0.40
3. Intermediation ratio (issues of financial institutions (indirect) to non-financial sectors ÷ issues of non-financial sectors)	0.33	0.47	0.63
4. New issue ratio (issues of non-financial sectors ÷ investment)	0.51	0.66	0.64
5. Share of the rest of the world in total financing	—0.08	0.01	0.02

Total debt in the economy is classified into indirect claims issued by financial institutions, primary issues raised by non-financial sectors, and the claims of the Rest of the World sector. FIB indicates the role of debt in investment activity. The rise in the ratio points out the growing complexity of the financial system accompanied by modernization and growth. The intermediation ratio recorded a gradual increase indicating the relatively growing importance of financial institutions and implicitly the reliance on indirect financing by investing sectors. In the computing of the ratio, the inter-financial institutional claims issued/held are not taken into account. The new issue ratio points out the significant role of non-financial institutions in raising external finance.

Sectoral Flows

Statements II and III give some idea of the saving-investment gap in different producing sectors and the total borrowing and lending operations needed to fill the deficit or to transfer the excess of saving over investment to needy sectors for the first plan period (Statement II, 1951–52 to 1955–56) and for the latest available four-year period (Statement III, 1969–70 to 1972–73). Statements II and III show sector-wise sources and uses, by instruments, and indicate how various issues finance the deficits or how claims are purchased by the surplus sector (the household is the only surplus domestic sector). Statement I shows the "discrepancy," which is rather an inconvenient item but which cannot be avoided, as is explained in the section on Limitations. With the passage of time, in relative terms, discrepancies have been reduced. It must be made clear that it is not that the deficit sectors have only debt liabilities and the surplus sectors only loans and advances as assets. Both these types of sectors have external liabilities and financial assets. But when these are netted out, it is the deficit sector which on balance issues claims and the surplus sector which holds them as assets (*i.e.,* claims on the borrowing sector). Banks and OFIs being financial institutions, their saving or investment in absolute terms is very small. The same is even more true when they are viewed in relation to the changes in assets and liabilities which, by and large, reflect their scale of operations. It may not as such be unrealistic to abstract and assume that financial intermediaries have in general no saving-investment gap. This assumption does not detract from the analysis; even when it is relaxed, the analysis can be taken care of without affecting the conclusions. Obviously, currency and deposits on the liabilities (sources) side and loans and advances on the assets (uses) side are the major financial issues and claims through which funds flow to and from the banking sector. With the increasing monetization of the economy, this scale is bound to increase. Households are the main holders of currency and deposits as net assets.

In recent years, the ratio of government saving to NNP is about 2 percent and that of investment to NNP is around 6.5 percent. The ratio of the deficit to NNP is thus about 4.5 percent. As a sector directing the entire economy, its scale of borrowing and lending is quite huge, and much of its borrowing comes from banking and OFI as well as the ROW sector, the first two holding securities as claims on the government sector. Much of this gap shows the needs of government non-departmental undertakings, and there is a flow of funds from government to government undertakings. Recently, government undertakings are taken out as a seperate sector (though this is not shown in the tables here), three-fourths of whose needs for external funds were met by government in the period 1969–70 to 1972–73. A more recent trend is the increasing reliance of the government undertakings on the banking sector for both short-term and long-term funds. Although the Rest of the World sector provides funds to government on a substantial scale, the need for foreign exchange by the other sectors, including the public sector undertakings, is usually met through government. This feature comes out better in the inter-sector flow-of-funds matrix (Table 3).

Table 3. Financial Transactions: Matrix for the Third Plan Period (1961–62 to 1965–66)   (Unit: Million rupees)

Lending sector Borrowing sector	Banking	Other financial institutions	Private corporate business	Government	Households	Rest of the world	Total
Banking	—	—	6910	12660	—	—	19570
Other financial institutions	540	—	3500	5480	—	—	9520
Private corporate Business	1630	250	5400	—	—	—	7280
Government	—	—	720	22280	—	—	23000
Households	16800	8960	2770	5880	30050	—	64460
Rest of the world	600	310	380	21330	—	—	22620
Total	19570	9520	19680	67630	30050	—	146450

The private corporate sector's saving-investment proportion of NNP is about 1.2 to 1.5 percent, having reached its peak at 2.3 percent during the third plan period (1961–62 to 1965–66). The dependence of the private corporate sector on banking, OFI, and government to close the gap has increased even in relative terms, whereas its dependence on the household sector has, relatively speaking, declined. Increased dependence on government is largely due to the cooperative non-credit societies and enterprises which depend for loans and advances on government to a very large extent.

Thus, the household sector emerges as the sole surplus domestic sector. The ratio of saving to NNP is about 11 percent, whereas investment to NNP is around 6 to 7 percent; the net result is a surplus of savings over investment of about 4 to 5 percent. Earlier in the first plan period this surplus was about 2 percent of the NNP. Put differently, the household sector meets 60 percent of its own investment needs and passes on 40 percent of its savings to other sectors, either directly or indirectly through the financial or government sectors. Currency and deposits are its main assets, and in the total financial surplus of the sector these assets rose from 36 percent in the first plan period to about 86 percent in the period 1969–70 to 1972–73. Small savings have declined in relative terms, although fund increases are larger in absolute amount. Insurance and provident funds also show higher annual increases. Loans and advances as well as securities are showing declines, indicating liquidation, repayment, or lending to other sectors.

An interesting exercise is the construction of an inter-sector transaction matrix, as shown in Table 3. Although some problems are involved in constructing this matrix, it provides a framework for financial planning. This aspect is discussed in the section on Applications.

Uses and Applications

Financial flow of funds forms one integral part of the system of national accounts and is linked with the capital finance accounts of the nation which show the saving and investments of the various sectors with a balancing entry of net surplus or deficit resulting in the acquisition of financial assets or liabilities. This balancing entry for each sector is the starting point of the opening entry. The flow-of-funds accounts reveal the lending and borrowing patterns of the individual sectors. This main purpose is served even when national accounts are somewhat modified to suit the special needs of the developing countries. As can be seen, the ultimate economic entity here, as in the case of modified national accounts, is the household and not the individual. For developing countries, the interesting aspect of the study is the manner in which the financial infrastructure and its pattern and scale develop in the organized part of the money market to suit economic development and the way each sector reacts to the various types of instruments. As has already been mentioned, the dominance of one or the other sector (*e.g.* government or public sector undertakings) in economic development can be clearly brought out. The impact (or at least the effects) of fiscal and monetary policies in directing the available surplus resources—domestic as well as from abroad—to desired ends can be better appreciated if flow-of-funds tables are available. This aspect is of particular importance to economies which are wholly or partially planned.

While all this applies to the organized part of the economy, one should admit that at present the flows do not reveal the patterns or the scale of unorganized financing agencies included in the household sector. As the economy develops and becomes more specialized, the picture might unfold, but at present one draws a blank. Many of these flows cancel out as intra-household sector flows. Some information on a "stock" basis becomes available in India at long intervals of time. For instance, the debt and investment surveys carried out every ten years since 1951–52 have revealed that the percentage of rural debt financed by non-institutional agencies like landlords and agricultural and professional money-lenders was as high as 74.5 percent in 1952, 68.5 percent in 1962, and 45.6 percent in 1971. While the importance of non-institutional financing in the rural economy has declined, it is still quite high. With the abolition of rural debt of small and marginal farmers and of weaker sections of the society to private credit agencies, more funds must be sought from the organized financial agencies. The changing patterns will reveal whether the sought-after reforms have any effect and, if so, to what extent organized financial agencies are replacing unorganized agencies.

An important application of considerable importance relates to financial planning. For an economy where a planning mechanism works and investment and saving patterns are (sectorally) projected, it becomes important to ascertain whether, in the light of the behavioristic pattern of disposition of surplus funds, the projected sectoral saving and investment patterns are consistent. A mathematical model of the input-output type (Divatia, 1969) was constructed, and the results have brought out the fact that, given an intersectoral flow-of-funds matrix, a given sectoral saving pattern has a unique sectoral investment pattern; any attempt to establish another investment pattern would be inconsistent with the given saving pattern, and vice versa. This exercise was carried out with the help of a 6×6 matrix, rows and columns representing the six sectors already mentioned. One has to know about the sectoral saving pattern to be able to plan an investment pattern, given the flow-of-funds matrix, and vice versa. If this is not possible, the question for planners may be what should be the flow-of-funds matrix (*i.e.,* the structural coefficients) and the constraints on the elements of the matrix so that the given I and S sectoral patterns can be brought into consistency. This problem has yet to be solved. In the case of India, this model has been used to compare the planned savings and investment patterns with the estimates based on the model.

The estimates suggested that if the investment (sectoral) pattern projected in the third plan was to be achieved with the prevailing flow-of-funds matrix, then in the savings pattern more reliance would have had to be placed on ROW sector than the plan envisaged. In other sectors domestic savings were likely to be much lower than the plan estimated. Alternatively, if the savings pattern and the matrix were to be taken as fact, then investments would have to be much higher in the private corporate sector than what the plan envisaged and much lower in the government and household sectors.

The changes occurring in the structural coefficients are themselves of interest. The matrix which evolved enables one to grasp these changes readily. For instance, in regard to the plan it is of interest to compare the third plan values with the values worked out on the basis of the financing of the fourth plan investment targets.

As for the household sector, its investment depends entirely on its own savings (in net terms); with its surplus, it is a net lender rather than a borrower. It is, therefore, safe to assume the structural coefficient of demand for funds to be unity in the diagonal cell, household-household, for both these periods. In regard to the government and private corporate sectors, the figures in Table 4 emerge.

Structurally, therefore, in the fourth plan, the relative reliance of the private corporate sector on banking, government, and the house-

Table 4. Structural Coefficients of the Private Corporate Sector and the Government Sector

Lender	Private corporate		Government	
	4th plan	3rd plan	4th plan	3rd plan
Banking	0.287	0.339	0.161	0.187
Other financial institutions	0.292	0.174	0.204	0.081
Private corporate business	0.242	0.288	—	—
Government	0.019	0.058	0.388	0.334
Household	0.110	0.134	0.018	0.084
Rest of the world	0.050	0.007	0.229	0.314
	1.000	1.000	1.000	1.000

hold sector is proposed to be reduced, and that on other financial institutions and the rest of the world increased.

In the case of the government sector, its relative reliance on other financial institutions and its own savings is proposed to be increased, but reduced vis-à vis banking, the household, and the rest of the world.

What actually happens in reality can be measured only when the complete data in regard to flow-of-funds and saving-investment patterns become available. It may be added here that Dr. Pani and his associates in the RBI (Department of Statistics, 1972, 169–186) later developed a more disaggregated sectoral matrix of 11 × 11 order, and considered gross instead of net flows. The results were quite close to those obtained by the use of the 6 × 6 matrix.

These are some of the uses to which the flow-of-funds accounts can be put. Their utility will increase if financial balance sheet data (sectoral and issue-wise) are available and still more if the quality of investment data improves.

Limitations

The limitations of these data can be broadly grouped into four categories: (1) problems in sectoring, (2) valuation differences, (3) timing differences, and (4) the time lag and other deficiencies in the data. The first limitation has been described in some detail in the case of the household sector which, though most important as the only surplus sector, is not homogeneous. Most of the estimates derived for it are residuals of totals less independent estimates for other sectors. Financial savings, investment, and hence the gap or the surplus available thus come out as residuals. Secondly, it is at least necessary to have separate accounts for sub-sectors for small trade and industries (operating on an establishment basis), moneylending activities under license, and the non-profit-making institutions so that the household sector can be set up in as homogeneous a manner as possible. These attempts would, however, need much more data on a regular basis; steps need to be taken in this direction not only for flow-of-funds accounts but even for national income accounts. Furthermore, it may be added that in an economy such as India's, "households" rather than "persons" is the preferred economic entity.

Valuation limitations arise because the pricing of claims by the holder differs from that by the issuer. The former prices the claims at the market price whereas the issuer prices the same instrument at issue price. Associated with this is the difficulty of adjusting capital gains or losses.

These gains or losses even out at the national level, but not necessarily at the sectoral level. Investment figures at the sectoral level do not necessarily exclude secondhand fixed assets, whereas estimates of overall investment based on the commodity flow method generally exclude secondhand machinery and equipment. For these reasons the savings-investment gap does not usually tally with lending-borrowing differences. One has therefore to make do with the discrepancies.

Timing differences arise because all economic entities, even within a given sector, and certainly those belonging to different sectors, do not generally have common accounting periods. Thus, within the private corporate sector accounting years of companies are different, and the flows worked out do not strictly pertain to the accounting year but indicate the approximate magnitude of flows. For commercial banks, on the other hand, January to December is the common accounting year. Hence, the flow measured as "use" or lending to the corporate sector will not tally with the flow from the borrower's or the "sources" end, i.e., the corporate sector end.

Time lags in the data make for delays in completing the flow-of-funds accounts. While in developed countries even quarterly flows are available with a three- to six-month time lag, annual flow accounts for India have a time lag of at least three years. Much can be done to rectify this defect if coordinated steps are taken to ensure data availability in good time.

In the foregoing only some salient aspects of flow-of-funds accounts are stated. For want of space details have been omitted. The main

Statement I. Flow of Funds in the Indian Economy

(Unit: Million rupees)

	First plan period (1951–52 to 1955–56)			(1969–70 to 1972–73)		
	Private corpor- ate bu- siness	Govern- ment	House- holds	Private corpor- ate bu- siness	Govern- ment	House- holds
1. Saving	1780	6140	25467	7290	28908	153921
2. Investment	4040	14190	16530	23160	92156	92370
3. Investment-saving gap	2260	8050	8937[a]	15870	63248	61551[a]
4. Borrowings	4929	9657	3336	15441	88464	26596
5. Lending	770	826	12273	2165	20210	88147
6. Financial deficit/surplus	4159	8831	8937	13276	68254	61551[b]
7. Discrepancy [(3)–(6)]	—1899	—781	—	2594	—5006	—

[a] Derived as (1–2)
[b] Denotes surplus.

Statement II. Financial Flows in the Indian Economy, First Plan Period (1951–52 to 1955–56)

(Unit: Million rupees)

Sector	Banking		Other financial institutions		Private corporate business		Government		Rest of the world		Households		Total	
	Sources	Uses	Sources	Uses	Sources	Uses	Sources	Uses	Sources	Uses	Sources	Uses	Sources	Uses
1. Banking	—	—	93	187	1188	560	2789	−919	−1101	−717	1713	3848	4682 (21.1)	2959 (14.9)
2. Other financial institutions	85	11	—	—	399	—	1440	75	—	—	354	2033	2278 (10.3)	2119 (10.7)
3. Private corporate business	491	1004	—	417	—	—	−5	374	—	217	81	2829	567 (2.5)	4841 (24.4)
4. Government	−355	2414	120	1294	374	83	—	—	−467	484	1188	3563	860 (3.9)	7838 (39.6)
5. Rest of the world	−490	−1123	113	55	81	—	922	−54	—	—	—	—	626 (2.8)	−1122 (−5.6)
6. Households	3848	1713	2033	354	2829	81	3563	1188	—	—	—	—	12273 (55.2)	3336 (16.8)
7. Items not elsewhere classified	101	—	40	—	58	46	948	162	−217	−365	—	—	930 (4.2)	−157 (−0.8)
Instruments					—									
1. Currency and deposits	3275	479	—	187	75	559	−12	−994	—	−72	—	3256	3338 (15.0)	3415 (17.2)
2. Investments	198	624	183	1579	2078	89	4019	15	12	1	—	2652	6490 (29.2)	4960 (25.0)

Statement II. (continued)

	Banking		Other financial institutions		Private corporate business		Government		Rest of the world		Households		Total	
	Sources	Uses	Sources	Uses	Sources	Uses	Sources	Uses	Sources	Uses	Sources	Uses	Sources	Uses
a) Government securities	—	1930	—	1205	—	82	3996	—	6	—52	—	731	3996 (18.0)	3896 (19.7)
b) Others	198	—1306	183	374	2078	7	23	15	12	53	—	1921	2994 (11.2)	1064 (5.3)
3. Loans and advances	60	2658	81	457	2472	81	981	1698	—565	151	3336	804	6365 (28.7)	5849 (29.5)
4. Small savings	—	—	—	84	—	—	2398	—	—	—	—	2314	2398 (10.8)	2398 (12.1)
5. Life insurance fund	—	—	1263	—	—	—	—	—	—	98	—	1165	1263 (5.7)	1263 (6.4)
6. Provident fund	—	—	832	—	—	—	1004	—	—	—	—	1826	1836 (8.3)	1836 (9.3)
7. Trade debt or credit	—	—	—	—	246	—	85	28	—	—	—	246	331 (1.5)	274 (1.4)
8. Foreign claims not elsewhere classified	13	258	—	—	—	—	342	—55	—	—	—	—	355 (1.6)	205 (1.0)
9. Other items not elsewhere classified	134	—	40	—	58	41	840	134	—1232	—559	—	—	—160 (—0.8)	—384 (—1.9)
Total	380	4019	2399	2307	4929	770	9657	826	—1785	—381	3336	12273	22216 (100.0)	19814 (100.0)

* Figures in brackets represent percentages of the total.

Statement III: Financial Flows in the Indian Economy, Fourth Plan Period: 1969–70 to 1972–73

(Unit: Million rupees)

	Banking		Other financial institutions		Private corporate business		Government		Rest of the world		Households		Total	
	Sources	Uses	Sources	Uses	Sources	Uses	Sources	Uses	Sources	Uses	Sources	Uses	Sources	Uses
Sector														
1. Banking	—	—	2749	4734	6138	1907	36089	1927	920	—159	21076	52621	66372 (29.0)	61418 (26.7)
2. Other financial institutions	5156	2156	—	—	2707	—	13028	670	—8	435	1729	21106	22612 (9.8)	24387 (10.6)
3. Private corporate business	1959	10285	19	4670	—	—	445	3002	—36	1310	142	4989	2529 (1.1)	21636 (9.4)
4. Government	7589	40803	762	15788	2318	82	—	—	1917	16857	3649	9431	16235 (7.0)	82961 (36.0)
5. Rest of the world	—1431	735	507	—3	—795	—	15910	2071	—	—	—	—	14191 (6.2)	2803 (1.2)
6. Households	52621	21076	21106	1729	4989	142	9431	3649	—	—	—	—	88147 (38.2)	26596 (11.5)
7. Items not elsewhere classified	5841	1462	728	15	84	—56	13361	8890	—50	334	—	—	20144 (8.7)	10650 (4.6)
Instruments														
1. Currency and deposits	60584	—595	—	2075	646	1993	491	444	—	2973	—	52836	70721 (26.3)	59726 (25.9)
2. Investments	5669	37832	2149	13147	2781	116	38915	2944	764	202	—	—1410	50278 (21.9)	52831 (22.9)

Statement III. (continued)

	Banking		Other financial institutions		Private corporate business		Government		Rest of the world		Households		Total	
	Sources	Uses	Sources	Uses	Sources	Uses	Sources	Uses	Sources	Uses	Sources	Uses	Sources	Uses
a) Government securities	—	36289	—	8750	—	66	38345	—	—	161	—	—2989	38345 (16.6)	42277 (18.3)
b) Others	5669	1543	2149	4397	2781	50	570	2944	764	41	—	1579	11933 (5.2)	10554 (4.6)
3. Loans and advances	675	37772	2915	7746	10230	142	21078	12989	321	13924	26026	3553	61246 (26.5)	76126 (33.0)
4. Small savings	—	—	—	4362	—	—	8443	—	—	—	—	4081	8443 (3.7)	8443 (3.7)
5. Life insurance funds	—	—	9316	—	—	—	334	—	—	—23	—	9673	9650 (4.2)	9650 (4.2)
6. Provident funds	—	—	10785	—	—	—	6936	—	—	—	—	17721	17721 (7.7)	17721 (7.7)
7. Trade debt or credit	—	—	—7	—	1700	—	6833	—	—	—	—	1693	8526 (3.7)	1693 (0.7)
8. Foreign claims not elsewhere classified	—165	46	—	—	—	—	—	1711	1711	—	—	—	1546 (0.7)	1757 (0.8)
9. Other items not elsewhere classified	5972	1462	710	—397	84	—86	5434	2121	—171	—601	570	—	12599 (5.4)	2499 (1.1)
Total	72735	76517	25869	26933	15441	2165	88464	20209	2625	16475	26396	88147	230730 (100.0)	230446 (100.0)

ᵃ Figures in brackets represent percentages of the total.

attention is given to financial instruments, sectoral flows, and uses, and almost nothing is stated about methods. For more detail, some articles quoted in the bibliography may be of use. For the developing countries, especially where unorganized producer and financial entities exist within the household sector, it seems necessary to strive for more data before this sector can be made more homogeneous. This improvement may yield more knowledge about flows which are now being treated as intra-household. Meanwhile, the flow-of-funds accounts will continue to reflect the role that financial institutions in the organized sector play in the economic development of a country.

References

Bank of England. *An Introduction to Flow of Funds Accounting,* 1952–70, 1972.
Bein, A. D. "Surveys in Applied Economics. Flow of Funds Analysis," *The Economic Journal,* December 1973.
Bhatt, V. V. "Saving and Flow of Funds Analysis A Tool for Financial Planning," *Review of Income and Wealth,* March 1971.
Board of Governors of the Federal Reserve System. *Flow of Funds Accounts 1945–68,* 1970.
Central Statistical Organisation, Government of India. *Report on the Working Group of Flow of Funds,* 1963.
Cohen, J. "Coplands Money Flows after Twenty-five Years: A Survey," *Journal of Economic Literature,* March 1972.
Divatia, V. V. "An Operational Technique of Financial Planning," *Reserve Bank of India Bulletin,* September 1960.
Divatia, V. V. and Venkstachalam, T. R. "Flow of Funds Accounts," *Reserve Bank Staff Occasional Papers,* December 1976.
Fry, M. J. "An application of the Stone Model of Financial Planning in Turkey" (mimeo). Paper presented at Eleventh General Conference of International Association for Research in Income and Wealth, 1969.
Goldsmith, R. W. *Financial Structure and Development.* 1969.
Goldsmith, R. W. *Determinants of Financial Structure.* OECD, 1971.
Pani, P. E. *The Use of Financial Flow Accounts in Planning* (mimeo), 1972.
Polkoff, Murry, *et al.* (eds.). *Financial Institutions and Markets.* 1970.
Reserve Bank of India. "Financial Flows in the Indian Economy," *RBI Bulletin,* March 1967, February 1972, and August 1975.
Wallich, H. C. "Uses of Financial Accounts in Monetary Analysis," *Review of Income and Wealth,* December 1969.

Theoretical Issues in Production Accounting

Kazuo Sato

This paper is concerned with theoretical issues in measuring real national product. We are interested in identifying what is really being measured from the viewpoint of economic theory. We do not discuss the feasibility of measurement that may emerge from our theoretical examination. It seems to us that establishing theoretical foundations is a precondition for meaningful measurement.[1] As measurements are almost always imperfect and approximate, we must know what is being approximated.

National income in constant prices is expected to measure economic welfare when approached from the expenditure side and economic efficiency when approached from the production side. The two measurements are, of course, interdependent. If environmental pollution must be substracted from GNE as social cost, it must affect economic efficiency in the production process of the economy. This important aspect is abstracted from in this paper.

The issues to be examined below have been discussed over and over again, and it is unexciting and trite to rehash them unless a fresh point

[1] In his summary of proceedings of the 1958 Conference of Studies in Income and Wealth dealing specifically with the real production accounts, Kendrick observed:

> Productivity remains one field in which economic statistics have run ahead of economic theory. Unaided by the theoretician with respect to the proper treatment of certain of the more difficult aspects of productivity measurement, especially the problem of measuring real capital stock and input, the statistician has had to proceed using the most reasonable concepts and conventions he could devise. The results have been useful, but certainly current estimates are amenable to improvement, and both makers and users could profit by devoting more thought to their meaning and interpretation (Kendrick, 1961: 3).

Since that time, economics has made considerable progress in the field of production analysis. However, theory and practice have not been happily married as yet.

of view is introduced. In this paper, I approach these issues from the side of production analysis, trying to offer a new view. A systematic approach like this enables us to clear up a number of ambiguities and misconceptions still remaining in this field.

In what follows, we start from real value added and then proceed step by step through real quasi-rents, total factor productivity, capital measurement, and macro production functions. Capital letters denote quantities and small letters prices or deflators:

J efficiency-corrected capital stock
K, k conventional capital stock
$L,$ labor inputs
M, m materials or intermediate inputs
Q, q gross output
R, r real quasi-rents
T total factor productivity
T' quasi-rent productivity of capital
V, v real value added
X, x primary inputs
Y, y GNE
t time or technology level

Other symbols are explained in the text as they appear.

Real Value Added[2]

For the sake of expository simplicity, we consider a closed economy and disregard government transactions. We begin our analysis by considering real value added of industries, *i.e.*, output net of intermediate inputs.

For the economy as a whole, we have a national income identity between expenditure and production in current prices:

$$\sum_{j=1}^{n} y_j Y_j = \sum_{i=1}^{n} v_i V_i \qquad (1)$$

where $y_j Y_j$ is the final demand for sector j's output and $v_i V_i$ is the value added of sector i. The identity should also hold in constant prices. In the base-year prices, we have

$$\sum_{j} y_j^0 Y_j = \sum_{i} v_i^0 V_i \qquad (2)$$

[2] This section is based on (Sato, 1976).

where superscript O denotes the base-year value. Since value added is the difference of gross output and intermediate inputs

$$v_i V_i = q_i Q_i - m_i M_i, \qquad (3)$$

we have

$$v_i^0 V_i = q_i^0 Q_i - m_i^0 M_i \qquad (4)$$

as the Laspeyres formula for real value added. Dividing V_i into $v_i V_i$, we obtain the implicit deflator v_i, which is in the Paasche form. This is the well-known double-deflation method since output value and input value are separately deflated to yield the real value added as their difference.[3] In fact, this is the only method that preserves consistency in aggregation in constant prices when real GNE is derived by the Laspeyres formula.[4] However, one can readily observe that double-deflated value added can behave perversely. This arises when M_i/Q_i changes a great deal from its base-year value as a result of technical change, price-induced substitution, changes in output mix, or changes in composition of firms in the industry. When intermediate inputs account for a large fraction of total gross value of production, $v_i^0 V_i$ may even become negative while $v_i V_i$ is positive. Consequently, some argued that the concept of real value added is meaningless and should be abandoned (Rymes, 1981) or that different deflation procedures should be adopted (David, 1966; Fenoaltea, 1976).

First of all, we point out that the potential perversity of real value added that is derived by the double-deflation method does not imply the invalidity of the concept of real value added. It simply means that the formula is inappropriate. It was argued by a few (e.g. Christensen and Jorgenson, 1970) that real GNE should be computed by the Divisia formula since it is theoretically the most preferred among index-number formulas. The Divisia index is derived by changing weights continually. Thus, on the expenditure side, aggregate real GNE is obtained in the form of

$$\frac{dY}{Y} = \sum_j \alpha_j \frac{dY_j}{Y_j} \qquad (5)$$

where $\alpha_j = y_j Y_j / \sum_k y_k Y_k$ is the expenditure share of sector j. Consistency is maintained by defining another Divisia index:

[3] Both Q and M are vectors and have to be derived as indexes.
[4] Data availability frequently makes the method inoperative in a number of industries. Hence, the consistency in aggregation is not strictly maintained in practice.

$$\frac{dV}{V} = \sum_i \beta_i \frac{dV_i}{V_i} \tag{6}$$

where $\beta_i = v_i V_i / \sum_k v_k V_k$ is the value-added share of sector in total GNP. This is because

$$\frac{dY}{Y} = \frac{dV}{V}. \tag{7}$$

Since the Divisia index of the Divisia indexes is a Divisia index, we have to define dV_i / V_i as a Divisia index by

$$\frac{dV_i}{V_i} = (1 + \mu_i)\frac{dQ_i}{Q_i} - \mu_i \frac{dM_i}{M_i} \tag{8}$$

where $\mu_i = m_i M_i / v_i V_i$. Similarly, dQ_i / Q_i and dM_i / M_i have to be derived as Divisia indexes. The dual to (8) is the Divisia index of the implicit deflator

$$\frac{dv_i}{V_I} = (1 + \mu_i)\frac{dq_i}{q_i} - \mu_i \frac{dm_i}{m_i}. \tag{9}$$

The Divisia indexes (V_i, v_i) never become negative, provided that the nominal value added $v_i V_i$ is positive. Hence, real value added is immune from perversity when measured as a Divisia index. It can be easily seen that the Laspeyres index of real value added is a lower bound to the true index. The negativity of the Laspeyres index does not imply the negativity of the true index. Hence, we are not obligated to renounce the concept of real value added.

What is the minimum required assumption to justify the Divisia index of real value added? As is well known, it is the equality of the marginal products of intermediate inputs and their real prices. We examine this point below. We omit industry subscripts henceforth.

Imagine that there is a production function

$$Q = F(X, M) \tag{10}$$

where X is a vector of primary inputs. Our assumption is that

$$F_M = \frac{m}{q} \quad \text{and} \quad \frac{\mu}{1 + \mu} = \frac{mM}{qQ} = \frac{M}{Q} F_M. \tag{11}$$

(8) is now rewritten as

$$vdV = q(dQ - F_M \, dM). \qquad (12)$$

At the base year, $v = q = 1$, so that

$$dV = dQ - F_M dM. \qquad (13)$$

This simple relation shows that real value added, as measured in the Divisia form, is gross output less the contribution of intermediate inputs, the contribution being measured by their marginal productivity. The residual, which is real value added, may then be attributed to the contribution of primary inputs.

Let the production function be such that X is separable from M, i.e.,

$$Q = F(\phi(X), M) \qquad (14)$$

and F is linear homogeneous in ϕ and M, i.e., F is subject to "X-generalized" constant returns to scale. Then, (13) reduces to

$$dV = F_\phi \phi' dX \text{ or } V = \phi(X). \qquad (15)$$

In this case, V is completely attributed to X and is independent of M. When the separability condition is not satisfied, V is not determined by X alone. It depends also on M. Even if X is unchanged, V can differ when M is changed. In other words, the Divisia index is not uniquely associated with X. The uniqueness of V is a desirable property if V is to be explained solely by X. But the non-uniqueness of V does not make it meaningless.[5]

When the marginal product of M and its real price are unequal because of imperfect competition and other market distortions, the real value added can still be economically meaningful if their ratio is stable. However, when the ratio changes, the real value added is biased significantly (e.g. at the time of rapid price changes).

Observe that one assumes nothing about primary inputs. Measurement of real value added has nothing to do with the marginal condition for primary inputs nor with the measurability of primary inputs per se. Since there is a serious conceptual problem as to the measur-

---

[5] Some argue that real value added is meaningful in this case only (Arrow, 1974), but this is an overstatement. It is so only for econometricians attempting to estimate value-added production functions. While the omission of M constitutes a misspecification, its significance can be assessed by comparing Allen partial elasticities of members of X with M. (Separability is equivalent to the equality of these elasticities as Berndt and Christensen (1973) demonstrated. Empirical evidence is still scanty.)

ability of capital inputs, as we shall note presently, it is better not to subtract capital consumption allowances from value added. The same should apply to interest cost paid to financial institutions unless services of financial borrowings can be considered as intermediate inputs.

A few alternative deflation procedures are suggested in the literature. Taking the possible perversity of the double-deflated real value added seriously, David proposed single deflation, namely, deflating nominal value added by the gross output price index (David, 1966). Thus, his measure yields V' defined by

$$v^0 V' = \frac{qQ - mM}{q/q^0} = q^0 \left(Q - \frac{m}{q} M \right) \tag{16}$$

When the marginal condition (11) is assumed, the parenthetical expression is $(Q - F_M M)$, which can be regarded as the contribution of X to production. This is the theoretical defense which David invoked. While it eliminates the potential negativity of real value added, it does not satisfy the consistency in aggregation. Hence, it is not acceptable from the national-accounting viewpoint. On the other hand, Fenoaltea (1976) suggests using a single deflator for all industries. It is true, nevertheless trivial, that this procedure expresses value added in real terms while maintaining consistency in aggregation. He argues that the wage unit is exactly such a deflator,[6] but because it eliminates efficiency growth, he suggests taking the implicit GNE deflator. Real value added measured in this way contains the sectoral terms-of-trade effect. When some good becomes relatively cheaper because of, say, technical change, the contribution of the producing industry to total real added value is understated if this method is employed. In other words, the function of real value added as a measure of economic efficiency is eliminated. Therefore, this method cannot be accepted either.[7]

While the Divisia form is theoretically preferable in computing real value added, it is likely that the double-deflation method (for that matter, even the single-deflation procedure in some sectors) will remain the officially favored one insofar as GNE in constant prices is

[6] This suggestion shows up in the literature from time to time.

[7] However, in the absence of appropriate deflators, international comparisons of sectoral output are often conducted by this procedure. So far, purchasing power parity estimates are limited to the expenditure side. In the most recent large-scale attempt on this subject (Kravis et al., 1975: 19), the authors note that "the interest in—and significance of—comparisons on the production side would be great," but lament that "the statistical difficulties of performing such comparisons are much greater than the case of the expenditure comparisons."

based on the Laspeyres formula. The divergence between the two indexes depends on relative-price changes and technical changes that affect the input-output ratio. It can be substantial at the industry level. But so long as m/q is stable, the two do not diverge much and our distinction becomes merely academic.

Real Quasi-rents

Real value added is gross output less the contribution of intermediate inputs on the assumption that their marginal products and their real prices are equal. The procedure can be extended to all inputs which are variable in the short run, namely, materials and labor. If all labor inputs are of this nature, there is no formal difference between men and materials. Needless to say, not all labor inputs are variable in the short run. Quite like machines, some of them are almost fixed inputs. Even those which eventually become variable may not be adjusted very quickly. Therefore, it is probable that the marginal condition is not always adhered to. Nonetheless, if we take a fairly long time, labor inputs are adjustable and the marginal condition should be approximately satisfied.

When wages are deducted from value added, we get quasi-rents

$$rN = qQ - mM - lL \tag{17}$$

where L is labor. We can compute real quasi-rents (R) and the deflator (r) in exactly the same way as real value added in the Divisia form by combining M and L. It is assumed that rR never becomes negative when the marginal condition holds for both M and L. With this, all that has been said about real value added can be applied to real quasi-rents. Real quasi-rents are gross output less the contributions of intermediate and labor inputs to production and may be considered as the contribution of non-labor primary inputs which we may call, for simplicity, capital inputs. While the marginal conditions are assumed for intermediate and labor inputs, no such assumption is made about capital inputs. Further, real quasi-rents are measured even if we know nothing about capital inputs nor about how they are paid. Capital is assumed to be paid the residual, *i.e.*, quasi-rents.

Unlike real value added, there is no way to measure real quasi-rents other than in the Divisia form because relative prices do not remain constant. The Divisia index of real quasi-rents is unique (*i.e.*, independent of L and M) if and only if the production function is given by

$$Q = F(\psi(K), L, M), \tag{18}$$

i.e., if capital inputs (K) are separable from labor and materials inputs and F is K-generalized constant returns to scale. In this case, we have

$$R = \psi(K). \tag{19}$$

R coincides with K if ψ is homogeneous to the first degree in K. In other words, in the absence of economies of scale and technical change, we can measure K from the production side even if we don't know individual elements of K. Unfortunately, the point is academic since the required condition is hardly likely to be found in reality.

Real quasi-rents are free from measurement problems of capital inputs and represent the limit to which we can go without information on capital inputs. Beyond this limit, we can no longer evade measuring capital inputs.

The concept of real quasi-rents may be unfamiliar, but it has been employed by Denison in his well-known paper (Denison, 1957) on quality change and capital measurement. As an example, consider old and new machines. Assume fixed proportions which vary between the vintages. Can we say how many old machines are equivalent to one new machine? In his Method 3, Denison suggests comparing "the contribution of capital to production" by subtracting the contribution of labor from gross output (since intermediate inputs are already netted out, this is value added). Denoting the two vintages by 0 and 1, the contribution in question is given in the base-year prices by

$$\begin{cases} \left(\dfrac{V}{K}\right)_0 - \dfrac{l_0}{v_0}\left(\dfrac{L}{K}\right)_0 \text{ for vintage 0,} \\[2mm] \left(\dfrac{V}{K}\right)_1 - \dfrac{l_0}{v_0}\left(\dfrac{L}{K}\right)_1 \text{ for vintage 1.} \end{cases} \tag{20}$$

According to Denison, the ratio of the latter to the former serves as the required conversion factor of vintage 0 into vintage 1. His suggestion is thus based on comparisons of quasi-rent productivity in base-year prices.[8]

Total Factor Productivity

While real value added is meaningful by itself, its significance is more

---

[8] Denison rejects this method because of practical considerations, not on theoretical grounds.

fully appreciated when it is compared to the primary inputs that produce. As we have noted, real value added can be identified with the index of primary inputs.

For the production function

$$Q = F(X, M),\tag{10}$$

we get

$$\frac{dQ}{Q} = \frac{F_X X}{F}\frac{dX}{X} + \frac{F_M M}{F}\frac{dM}{M}.$$

Noting that

$$\frac{F_M M}{F} = \frac{\mu}{1 + \mu},$$

we obtain

$$\frac{dV}{V} = (1 + \mu)\frac{dQ}{Q} - \mu\frac{dM}{M} = \frac{F_X X}{F - F_M M}\frac{dX}{X}.\tag{21}$$

This equation shows the relation between the real value added index and the primary input index. If F is homogeneous to the first degree in X and M, the multiplier of dX/X is unity. Then, the real value added index coincides with the primary input index. When F is subject to increasing (decreasing) returns to scale, the multiplier is greater (less) than the primary input index. Thus, the real value added index is the composite of the primary input index and (dis) economies of scale. The multiplier is independent of M only if (14) specifies F.[9]

The Divisia index of total factor productivity results from

$$\frac{dT}{T} = \frac{dV}{V} - \frac{dX}{X}\text{ or }T = \frac{V}{X}.\tag{22}$$

With (21), we get

$$\frac{dT}{T} = \frac{F_X X + F_M M - F}{F - F_M M}\frac{dX}{X}.\tag{23}$$

With no technical change, T measures the contribution of economies of scale.

---

[9] Note that dX/X is a Divisia index with factor shares as weights. They are independent of M only if the separability condition is satisfied.

Total factor productivity is more interesting and important when technical change occurs. Thus, let our production function be

$$Q = F(X, M, t) \tag{24}$$

where t denotes the technology level. We can easily show that real value added in the presence of technical change is unique, *i.e.*, independent of M if and only if (24) is given by

$$Q = (\phi(X, t), M), \tag{25}$$

where F is homogeneous of the first degree in ϕ and M. (M-augmenting technical change violates the required condition.) Then, we have

$$V = \phi(X, t). \tag{26}$$

Total factor productivity is obtained by

$$\frac{dT}{T} = \frac{dV}{V} - \frac{dX}{X} = (1 + \mu)\frac{dQ}{Q} - \mu\frac{dM}{M} - \frac{dX}{X}. \tag{27}$$

Hence, it is real value added less the contribution of tangible primary inputs (excluding economies of scale) or, equivalently, gross output less the contribution of tangible inputs.[10] This observation suggests that total factor productivity is, in principle, no different from real value added and real quasi-rents. Real value added is gross output less all intermediate inputs, real quasi-rents are gross output less all variable inputs, and total factor productivity is gross output less all tangible inputs. This makes total factor productivity an index of the contribution of intangible inputs, namely, economies of scale and technical change.

What we have said about real value added applies *in toto* to total factor productivity. If we derive T from (26), then its uniqueness (*i.e.*, independence from X) requires that

$$V = T(t)f(X), \tag{28}$$

where f is linear homogeneous. Thus, T is unique if and only if the value-added production is linear homogenous and technical change is Hicks-neutral. If technical change is of any other type, T is no longer unique. (This point was emphasized by Nelson (1973) and Usher (1974)). If we derive T from (24), we readily observe that t must be separable

---

[10] Strictly speaking, this refers to $(1/1 + \mu)(dT/T)$.

from X and M (*i.e.*, Hicks-neutral) and F linear homogeneous in X and M. (Relation (28) is a special case.)

Our argument indicates that there are two alternative ways to look at total factor productivity. In the first we regard total factor productivity as gross output less the contribution of tangible inputs. In this case, the only meaningful formula is the Divisia index. Both the Laspeyres and Paasche formulas are inapplicable because intangible inputs are paid nothing. In the second, total factor productivity is the ratio of real value added to the index of primary inputs. In this case, we can apply, say, the Laspeyres formula to the numerator and the denominator separately.[11]

How is X to be derived? As X is a vector, its elements have to be aggregated into an index with weights which are the percentage shares of value added in the Divisia formula. They come from the distribution accounts:

$$vV = \sum_{j=1}^{k} x_j X_j. \qquad (29)$$

Denoting $\gamma_j = x_j X_j / vV$, we obtain

$$\frac{dX}{X} = \sum \gamma_j \frac{dX_j}{X_j}. \qquad (30)$$

There is an implicit assumption that the marginal products of primary inputs are equated to their respective real prices (x_j/v) in the case of constant returns and are in proportion to the latter in the case of non-constant returns. This procedure involves an untested assumption. If labor receives its marginal product and capital the residual, the assumption does not hold except in the constant returns case.

Productivity accounting makes a great deal more assumptions about the production function and market pricing. Recall that real value added is meaningful whether or not primary inputs are paid their marginal products or whether or not they can be quantified. Measurability of total factor productivity is concerned with the realism of these assumptions.

In an ideal situation in which all inputs are homogeneous and paid their marginal products, no problem arises as to the quantity measurement. We can construct the Divisia index of all or some primary inputs. By assuming that workers' wages are equal or in proportion to

---

[11] The first approach was followed by Solow (1957) and the second approach by Kendrick (1961).

their marginal products, we can construct the sub-index of labor inputs. Similarly, the sub-index of capital inputs is obtained. This sort of subaggregation requires no assumption of functional separability within the production function.

As for labor inputs, it is known that interoccupational and inter-industry wage structures are relatively stable. Hence, one can aggregate labor inputs as a composite good on the strength of Hicks' aggregation theorem, even if real wages and the marginal products of labor moment-arily deviate from each other over the course of business cycles.

The difficulty is with the quantification of capital inputs. First of all, no separate payments are made to individual capital items unless they are rented by users. Since most of business plant and equipment is owned by users, imputations become necessary. Imputations are relatively straightforward if capital items are homogeneous, *i.e.*, if all items that are classified to a given category are alike and perfect substitutes among themselves. In this case, the capital input index can be readily constructed by combining quantities of these categories with weights equal to their imputed shares of quasi-rents. As we are con-cerned with equilibrium situations, these shares are derived from the imputed normal "flow" prices (the product of capital goods prices and the sum of normal rates of return and depreciation).[12]

Unfortunately, it is this assumption of capital "malleability" that is least realistic. The term capital goods can cover many items of different specifications. These specifications can change even without technical change. When techniques are made more capital-intensive for a given technology, the capital-labor ratio is increased because more expensive machines are adopted rather than increasing the number of machines per operative. Since machines run for many years, different specifica-tions for a machine coexist. They have to be reduced to common units if we wish to get an aggregate input index of this machine. The situa-tion is further complicated as technical change shifts the production function. The machine's quality is improved even if specifications are unchanged. We have now to reduce machines of different specifications

---

[12] This procedure is followed by Christensen and Jorgenson (1969) in constructing the capital input index for the U.S. economy.

Needless to say, capital consists of a few broadly different types of assets: land, fixed reproducible assets, inventories, and financial assets. There must be substitution relationships which will help establish an equilibrium. Financial assets are usually left out of K, but insofar as they are indispensable to the production process, should they not be included in K?

Fixed capital stock is paid interest and depreciation, while inventories are paid in-terest alone. If depreciation is excluded from the returns to the former (as in the case where net value added is taken), inventories tend to get too much weight in comput-ing the primary input index.

and of different qualities into common units. To do this, we have to know the marginal products at the same instant. We can then apply them as weights to aggregate them into an index. Such an aggregate index is invariant if and only if these marginal products maintain constant proportions. Otherwise, weights have to be changed whenever the marginal proportions change. Such an index is apparently of limited value if not useless. This heuristic argument makes it obvious that a necessary condition for the existence of an invariant aggregate index of an input consisting of "heterogeneous" items is the constancy of the ratios of their marginal products. This condition provides a rigorous definition of capital malleability.

When capital is nonmalleable, heterogeneous items can no longer be summed up into an index which is invariant. In other words, these items have to be listed separately in a vector which cannot be represented by an index. In this case, each item can start from zero. Then, dX_j/X_j is undefinable since $X_j = 0$. We cannot construct the Divisia index. This means that we have to look for an alternative way to measure total factor productivity.

Quasi-rent Productivity

The first interpretation of total factor productivity, as we mentioned, starts from the real value-added production function $V = \phi(X, t)$ and defines $T = V/X$. We can apply the same interpretation to real quasi-rents. That is, from $R = \psi(K, t)$, we define

$$T' = R/K, \tag{31}$$

which may be called the quasi-rent productivity of capital. T' is quite analogous to T. We note that

$$\frac{dR}{R} = (1 + \nu)\frac{dV}{V} - \nu\frac{dL}{L} \tag{32}$$

where $\nu = lL/rR$. The Divisia index of T' is then

$$\frac{dT'}{T'} = \frac{dR}{R} - \frac{dK}{K} = (1 + \nu)\frac{dV}{V} - \nu\frac{dL}{L} - \frac{dK}{K}$$
$$= (1 + \nu)\left(\frac{dV}{V} - \frac{dX}{X}\right)$$

so that

$$\frac{dT'}{T'} = (1 + \nu)\frac{dT}{T}. \tag{33}$$

We have $1 + \nu = \nu V/rR$, *i.e.*, the reciprocal of capital's share of value added. Thus, the quasi-rent productivity is much larger than total factor productivity.

What should make T' a useful concept is that R is free from measurement errors in K. Any error in K is transmitted to T'. Let $g(z)$ be dz/z and the asterisk denote the true value. Then,

$$g(T') - g(T')^* = g(K)^* - g(K)$$

so that the percentage error in $g(T')$ is

$$\frac{g(T') - g(T')^*}{g(T')^*} = \frac{g(K)^* - g(K)}{g(K)^*} \frac{g(K)^*}{g(T')^*}. \tag{34}$$

The error in $g(T')$ depends on the error in $g(K)$ and the relative size of $g(K)^*$ and $g(T')^*$. By (33), $g(T)$ has the same percentage error as $g(T')$.

We note that the Divisia index of K can be obtained when capital is malleable. Consider the well-known vintage model. Each year's investment is associated with its own production function. Let $I_\tau(\tau)$ be the fixed capital formation at year τ, $I_\tau(t)$ its remainder at year $t(\geq \tau)$. Assume that technical change is embodied in capital goods and completely capital-augmenting. Then, the vintage production functions are

$$V_\tau(t) = F(A(\tau)I_\tau(t), L_\tau(t)). \tag{35}$$

Suppose that labor is homogeneous and the marginal product of labor is equated to the real wage rate, l/v, across vintages. It can be shown that no vintages become economically obsolete so long as the latest vintage earns positive quasi-rents. Also, assuming the F is homogeneous to the first degree, it can be demonstrated that the marginal products of capital are in proportion to $A(\tau)$ regardless of the level of l/v. Hence, in our definition, capital is malleable even though capital stocks are distinguished by vintage. (35) is aggregated over vintages (Fisher, 1965) into

$$V(t) = F(J(t), L(t)) \tag{36}$$

where $V(t) = \sum_{\tau=t}^{-\infty} V_\tau(t)$, $L(t) = \sum_{\tau=t}^{-\infty} L_\tau(t)$, and

$$J(t) = \sum_{\tau=t}^{-\infty} A(\tau)I_{\tau}(t), \tag{37}$$

which is the efficiency-corrected capital stock introduced by Solow (1962). We can readily see that

$$R = J. \tag{38}$$

Thus, if quality change is attributed to individual vintages in aggregating, no residual is left over. Hence, K has to be defined conventionally by

$$K(t) = \sum_{\tau=t}^{-\infty} I_{\tau}(t). \tag{39}$$

So far, we have assumed that there is no problem in identifying capital goods in physical units. But how can we identify one unit of one vintage and an equal unit of another vintage? Apparently, the two vintages must be comparable in terms of physical specifications which are independent of actual performance differences. In other words, we assume the existence of a standard machine with unchanging specifications. If specifications change, we should be able to compare new specifications to old specifications through, say, hedonic price indexes. Quality change should not influence this comparison.[13]

The Vintage Effect and Bias in Total Factor Productivity

As we noted, the procedure of the preceding section works only when technical change is purely capital-augmenting. What happens when technical change is not of this type? Let us consider a special example.

There are two vintages of machines, α and β. Both are subject to fixed proportions. β is more efficient in the sense that

$$\left(\frac{V}{K}\right)_{\alpha} \leqq \left(\frac{V}{K}\right)_{\beta}, \quad \left(\frac{V}{L}\right)_{\alpha} \leqq \left(\frac{V}{L}\right)_{\beta}.$$

Let us assume that we know how to count these machines in common units. Initially, machines were type α only. But, later, β machines are

---

[13] This is Denison's Method 1 which counts machines by production cost (Denison, 1957). The difference of capital goods from consumer goods is that, for the latter, quality change is included in specifications.

added. Let the stock of machines be K_α in the base year and $K_\alpha + K_\beta$ in the current year. Note that we cannot employ the Divisia formula. Thus, we go to (20) to define quasi-rent productivity and compare the productivity of α alone and that of α and β together. For a given real wage rate l/v, the productivity ratio is given by

$$\frac{T'_{\alpha+\beta}}{T'_\alpha} = \frac{\dfrac{K_\alpha}{K_\alpha^+ + K_\beta}\left(\dfrac{V}{K}\right)_\alpha\left(1 - \dfrac{l}{V}\left(\dfrac{L}{V}\right)_\alpha\right) + \dfrac{K_\beta}{K_\alpha + K_\beta}\left(\dfrac{V}{K}\right)_\beta\left(1 - \dfrac{l}{v}\left(\dfrac{L}{V}\right)_\beta\right)}{\left(\dfrac{V}{K}\right)_\alpha\left(1 - \dfrac{l}{v}\left(\dfrac{L}{V}\right)_\alpha\right)}$$

$$= \frac{K_\alpha}{K_\alpha + K_\beta} + \frac{K_\beta}{K_\alpha + K_\beta}\frac{(V/K)_\beta}{(V/K)_\alpha}\frac{1 - \dfrac{l}{v}\left(\dfrac{L}{V}\right)_\beta}{1 - \dfrac{l}{v}\left(\dfrac{L}{V}\right)_\alpha}. \tag{40}$$

This ratio is independent of the prevailing prices if and only if $(V/L)_\alpha = (V/L)_\beta$, i.e., if the vintages differ only in their average capital productivity. This is the case of pure capital augmentation. In this special case, we get

$$\frac{T'_{\alpha+\beta}}{T'_\alpha} = \frac{K_\alpha}{K_\alpha + K_\beta} + \frac{K_\beta}{K_\alpha + K_\beta}\frac{(V/K)_\beta}{(V/K)_\alpha}\frac{1 - \dfrac{l}{v}\left(\dfrac{L}{V}\right)_\beta}{1 - \dfrac{l}{v}\left(\dfrac{L}{V}\right)_\alpha}, \tag{41}$$

which is greater than 1 as $(V/K)_\beta > (V/K)_\alpha$. It depends on the proportion of the two vintages in the machine population but not on l/v. This implies not only that α and β can be uniquely converted into common efficiency units, but also that quasi-rent productivities are unambiguously derived. Since quality change has to be separated from quantity change, we do not combine K_α and K_β in efficiency units. We simply assume that one machine of α is equal to one machine of β. Once this aggregation is completed, we have the capital input index. Hence, we can compute the Divisia index of total factor productivity from V/X since X can be obtained. Equivalently, we can apply (33) to convert T' into T. The two methods yield the same number.

The same point can be made in another way. Quasi-rent productivity is

$$\Pi = \frac{vV - lL}{K} = v\,\frac{L}{K}\left(\frac{V}{L} - \frac{l}{v}\right). \tag{42}$$

If $(V/L)_\alpha = (V/L)_\beta$, we always get

$$\Pi_\beta/\Pi_\alpha = (L/K)_\beta/(L/K)_\alpha > 1. \qquad (43)$$

Although vintage β is more efficient than α, the difference remains constant. In this case, Π_β/Π_α represents the quality change. If we use this as the conversion factor in constructing the capital stock, all the quality change is converted into quantity change and, as a result, technical change is eliminated. Thus, no valuation adjustment is made to different vintages.

Now, the question is what to do when the condition is not met. It is likely that the condition is not even approximated. The case above implies rising capital productivity, stationary labor productivity, and falling capital intensity in a growing industry. But the actual observation is more like stationary capital productivity, rising labor productivity, and rising capital intensity. Then, technical change must be predominantly labor-augmenting. Can we still employ the same procedure?

We have just noted that there are two alternative ways to arrive at total factor productivity. Since we already pointed out that there is no Divisia index of the capital inputs when capital is not malleable, we have to go through the quasi-rent productivity index to get to total factor productivity.

(40) shows that with $(V/L)_\alpha < (V/L)_\beta$, the quasi-rent productivity index increases as l/v is increased, even though there is no physical change in production. l/v tends to rise over time as productivity improves in the economy as a whole. Hence, the index tends to be understated in base-year prices and overstated in current-year prices. This implies that total factor productivity is also not unique in general.[14]

One can look at Π_β/Π_α. With $(V/L)_\alpha \neq (V/L)_\beta$, Π_β/Π_α is no longer constant. A rise in l/v implies that α loses its revenue productivity relative to β although its physical productivity is unchanged. This corresponds to nonconstancy of the marginal-products-of-capital ratios when factor proportions are variable. Hence, there is no way to construct an invariant efficiency-corrected capital input index. Put technically, the Divisia index is no longer unique.

Essentially, this nonuniqueness of the Divisia indexes (both T, T', and K) is no different from the nonuniqueness of all other index numbers. The fact that T' depends on which year is used as the base is analogous to the Laspeyres and Paasche indexes of the cost-of-living index. In such instances, one takes some average of the two, say, Fisher's ideal index, in the hope of approximating the "true" index (even

---

[14] In a vintage model, Hicks neutrality no longer ensures the uniqueness of T.

though there is no unique true index). In the present instance, we have argued that the quasi-rent productivity index understates weights in the base year and overstates weights in the current year.

By analogy, we may take their geometric mean as an approximation to the Divisia index of T'. From this index, we can then estimate total factor productivity T by means of (5.3). We think that this is the most we can do where capital is nonmalleable.

As far as I know, this procedure has never been employed in computing total factor productivity (apart from its feasibility). All studies of total factor productivity depend on the conventionally measured capital input index. Since the deterioration of the earning capacity of old vintages, i.e., economic obsolescence, is not taken into account, the growth rate of the capital input index tends to be overestimated. We can readily see that this results in the underestimation of total productivity growth. The more biased technical change is toward labor-augmentation and the more rapid technical change is, the faster vintages become obsolete (i.e., lose quasi-rent productivity), and, hence, the more understated total factor productivity growth is in the conventional method.[15] This underestimation can be sizable as indicated by the numerical example given in the Appendix. Since technical change is likely to be predominantly labor-augmenting, we must expect a considerable underestimation of total factor productivity growth.

We note that this bias is in addition to the non-uniqueness of T when technical change is not Hicks-neutral in a macro value-added production function in which the capital input index appears (assuming, implicitly, capital malleability) (Nelson, 1973; Usher, 1974).

Macro Production Functions

We have examined the concepts of real value added, real quasi-rents, quasi-rent productivity, and total factor productivity. Our analysis is based on the major premise of the equality of the marginal products and real prices of factor inputs that are to be deducted from gross output. When the premise is not satisfied, subsequent measurements run aground.

---

[15] It may be argued that this underestimation is removed because the depreciation rate takes into account gradual economic obsolescence. This is probably so in a steady state in which the bias and rate of technical change remains stationary. But as they are not constant out of the steady state, we cannot completely eliminate the problem.

Marginal productivity theory has been under attack for some time, but we may point out that our analysis is immune from such attacks. We are not assuming that there is a simple macro production function with a nice property of differentiability. We only use it in our exposition to simplify our analysis. To make the point clear, imagine that our industry consists of many basic production units characterized by fixed factor proportions. Marginal products are undefinable for them. How do these units decide on production? They employ their capacity for production so long as they can earn non-negative quasi-rents. The marginal unit has zero quasi-rents.[16] Now suppose that an input price has risen. The marginal unit is losing money and goes out of business. At the margin, the marginal cost of this input and marginal revenue are equated. Therefore, for the industry as a whole, the marginal product of this input seems to be equated to its real price. In other words, even though we cannot define marginal productivity, we can still proceed as if the marginal productivity condition holds at the industry level so long as individual firms are rational in the short run. The macro production function which we employed is simply a shorthand way to express this relation.

In constructing Divisia or any other index numbers, however, we have to make a considerably stronger assumption. We have to compare two different time points, however close they may be. If we look carefully at our analysis, we notice that we implicitly assume that the macro production function remains "invariant". If the production function changes its shape between the two time points,[17] we lose continuity and the Divisia index is based on the continuity assumption. One might emphasize the stringency of maintaining the invariance of the macro production function.[18] However, on second thought, this is not really an insurmountable obstacle. Consider one source of shifts in the macro production function, namely, shifts in the efficiency distribution of firms in the industry. It is shown that the macro production function is invariant if and only if this distribution is invariant in its relative form (Sato, 1975). For instance, if more efficient firms increase their market shares, the macro production function changes its shape. This may seem to invalidate our analysis. But what we have to do is to account for the effect of resource shifts from less efficient to more efficient firms.

---

[16] Hence, quasi-rents are the vital decision variable. It is also for this reason that value added should be gross of capital consumption allowances.

[17] Technical change must be restricted to factor-augmenting types in order to keep the macro production function invariant in our sense.

[18] The condition is derived in (Sato, 1975). The necessity of the invariance of the macro production function is noted by Nadiri (1970: 1163).

When this is done, what remains refers to the macro production function which remains invariant by this adjustment.[19] The current procedure for deriving total factor productivity does not pay much attention to this aspect except for interindustry resource shifts. But, given sufficiently detailed data, this adjustment can be incorporated.

The macro production function that provides the basis for our analysis is an ex post function since capital stocks are already in existence even though we look at their changes over time. Nowhere in our analysis is there an explicit ex ante production function. This is both an advantage and a disadvantage.

It is an advantage because our analysis has nothing to do with the capital-theory controversy of the 1960s. Among other things, the controversy was concerned with the existence of a well-behaved aggregate production function in which capital can be uniquely divided between quantity and price. The well-known reswitching phenomenon was presented as *prima facie* support for the nonexistence of the aggregate production function. This, however, is a complete red herring as far as growth accounting is concerned. The typical capital-theoretic model is that of a static general equilibrium in which there is no distinction made between the ex ante and the ex post. The existence or nonexistence of an aggregate production function in this framework has nothing to do with our purely ex post macro production function.[20]

The disadvantage is that we cannot estimate an ex ante production function from time-series data. All that the macroeconometrician can do is to estimate ex post functions (this does not apply to cross-section production functions). There is a mistaken notion that *ex ante* functions are estimated from time series.

Concluding Remarks

In this paper we have examined a number of theoretical issues in real production accounting. Our step-by-step approach indicates that real value added, real quasi-rents, and total factor productivity are all members of the same genus. The conditions required for their conceptual validity or their uniqueness are of exactly the same type.

---

[19] This view is presented in contrast to Fisher (1969) who argues that there is no aggregate production function when the capital-augmentation condition is violated.

[20] The literature is confused on this point. See, *e.g.*, Rymes (1971) and Harcourt (1972), who reject the concept of total factor productivity. We also note that our own production function does not require factor substitutability along an ex ante production function, to which many economists object (Robinson, 1975; Hicks, 1975).

First, we take the concept of real value added. This is gross output less the contribution of intermediate inputs evaluated by their respective marginal products which are assumed to be equal to their real prices. Despite various critical comments on the concept, we argue that it is perfectly valid as an analytical concept. We show that its sometimes perverse behavior in the Laspeyres form vanishes in the theoretically desirable Divisia form. We note that no equilibrium assumption is made as to primary inputs, not even their measurability. This is one of the most important advantages of real value added.

We then move on to the concept of real quasi-rent which is gross output less the contribution of variable inputs or, equivalently, value added less the contribution of labor inputs, assuming that the marginal product of labor inputs are equated to their real wage rates. This concept is completely analogous to real value added although it does not seem to be emphasized in the literature. We note that it is a useful concept, in particular when we come to the problem of measurement of capital inputs.

Next, we treat total factor productivity, which forms the basis of growth accounting. Total factor productivity is again an extension of real value added in that it is gross output less all tangible inputs. Hence, it measures the contribution of intangible inputs, namely, economies of scale and technical change. The marginal productivity condition must hold for all tangible inputs including capital inputs. It is also observed that total factor productivity may alternatively be measured as the ratio of the real value added index to the primary input index. The most serious problem involved in measuring total factor productivity is how to reduce heterogeneous capital inputs into common units. Apart from the hypothetical case of capital malleability (which is extended to the case of capital-augmenting putty-putty vintages), it is impossible to obtain a convenient capital aggregate.

In this connection, quasi-rent productivity is suggested as a concept worth looking into. In the particular context of a vintage model, a proper procedure, it is suggested, is to aggregate heterogeneous capital goods with their relative quasi-rent productivities as weights. Except for the capital-augmenting case, these weights are not independent of the prevailing real wage rate. Hence, the resulting index of total factor productivity is not unique. However, one can look at it as a variant of the usual nonuniqueness of index numbers under nonhomothetic preferences. The Appendix gives a numerical exercise to clarify some of these points.

Finally, it is pointed out that all these measurement exercises assume the invariance of the macro production function. Although the macro production function is not likely to remain invariant over time, an approximate compensation can be seen in intra-industry resource shifts.

Appendix: Biases in Total Factor Productivity in the Vintage Context—A Numerical Example

Following the discussion in section 6, assume that there exist two vintages. The initial vintage is α. Three versions of the later vintage β are considered corresponding to Hicks neutrality ($\beta 1$), labor augmentation ($\beta 2$), and capital augmentation ($\beta 3$). Fixed proportions are assumed. Their specifications are given in Table 1. (The specifications of α and $\beta 1$ are those used by Denison (1957) in his numerical example.) At time 0, there are 20 machines of vintage α. At time 1, 10 machines of vintage β are added. Therefore, the conventional capital stock is 30 machines. Let l/v be 1/2 in the base year and 1 in the current year. We can compute quasi-rent productivity index T_1'/T_0' in base-year and current-year prices, respectively, by applying the formula (40). We compute their geometric mean as our final index. To derive total factor productivity index T_1/T_0, we apply the formula

$$\ln T_1/T_0 = \tfrac{1}{2}(\nu_0 + \nu_1) \ln T_1'/T_0', \qquad (A.1)$$

which is an approximation to the Divisia index where ν_t is the ratio of

Table 1. Hypothetical Specifications

(A) Specifications

Vintage	L/K	V/K	V/L
α	3	4	4/3
β_1 Hicks-neutral	3	8	8/3
β_2 L-augmenting	3/2	4	8/3
β_3 K-augmenting	6	8	4/3

(B) Quantities

Time	Vintage	K	L	V
0	α	20	60	80
	β_1	10	30	80
	β_2	10	15	40
	β_3	10	60	80
1	$\alpha + \beta_1$	30	90	160
	$\alpha + \beta_2$	30	75	120
	$\alpha + \beta_3$	30	120	160

quasi-rents to value added in time i. The result is given in col. (6) of Table 2.

Table 2. Quasi-rent and Total Factor Productivity

Case	l/v	$1 - v = lL/vV$		T'_1/T'_0		T_1/T_0	T_1/T_0		Bias
		0	1						
	(1)	(2)	(3)	(4)	(5)	(6)	(7)	(8)	(9)
$\alpha + \beta 1$	1/2	12/32	9/32	1.533	1.891	1.403	1.333	1.333	1.209
	1	24/32	18/32	2.333			1.333		
$\alpha + \beta 2$	1/2	12/32	10/32	1.100	1.284	1.133	1.121	1.095	1.398
	1	24/32	20/32	1.500			1.071		
$\alpha + \beta 3$	1/2	12/32	12/32	1.333	1.333	1.134	1.197	1.134	1.000
	1	24/32	24/32	1.333			1.075		
$\alpha + \beta 2$	5/6	20/32	12/32	1.278	1.385	1.130	1.073	1.073	1.783
	1	24/32	20/32	1.500			1.073		

(4): fixed weights.
(5): geometric mean.
(6): computed by (A.1).
(7): computed by (A.2), fixed weights.
(8): computed by (A.2), average weights.
(9): ((6)–1)/((8)–1).

An alternative is to compute the primary input index X_1/X_0 and then derive T_1/T_0 as $(V_1/V_0)/(X_1/X_0)$. This is the conventional method. Analogous to arithmetic indexes, we compute

$$\ln X_1/X_0 = \begin{cases} v_0 \ln K_1/K_0 + (1 - v_0)\ln L_1/L_0 \text{ (base-year weights)} \\ v_1 \ln K_1/K_0 + (1 - v_1)\ln L_1/L_0 \text{ (current-year weights)} \quad (A.2) \\ v \ln K_1 K/_0 + (1 - v)\ln L_1/L_0 \text{ (average weights)} \end{cases}$$

where $v = \frac{1}{2}(v_0 + v_1)$. The three values of T_1/T_0 corresponding to (A.2) are given in col. (7) and (8) of Table 2. The results can be summarized as follows:

(i) T'_1/T'_0 (unique in $\beta 3$ (capital-augmentation)). In other cases, the spread between the Laspeyres and the Paasche indexes is quite substantial; the Paasche figures exceed the Laspeyres.

(ii) T_1/T_0 (conventional). In $\beta 1$, $K_1/K_0 = L_1/L_0 = 3/2$. Hence, T_1/T_0 is unique regardless of l/v. In other cases, the Laspeyres figures exceed the Paasche values. Fisher's log-change index figures lie in between and are an approximation to the Divisia index.

(iii) T_1/T_0 (alternative). This coincides with the conventional index in $\beta 3$. In other cases, the conventional index understates. The ratio of the two $(T_1/T_0 - 1)$ increases with the tendency towards labor-augmenting technical change (col. (9), Table 2).

Empirically, the factor shares are stable. In the $\beta 2$ case, this results if l/v is 5/6 in the base year and 1 in the current year. We make the same computation and find that the Laspeyres and the Paasche index of T_1/T_0 (conventional) coincide; the alternative index is understated by a wide margin.

References

Arrow, K. J. "The Measurement of Real Value Added," in David, P. A., and Reder, M. W. (eds.), *Nations and Households in Economic Growth*. New York, 1974.

Berndt, E. R., and Christensen, L. R. "The Internal Structure and Functional Relationships: Separability, Substitution, and Aggregation," *Review of Economic Studies*, July 1973.

Christensen, L. R., and Jorgenson, D. W. "The Measurement of U.S. Real Capital Input, 1929–1967," *Review of Income and Wealth*, December 1969.

Christensen, L. R., and Jorgenson, D. W. "U.S. Real Product and Real Factor Input, 1929–1967," *Review of Income and Wealth*, March 1970.

David, P. "Measuring Real Net Output: A Proposed Index," *Review of Economics and Statistics*, November 1966.

Denison, E. F. "Theoretical Aspects of Quality Change, Capital Consumption, and Net Capital Formation," in *Studies in Income and Wealth, Problems of Capital Formation*, Vol. 19, Princeton, 1957.

Fenoaltea, S. "Real Value Added and the Measurement of Industrial Production," *"Annals of Economic and Social Measurement*, Winter 1976.

Fisher, F. M. "Embodied Technical Change and the Existence of an Aggregate Capital Stock," *Review of Economic Studies*, October 1965.

Fisher, F. M. "The Existence of Aggregate Production Functions," *Econometrica*, October 1969.

Harcourt, G. C. *Some Cambridge Controversies in the Theory of Capital*. London, 1972.

Hicks, J. R. "Revival of Political Economy: The Old and The New," *Economic Record*, September 1975.

Kendrick, J. W. "Introduction," in *Studies in Income and Wealth, Output, Input, and Productivity Measurement*, Vol. 25. Princeton, 1961.

Kendrick, J. W. *Productivity Trends in the United States*. Princeton, 1961.

Kravis, I. B., *et al. A System of International Comparisons of Gross Product and Purchasing Power*. Baltimore, 1975.

Nadiri, M. I. "Some Approaches to the Theory of Measurement of Total Factor Productivity: A Survey," *Journal of Economic Literature*, December 1970.

Nelson, R. R. "Recent Exercises in Growth Accounting: New Understanding or Dead End?" *American Economic Review*, June 1973.

Robinson, J. "The Unimportance of Reswitching," *Quarterly Journal of Economics*, February 1975.

Rymes, T. K. *On Concepts of Capital and Technical Change*. London, 1971.

Sato, K. *Production Functions and Aggregation*. Amsterdam, 1975.

Sato, K. "The Meaning and Measurement of the Real Value Added Index," *Review of Economics and Statistics*, November 1976.

Solow, R. M. "Technological Change and the Aggregate Production Function," *Review of Economics and Statistics*, August 1957.

Solow, R. M. "Technical Progress, Capital Formation, and Economic Growth," *American Economic Review*, May 1962.

Usher, D. "The Suitability of the Divisia Index for the Measurement of Economic Aggregates," *Review of Income and Wealth*, September 1974.

Appendix to Part I: Changes in the United Nations System of National Accounts

Yutaka Shimizu

The main impetus for the development of the System of National Accounts was the practical need for information about the working of the economic system as a whole and the way in which its various parts are related to one another. The practical need arose mainly from the great depression of the 1930s and the subsequent problems of economic mobilization and war finance raised by the Second World War. In the postwar period, the information was desired in order to throw light on problems of economic reconstruction and development or to assess economic change as a background for economic decision-making in connection with public policy.

The system was adopted largely by the developed countries at the beginning of the postwar period. However, as time passed, newly developing countries began to use the System as well. Extension of the coverage of estimates and improvement of its statistical reliability were rapid. As a result the System of National Accounts was able to contribute to the formulation of development policies by governments and at the same time to provide systematic knowledge about the development process.

The United Nations introduced the original System of National Accounts and Supporting Tables in 1953. It provided a coherent framework for recording and presenting data related to production, consumption, capital formation, and external trade in six areas or sectors of a nation's economy: (i) domestic production; (ii) national income; (iii) domestic capital formation; (iv) households and private non-profit institutions; (v) general government; and (vi) external transactions. Accounts for the last three sectors are divided into current and capital reconciliation accounts employing the savings figures obtained as a residual of current revenue (or receipts) and disbursements of individual income accounts.

The United Nations system also prescribed eleven supporting areas for data collection:

1. Expenditure on gross national product
2. Industrial origin of gross domestic product at factor cost
3. National income by type of organization
4. Distribution of the national income
5. The finance of gross domestic capital formation
6. Composition of gross domestic capital formation
7. Receipts and expenditure of households and private non-profit institutions
8. Composition of private consumption expenditure
9. General government revenue and expenditure
10. Composition of general government consumption expenditure
11. International transactions

This system was intended essentially to set out as clearly and concisely as possible a framework within which statistical information could be used to analyze the economic process comprehensively against the background of Keynesian theory.

With the passage of time more and more detail was added and simple aggregates were divided in order to meet the growing needs of economic analysis. More attention was given to estimates at constant prices and to expressing the main product flows and their components in these terms. Input-output studies (which subdivide production accounts to display the commodity flows between industries) and flow-of-funds tables (which show the flows of financial claims that enable the surplus savings of some groups of financing units to provide the funds needed by sectors whose capital expenditure exceeds their savings) were developed side by side in many countries. Construction of national and sector balance sheets was begun in several countries, and in a few cases complete systems of sector balance sheets were set up.

In addition, the construction of disaggregated models began as an aid to economic analysis and policy-making; at the same time, highly aggregated models were constructed using as their principal variables the main aggregates in the national accounts: output, consumption, saving, investment, etc. For many types of analysis and policy-making, it was not sufficient to work with aggregates alone; it was also necessary to look at many aspects of an economic system in greater detail.

Taking into account these changes, the United Nations introduced a second, revised System of National Accounts (Studies in Methods Series F No. 2, Rev. 3) in 1968; it integrated the original national accounts, input-output tables, flow-of-funds tables, balance of payment tables, and national balance sheets. This new system will here be called the Revised System of National Accounts. Its standard components are as follows:

I. Consolidated Accounts for the Nation
1. Gross domestic product and expenditure
2. National disposable income and its appropriation
3. Capital finance
4. All accounts-external transactions

II. Production, Consumption Expenditure, and Capital Formation Accounts
1. Commodities (to be prepared on an industry basis)
2. Other goods and services (to be prepared by government, private non-profit institutions, and households)
3. Industries (to be prepared on a commodity basis)
4. Producers of government services
5. Producers of private non-profit institutions
6. Domestic services of households

III. Income and Outlay and Capital Finance Accounts
1. Non-financial enterprises, corporate and quasi-corporate
2. Financial institutions
3. General government
4. Private non-profit institutions
5. Households, including private unincorporated non-financial enterprises

The expansion of the system naturally highlighted the structural as well as conceptual differences between the revised and the original System of National Accounts. An OECD publication[1] analyzes the discrepancies in detail.

Characteristics of the Revised System

The original system was basically the National Income accounts plus part of the balance of payments accounts. The revised system incorporated three other accounts and the entire balance of payments into the system. The revised system thus covers the commodity and monetary flows of a nation as well as its stock. The input-output tables and flow-of-funds accounts have been integrated on the basis of more specific

[1] OECD, *The Present System of National Accounts and Reconciliation Tables to the Previous Systems of National Accounts* (DES/NI/69.1), fourth revision, December 1972.

concepts, thus requiring a great deal of reformulation of the definitions used in the original system.

The revised system has introduced far more advanced functional classification. For instance, in the original system, the household sector was treated as a consuming sector (except for owner-occupied dwellings), together with private non-profit institutions. In the revised system, household activities are divided into consuming activities and enterprise (producing) activities. Private non-profit institutions have also been separated from the household sector; those mainly financed and operated by the government have been transferred to the government sector, and those serving households and mainly financed by the household sector and operated by households have been treated as an independent sector. The services produced by these institutions have been included in the commodity sector, and their operating surpluses have been registered under the functional classification accounts.

The basic features of the revised SNA can be summarized as follows:

1) The production accounts have been prepared on the basis of the nation as a whole, industries, producers of government services, private non-profit institutions serving households, and domestic services.

2) Consumption expenditure accounts have been prepared on the basis of government, private non-profit institutions serving households, and households.

3) Capital formation accounts have been prepared, by excluding household services, for each of the sectors which has a production account.

4) Income and outlay accounts have been prepared on the basis of the nation as a whole, non-financial enterprises, and quasi-corporate enterprises (defined as relatively large ordinary partnerships, sole proprietorships, and government enterprises which have complete profit-and-loss statements and complete balance sheet accounts on financial assets and liabilities as well as the real assets involved in the business; includes all unincorporated enterprises owned by non-residents), financial institutions, general government, private non-profit institutions serving households, and households (including non-corporate non-financial enterprises).

5) Capital finance accounts are also compiled with the same sector units shown in income and outlay accounts.

6) An external transaction account is prepared covering transactions with all other countries.

Production accounts, consumption accounts, and capital formation accounts are prepared on the basis of resident transactors in connection with commodity supplies and their uses. In the case of income and out-lay accounts and capital finance accounts, resident transactors have been classified on an institutional basis.

Another new feature of the revised system is that it recommends the use of the matrix form as the tabulation system. One advantage of this system is that within the closed system, each accounting item can be expressed in one figure; in the original SNA, a double entry-system, two identical figures were needed for the compilation of an account. A second advantage of the matrix form is that different transactors can be used in rows and columns. The use of commodity accounts by in-dustry in rows and activity accounts by commodity in columns in the production account is a good example of this type of matrix use. A third advantage is that two or more commodities produced by the same company will not be "mis-classified" under the dominant product of the industry.

Many more differences can be pointed out between the original system and the revised system. One major one is the difference in coverage of indirect taxes, and aonther is the treatment of imputed financial intermediary services.

In the original system indirect taxes are defined as follows: "When paid by businesses, indirect taxes are those chargeable to business ex-penses; when paid by private individuals, these taxes are those not levied regularly on income or wealth, and in the assessment of which no account is taken of the personal circumstances of the taxpayer." In the revised system, it is defined as only "those taxes assessed on producers in respect of the production, sale, purchase or use of goods and services which they charge to the expenses of production. Also included are import duties and the operating surplus, reduced by the normal margin of profit of business units and of fiscal and similar monopolies of government."

Although the method of calculating the imputed service charges of financial institutions (banks, life insurance companies, pension funds, etc.) remains the same, in the revised system these service charges have been treated as intermediary expenditure between financial institutions and enterprises.

Transition to the Revised System

More than a decade has passed since the United Nations introduced the Revised System of National Accounts. The new system has had a very wide impact both on the statistical agencies of various nations and on users of the national accounts. For the national accounts–compiling authorities, it was almost impossible to study the new system without referring to the old one. However, United Nations publications offered almost no information on ways of shifting from the original system to the revised one. Naturally confusion occurred among statistical agencies.

The problem was especially serious for statisticians in developing countries. Although one short chapter entitled "Adaptation of the Full System to the Developing Countries" was included in the original UN publication, modifying some aspects of the system, for most of the developing countries, which had finally mastered the old system after a hard struggle, it was almost impossible to adopt the revised system at once.

Even the developed countries had to study hard to introduce the new system. Japan switched over to the new system only in the fall of 1978. India has also moved into the revised system. Malaysia began in 1969 to make estimates on the basis of the new system. However, all the other countries in Asia are still compiling national accounts in conformity with the old system.

The United Nations has been well aware that universal adoption of the revised SNA will take time. Because of the difficulties many countries are experiencing in adopting the matrix form, for example, the UN has not been requiring that its questionnaires be completed in matrix form and has continued to accept data in double-entry as well as matrix form.

A review of the revised system has been going on[2]; examination of the experiences of various countries suggests that the introduction of the revised system might be facilitated by eliminating the distinction between quasi-corporate and other unincorporated enterprises and by better integrating the revised matrix with the accounts and tables of the basic system.

In any case, however, almost another decade will be needed before we can expect to see the internationally comparable data which were the aim of the international organization from the beginning.

---

[2] For example, J. W. van Tongeren, "A Review of Selected Aspects of the United Nations System of National Accounts in the Light of Countries' Experience," in *The Review of Income and Wealth* (Income and Wealth Series 25, Number 2), June 1979.

PART II

Measurement of Social Development

Micro-data Sets for the Measurement of a Socioeconomic Statistical System

Yoshimasa Kurabayashi

The vast and sweeping changes in both economic and social structures that most industrialized societies have experienced over the past decade demand fresh and plentiful statistical information, both economic and social, in order to review empirical studies of these changes and to structure appropriate policy responses.* The government statistical agencies and research institutions of industrialized societies are eager to collect, compile, and analyze the necessary statistics that respond to the issues. Their efforts have not resulted in a hotch-potch of scattered information. On the contrary, it is not difficult to discern a common characteristic underlying the attempts at collecting and compiling a coherent set of statistical information for the measurement of economic and social performance in the various societies.

As the social and economic activities in an industrialized society are closely interwoven, it is necessary for the statistical system to be designed to mutually interconnect these components. A few examples deserve to be noted in this connection. First, the United Nations proposal for a System of Social and Demographic Statistics, SSDS for short, exactly makes the point at issue, contending that its purpose is to provide a connected information system for social and demographic statistics

* This paper is a revised version of the paper presented to the Second Asian Regional Conference of IARIW under the title "A Socioeconomic Statistical System for Measuring a Society's Social and Economic Performance." The revision is based on the comments of the discussant of the paper and other participants. In particular, I am indebted to Professor M. Mukherjee, who acted as chairman of the session to which the original version of the paper was presented, for his helpful comments and encouragement. Comments from the discussant and other participants are acknowledged with the author's hearty thanks. Needless to say, the remaining shortcomings are the author's own.

which will be useful for description, analysis, and policy making in different fields of social life.[1] A second approach is the project that has been undertaken by the National Bureau of Economic Research under the guidance of Professor Richard Ruggles of Yale University. The methodology of the project emphasizes the direct relating of social indicators and social statistics to the national economic accounts, insisting that the hard core of the problem is the linkage between economic and social information.[2]

This article will discuss a synthetic approach to the measurement of economic and social performance in industrial societies, paying close attention to the economic and social conditions of Japan. The approach claims to be synthetic in the sense that it attempts to reach a synthesis between the United Nations system and the National Bureau of Economic Research project. Our approach and the United Nations system have in common the idea that a mutually connected system is basic for effective data collection and compilation. Our approach and the National Bureau of Economic Research project share a central concern with the building of a synthetic micro-data base to serve as the link between the social and economic data.

Design of a Socioeconomic Statistical System

In light of the inseparable connection between social and economic systems and the urgency of the issues confronting social scientists in industrialized societies, the time has come to design a system of collecting, classifying, and processing social statistics. This system should be comprehensive and coherent and at the same time parallel to a system of national accounts which provides an appropriate basis for the collection, classification, and processing of economic data. In what follows the system is referred to as a system of socioeconomic statistics, SSES for short, taking into account the fact that such a system of social statistics is closely interrelated with relevant economic statistics.

The structure of SSES is designed for sorting out the profile of social and community life in a society: basic activities in social and community

---

[1] In particular, see (United Nations, 1975).
[2] The research project has its origin in the 1971 Conference on the Measurement of Economic and Social Performance held at Princeton University under the joint sponsorship of the University's Department of Economics and the NBER (National Bureau of Economic Research) conference on Research in Income and Wealth. The scope and aim of the Conference are summarized in the introductory article by Moss (1973)

life together with the structure and changes in population and the structure and changes in manpower. The basic activities consist of the primary, secondary, and tertiary activities in social and community life. The primary activities are those which are necessary to meet the minimum necessities of subsistence such as sleeping and eating. The secondary activities encompass those which refer to learning and earning. The tertiary activities in social and community life are particularly important in industrialized societies, because they constitute those activities which arise from the growing increase in leisure hours, including recreational, cultural, and sporting activities. As Johan Huizinga once put it in his play-concept in culture, the culture of any society finds its completion and sophistication in the form of liberal disposal of leisure hours.[3]

The spectra of social and community life are closely associated with the structure of and changes in population, on the one hand, and those of manpower on the other. It is readily seen that the structure of and changes in population are basically dependent on the primary activities in social and community life. The structure of and changes in manpower are directly influenced by the secondary activities but the indirect effects of tertiary activity should not be ignored. Also, it is important that the spectra of social and community life not be isolated from several important social factors such as the effects of urbanization, the formation and composition of family and housing, and other living conditions which are in the social environment and protected by the public order. Moreover, the spectra of social and community life in contemporary industrialized society cannot be absolutely immune from the ecology of material flow which is the unavoidable product of brisk economic activity. The deterioration of the quality of life has drawn growing attention in industrialized societies over the past decade.[4]

The structure of SSES is illustrated in Figure 1. where the spectra of social and community life are arranged vertically beginning with the structure of and changes in population, which are placed in the upper panel, succeeded by the structure of and changes in manpower and basic activities. The following five dimensions of measurement can be distinguished in the diagram: (1) the framework of national accounts,

[3] The historical as well as cultural aspects of this point have been emphasized by Huizinga, whose work (1955) gives deep insight into the aspects of the play-concept in human life history.
[4] It should be noted that the SSES is closely associated with the balance of material flow with which its supply and disposition are concerned. Its design is not touched upon here.

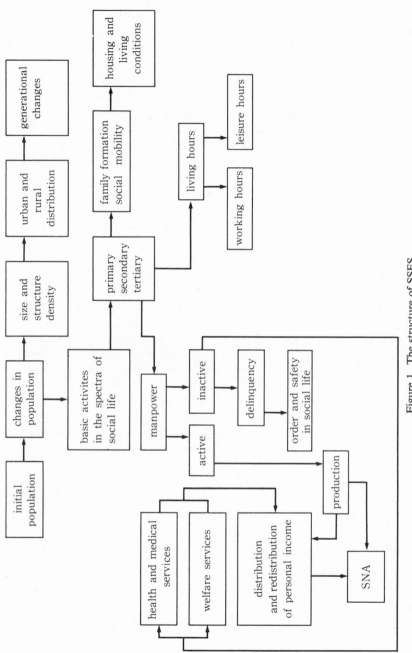

Figure 1. The structure of SSES

(2) the framework of demographic accounting, (3) the manpower balance, (4) time budgets, and (5) the system of social indicators. In what follows brief comments will be offered on the component dimensions of measurement.

Because SNA reference publications are widely available, it is not necessary to say much more about the framework of national accounts. The framework of demographic accounting is designed to illustrate the structure of and changes in population which are governed by such demographic factors as birth, death, and fertility rates as well as social factors like urbanization and housing conditions. Utilizing the framework of demographic accounting, it is possible to construct a variety of Markovian stochastic models for explaining changes in population flow, as the United Nations report has done. The manpower balance sheds fresh light on the important events of the secondary activity in the spectra of social and community life. Of particular note here is the fact that the advancement of education, both in breadth and in depth, substantially contributes to the quality of manpower and its earning capacity, which in turn govern the structure of and changes in manpower. Owing to the growing increase of leisure arising from the shortening of working hours in industrialized countries, considerable attention has recently been devoted to the allocation of living hours into working and leisure periods. In particular, the diversified and multiform uses of growing leisure time must constitute one of the most important aspects in the spectra of social and community life in post-industrial societies. In the following section these phenomena will be dealt with by emphasizing the design of a data base that is appropriate for the quantitative analysis of time budgets. The so-called "social indicators movement" has been one of the major developments in statistical analysis since the end of the 1960s. These measures are relevant for providing a measuring rod for social activities where it is not always easy to find a common and unified unit of measurement. Each social indicator tends to become individualized in the sense that it is connected with only a particular aspect of social activity and disregards the inextricable interrelation between activities. Thus, the system of social indicators acquires a special significance in the measurement dimensions of SSES for supplementing other component dimensions.[5]

Having briefly reviewed the component dimensions of measurement in SSES, we must again return to the framework of the national

---

[5] An attempt to develop the measurement of social indicators has been made by the Economic Planning Agency, Government of Japan. See, in particular, (Economic Planning Agency, 1974).

accounts. Undoubtedly, the primary purpose of the framework of national accounts is to collect, compile, and process economic data in a coherent and unified system. The framework of national accounts is especially relevant to the measurement aspects of the SSES because the production and formation of income and its distribution (both of which form the basic activities in the economy) are closely associated with the secondary activity in the spectra of social and community life as well as the structure of and change in manpower. A detailed system of the distribution of income and wealth that furnishes information concerning the distribution of personal income and wealth proves to be essential not only for the analysis of economic inequality, but also for the clarification of social justice. In this regard, it should be noted that the dynamics of manpower balance exercises a strong effect on the personal distribution of income and wealth.[6]

The Basic Survey of Social and Community Life as a Data Base

In the foregoing section we have discussed in some detail the structure of a socioeconomic statistical system that is proposed for measuring a society's social and economic performance. In this section we shall turn our attention to the measurement of SSES, taking into consideration the usefulness of establishing a data base for measurement. To this end, we shall utilize the "Basic Survey of Social and Community Life" (initiated and carried out by the Bureau of Statistics, Office of the Prime Minister) as an effective data base for the measurement of SSES with the intention of providing appropriate information for structuring social and community life.[7] Before we proceed to the measurement of SSES, a few remarks should be made concerning the nature and significance of a data base for the collection, compilation, processing, and storage of statistical information.

A data base structured on micro-economic units such as individuals,

[6] The development of a detailed statistical system of the distribution of income, consumption, and wealth has long been one of the major concerns of expert national income statisticians who have cooperated with the development of SNA; one attempt can be seen in (United Nations, 1972). This attempt especially attracts our attention because it paves the way for structuring a new system of micro-economic accounting essential for the measurement of economic inequality and justice. In this respect the necessity of a system of micro-economic accounting has also been referred to by Benard in his incisive work (1972).

[7] The first part of the Survey was carried out in the week beginning October 17, 1976. Partial results of the Survey are available, but many of the detailed results are still being compiled and processed.

households, and business establishments offers great potential not only for empirical studies of the economic and social behavior of these units, but also for a wide variety of applications for the linkage of social and economic data. When statistical surveys (including censuses) have been used for economic analysis, the data have often been compiled to emphasize vertical divisions according to different categories (*i.e.,* classes) and subcategories and often displayed in summary tables according to one- or two-way classifications. The construction of micro-data bases differs from this traditional approach, and the growing importance and potential of a micro-economic data base in the compilation of economic statistics has earned wide recognition for several reasons.[8]

First, the micro-data bases refer to a set of statistical information for separate and distinguishable agents, *e.g.* business establishments, government agencies, households, and private non-profit institutions. Second, it is important to recognize that the micro-data sets are produced from the amalgamation and integration of different statistical sources. Statistical data for separate agents generated from different statistical sources are merged into the micro-data bases with the help of the technique of data matching whose development is essentially owed to the potential of high-powered computers. Third, the collection, processing, storage, and retrieval of statistical information can be carried out on a consistent and systematic basis, which is of critical importance in obtaining statistical information cross-classified by multi-dimensional attributes. Fourth, it is worth noting that the multi-dimensional character of statistical data in the micro-data sets is of great importance for the compilation of social data. The construction of the micro-data sets is perhaps the most powerful apparatus for incorporating the social data into an integrated set of statistical information.

A data base is a device for the entering and processing of data in a computer system to perform various functions via a sequence of controlled computations. Data are organized within a data-base in units called files. Basically, a set of files consists of the following three bodies for the collection of statistical figures and other sources of information, both numerical and non-numerical: (i) the descriptor of files, (ii) the key directory, and (iii) filed data. The *descriptor of files* contains a set of information which describes the general characteristics of statistical

---

[8] The role of micro-data sets in the framework of national economic and social accounts has been taken up by Richard Ruggles and Nancy Ruggles in their joint work (1975). It is interesting to note that their idea to develop micro-data sets is closely associated with the design of micro-economic accounting proposed by Benard (1972).

figures stored in the files and can be drawn upon for the sequence of data processing and computation. It is often the case that the characteristics of statistical figures entered in the descriptor of files are supplemented by a set of information called the *key directory* which ensures the efficient enumeration and compilation of data characteristics. A set of information recorded in the form of data files is called *filed data* and constitutes one of the core components of a data-base. The structure of a set of files may be constituted by sequential files in which the filed data are essentially listed linearly, but if the amounts of information contained in a set of files are sufficiently large then a form of randomized files may be effective.[9]

The chief objectives of the Basic Survey of Social and Community Life (hereafter SSCL) are to collect statistical information concerning the basic activities in the spectra of social and community life in order to meet the growing concern in industrialized societies over the quality of social and community life. The 1976 SSCL was the first survey of its kind in Japan. The *Manual* prepared for the Survey states that the Survey will represent the communities' responses and the people's demands in the area of the basic activities, taking account of such social changes as the dawn of "the old-age society", the dominance of the nuclear family, the shortening of working hours, and changes in occupational structure. Such information is indispensable for policy making that gives priority to the promotion of adult and lifelong education, the improvement of welfare for workers, and the provision and upkeep of public facilities in local communities such as parks, athletic fields, libraries, museums, theaters, and orchestras. The SSCL is focused on both the individual and the household to which each individual belongs; about 75,000 sample households were chosen from 350 survey districts prescribed for Japan by the Bureau of Statistics on the basis of the 1975 Census of Population. The samples include resident foreigners, but exclude official diplomatic and consular representatives and members of the armed forces of a foreign country who are stationed in Japan.

The contents of SSCL are structured in a matrix form which is displayed in Table 1. In the matrix, rows are classified according to the basic activities in the spectra of social and community life, which consist of primary, secondary, and tertiary activities. These three basic activities are further subdivided: primary activity consists of (I.1) domestic life

---

[9] More details on structuring data-bases and data files are discussed in (Ura, 1973). The idea of developing individual data files for application to socio-demographic studies and the effective data linkage for the compilation of a system of national accounts was pioneered by Norwegian statisticians in the early 1960s and is referred to in (Nordbotten, 1971) and (Aukrust and Nordbotten, 1973).

and (I.2) living conditions; secondary activity consists of (II.1) learning and (II.2) earning; and tertiary activity consists of (III.1) leisure. Columns in the matrix are classified according to the unit of measurement: households, individuals, and disposable hours for individuals. The specific points to be queried in SSCL are entered as the elements of the matrix. For example, those queries which relate to the domestic life of households will entail surveys on sex, age, marital status, household composition, and relation to the household head.

Independent queries are made on household members classified by age: 15 and over, and under 15. It is interesting to note that this classification also serves to distinguish the manpower population (15 and over) from the rest of the population (under 15). Accordingly, the learning sub-category of secondary activity is substantially relevant for those who are aged less than 15, even though the extension of schooling years in the recent decade in Japan has strongly influenced the composition and age profile of the active work force. The earning sub-category of the secondary activity, on the other hand, essentially refers to those who are aged 15 and over.

A variety of information is collected from the queries concerning those who are 15 and over (here noted by $+15$) which is itemized as indicated below, the query serial number being indicated in parenthesis:

$+15(1)$, sex; $+15(2)$, relation to the household head;

$+15(3)$, age; $+15(4)$, marital status; $+15(5)$, school career, which is broadly subdivided into the categories (i) elementary education, (ii) intermediary education, and (iii) advanced education;

$+15(6)$, working status, which is subdivided into the categories (i) working for earnings, (ii) domestic work, (iii) schooling, and (iv) other;

$+15(7)$, occupations, which is subdivided into the categories (i) those who are employed, (ii) self-employed proprietors, (iii) those who work at home, and (iv) those employed by a family business. (i) is further broken down into (i.1) manual work, (i.2) professional practices, (i.3) clerical jobs, (i.4) administrative jobs, (i.5) sales and services, (i.6) transportation, communication, and security jobs. (ii) is further broken down into (ii.1) agriculture, forestry, and fisheries, (ii.2) manufacturing and services, and (ii.3) independent professional work;

$+15(8)$, size of enterprise, which categorizes those who are working for earnings by size of firm measured by the following number of employee groupings: (i) 1–4, (ii) 5–29, (iii) 30–99, (iv) 100–299, (v) 300–499, (vi) 500–999, (vii) over 1,000 employees, and (viii) government institutions;

$+15(9)$, working hours per week, divided into 7 categories: (i) less than 15, (ii) 15–34, (iii) 35–42, (iv) 43–48, (v) 49–59, (vi) over 60, and (vii) not fixed constantly.

+15(10), holidays per week.

For those younger than 15 years of age (here noted as –15), a set of information is collected from independent queries as indicated below, the query number indicated in parenthesis:

–15(1), sex; –15(2), relation to the household head; –15(3), age; –15(4) schooling status, which is divided into the categories (i) children's nursery, (ii) nursery-school, (iii) primary school, (iv) secondary school, and (v) no schooling;

–15(5), study outside of schools, which is further divided into (i) types of institutions and (ii) types of lessons. (i) is classified into the subcategories (i.1) teaching institutions, (i.2) private teachers, (i.3) others, and (i.4) no lessons. (ii) is classified into the subcategories (ii.1) extra schooling tuition, (ii.2) abacus calculation, (ii.3) art of calligraphy, (ii.4) foreign languages, (ii.5) music, (ii.6) sports, and (ii.7) other.

Queries concerning housing conditions and living space are centered on the household. Housing is divided into the categories (i) owner-occupied dwellings, (ii) rental dwellings owned by public corporations, (iii) privately owned rental dwellings, (iv) rental dwellings furnished by institutions for their employees, (v) rental rooms, and (vi) boarding dwellings. Space is measured by the number of rooms in the dwelling. Annual earnings take the individual household as the earning unit and are classified into 12 income classes, the unit of measuring being millions of yen: (i) less than 1, (ii) 1.00–1.49, (iii) 1.50–1.99, (iv) 2.00–2.49, (v) 2.50–2.99, (vi) 3.00–3.49, (vii) 3.50–3.99, (viii) 4.00–4.99 (ix) 5.00–5.99, (x) 6.00–7.99, (xi) 8.00–9.99 and (xii) over 10.

One of the outstanding characteristics of the SSCL is that a substantial number of its queries are addressed to the behavior of individuals who participate in the spectra of social and community life. The *modus operandi* of the participation contained in the queries comprises all facets of the basic activities in the spectra of social and community life, ranging from primary to tertiary activity. Thus, in connection with living conditions, the queries on medical and hospital care in Table 1 are classified according to (i) type of medical establishments and (ii) the type and amount of medical services. The type of medical establishment (i) is further subdivided into (i.1) hospitals, (i.2) medical clinics, (i.3) medical clinics attached to workplaces, (i.4) dental clinics, and (i.5) other medical establishments. The use of medical services (ii) is further subdivided into the categories (ii.1) inpatients and (ii.2) outpatients. The sub-classification of the frequency of use of medical services (ii) differs according to inpatients and outpatients. In the case of inpatients, frequency is classified into (1) not hospitalized, (2) less than one week, (3) over one week but less than one month, (4) over one month but less than three months, and (5) over three months. In the case of outpatients, the frequency is classified, similarly, by time according to the number of days of medical treatment grouped as follows: (1) no medical treatment, (2) 1–2, (3) 3–5, (4) 6–10, (5) 10–30, and (6) over 30.

We must consider whether extra school lessons are to be treated as part of the learning which is considered a secondary activity or whether these lessons are part of increased leisure time and should be associated, accordingly, with tertiary activity. The SSCL queries concerning extra school tuition definitely corroborate my view that these lessons constitute an important aspect of learning as an integral part of secondary activity. The queries on extra school tuition for general education concerned (i) types of learning facilities cross-classified by (ii) frequency of attendance, (iii) goals, and (iv) subject matter. The types of learning facilities are (i.1) vocational and training schools, (i.2) open classes and lectures, (i.3) lectures for the public, (i.4) radio and TV educational programs, and (i.5) other. The frequency of attendance is subdivided into the categories (i) daily, (ii) 2–3 days per week, (iii) 1 day per week, (iv) 2–3 days per month, (v) 1 day per month, (vi) more than 30 days per year, but intermittently, (vii) 15–30 days per year, but intermittently, and (viii) less than 10 days per year, but intermittently. The aims of learning are subdivided into the categories (i) vocational, (ii) selection or change of vocation, (iii) preparation for entrance examination, (iv) license or certificate qualification, (v) daily life, and (vi) other. The subjects of learning are divided into the categories of (i) technology and electronics, (ii) business practices and commercial businesses, (iii) education and welfare, (iv) medical and health services, (v) domestic services and home economics, (vi) foreign languages, (vii) current affairs, and (viii) liberal arts and other.

In order to ascertain the individual's approach to his leisure, different questionnaire items were designed for the SSCL, consisting of queries on (1) entertainment and cultural activities, (2) sports, (3) voluntary services, and (4) traveling. Queries on entertainment and cultural activities were cross-classified according to (i) types of entertainment and cultural activities, (ii) frequency of participation, (iii) community activities for the individual, and (iv) community recreation facilities. Types of entertainment are further itemized into flower arrangement, tea ceremony, cinema, performing musical instruments, and gardening. The frequency of participation in the various types of entertainment and cultural activities are the same as those for the learning activities mentioned earlier. The individual's involvement in community entertainment and cultural activities is categorized by joint participation with (i) family, (ii) work associates, (iii) school associates, (iv) neighbors, (v) friends, (vi) others, and (vii) no companions.

Queries were also made to determine whether the individual belongs to particular clubs or groups for entertainment and cultural activities. It is apparent that these categories are intended to furnish information on the extent to which communities are involved in people's entertainment and cultural activities. The query concerning the individual's participation in community entertainment and cultural activities is also made from the point of view of location. In this regard, facilities are classified according to (i) the individual's home and the surrounding area, (ii) workplace, (iii) school, (iv) public facilities, (v) private facilities, and (vi) other.

Similar sorts of information on sports are collected from queries concerning (i) types of sport, cross-divided into (ii) the frequency of participation, (iii) community sporting activities, and (iv) the facilities where different sorts of sports are exercised. Sport is classified into baseball, volleyball, table-tennis, judo, swimming, hiking, and golf. The frequency classification for participation in sport, the community associations, and the location of facilities is the same as that for entertainment and cultural activities.

Voluntary services are defined as the provision of the individual's effort, skill, and time for the advancement of the community's welfare without remuneration. Voluntary services are classified as (i) social services, (ii) community services, (iii) the administration of community organizations, (iv) the administration of PTAs (parent-teacher associations), (v) the administration of other social organizations, (vi) public activities for social and community services, and (vii) other. In addition to information on the types of voluntary activity, queries were also made to determine the frequency of participation in community activities and the provision of volunteer services. In each case frequency categories are the same as those for entertainment, cultural activities, and sports.

Independent queries concerning travel furnish significant information on the use of leisure time. As standards of living have risen in Japan, so has the desire to travel more frequently and to more distant places. Travel has been divided, according to purpose, into the categories of (i) sightseeing and recreation and (ii) other. This information is supplemented by queries on the frequency of travel (over the previous 12 months) and the size of the traveling party. The annual frequency of travel is subdivided into six classes: (1) once, (2) twice, (3) three times, (4) four times, (5) 5–9 times, and (6) more than 10 times. The nature of the traveling party is considered under the following categories: (1) family, (2) work associates, (3) school associates, (4) neighbors, (5) friends, (6) other, and (7) alone. In addition, queries were also made into the facilities used during travel. The facilities are classified into the following categories: (1) state-managed inns, (2) youth hostels, (3) lodgings owned and operated by government and private institutions, (4) hotels and inns, (5) private pensions, and (6) other.

In Table 1 (last column under Individuals) we note that an independent query has been made concerning the use of public facilities for the purpose of disclosing the frequency of the individual's utilization of private and public facilities when participating in various cultural and community activities. The private and public facilities used are classified into the categories (i) public halls and public cultural centers, (ii) libraries, (iii) museums and cultural display centers (both private and public), and (iv) youth centers. The annual frequency of their utilization is divided into the categories of (i) 1–2 days, (ii) 3–5 days, (iii) 6–10 days, (iv) 10–30 days, and (v) more than 30 days.

Table 1. The Contents and Structure of SSCL

	Households	Individuals	Disposable hours
I. Primary activity			
1. Domestic life	Sex, age, marital status, household composition, relation to household head		Sleeping, personal care, meals, housekeeping, shopping, resting, other
2. Living conditions	Housing conditions and living space	Medical and hospital care	Medical and hospital care
II. Secondary activity			
1. Learning	School career	Extra school tuition	Learning and study
2. Earning	Working status and occupation, working hours, weekly holidays, annual earnings		Commuting, working
III. Tertiary activity			
1. Leisure		Entertainment, recreational and cultural activities, voluntary activities	Entertainment, recreational and cultural activities, voluntary activities
		Use of public facilities	

One of the most important contributions of the SSCL is the fresh start it has given to the compilation of individual (for age 15 and older) time budgets for living hours.[10] As is noted in the column for disposable hours in Table 1, the disposal of living time can be arranged according to basic activities of the individual in the spectra of social and community life, here classified into the 17 headings presented, with definitions, in Table 2.

Table 2. Classification of Individual Time Budgets for Living Hours

(1)	Sleeping	Evening and other sleeping
(2)	Personal hygiene	Washing, bathing, dressing, other
(3)	Eating out	Meals taken outside the home (social engagements included under item 12)
(4)	Housekeeping	Cooking, washing, cleaning, child care, other
(5)	Shopping	
(6)	Commuting	Work and school
(7)	Other short trips	Travel other than commuting for school and work; job-related trips (*i.e.*, salesmen's travel) are excluded
(8)	Working	Work performed for remuneration; also includes the unpaid work of proprietors
(9)	Learning and study	Includes extra-school learning as well as learning and study in school. Work-enhancing study taken outside the workplace and approved by the employer is excluded here and included in (8)
(10)	Cultural and entertainment	
(11)	Sports	
(12)	Social engagements	Activities aimed at maintaining good personal and social relations including receiving guests and attendance at parties and meetings
(13)	Voluntary activities	
(14)	TV, radio, and newspapers	Recreational use of television, radio, and newspapers
(15)	Resting and relaxing	At home as well as at the workplace
(16)	Medical care	
(17)	Other	

The questionnaire requests the individual to indicate his time disposal in ten-minute units for a specified two days in a particular week. The two days are chosen so as to take into account different patterns of be-

[10] For the design of time budgets and their data collection, see (United Nations, 1975).

havior between weekdays and Sundays. The hours at one's disposal are arranged to total 24.

Detailed information on receipts and expenditures for urban households (including transfer income and payments and some financial transactions) is available from the Family Income and Expenditure Survey (hereafter FIES, Bureau of Statistics, Office of the Prime Minister) on a monthly basis. It would be quite interesting to construct a data base for separate household units which merged social data obtainable from the SSCL with data derivable from the FIES. Such an experiment is now being conducted to achieve the statistical matching of SSCL data with FIES data. The experiment is only preliminary because the conducted samples are limited to the Tokyo metropolitan area, drawing approximately 1,000 samples from SSCL and 500 samples from FIES. The scope and methodology of this experiment will be discussed in a forthcoming paper.[11]

Experimental Work on Compiling a Micro-Data Base

In this section, I shall give a brief summary account of my experiments for compiling a micro-data base which will be termed the AUD Data File. This AUD Data File has been compiled in order to achieve two objectives, the first of which concerns the potential use of a micro-data set stored on computer tapes or disks and then transmitted directly from the tapes for further processing. As data tapes contain personal information, government agencies which are responsible for conducting such statistical surveys are concerned with the protection of privacy and may not be willing to release the personal data for public use, even for experimental work. Thus, the compilation of a micro-data base is often subject to the limits imposed by the need to protect personal privacy. Use of the AUD Data File is free from the danger of violating privacy, however, for the data file contains no records or codes from which an individual can be identified.[12]

The second objective is to ease the merging of the AUD Data File with samples of the SSCL. The statistical matching of the SSCL data

[11] For technical details on the techniques of data matching and data merging to construct such a synthetic data base, it will be useful to refer to the works of Okner (1974), Ruggles and Ruggles (1974), and Alter (1974). The experiment in constructing a merged data file using the technique of interval analysis is discussed by Wolf (1977).

[12] I will not deal here with the issue of privacy and the use of the micro-data base. This point has been dealt with thoroughly in the works of Miller (1971), Dunn (1974), and others.

with the AUD Data File will provide synthetic statistical information to shed new light on leisure preferences and the disposal of limited time. The SSCL data contain plenty of information on one aspect of cultural activity closely associated with the disposal of leisure hours. This information will be matched with the AUD Data File to produce a more detailed and synthetic set of statistical information.

The AUD Data File consists of information collected from questionnaire forms distributed to attendants at the June 1977 subscription concerts of the NHK Symphony Orchestra (Tokyo).[13] Approximately 5,000 sheets (samples) were collected; the response ratio was about 30 percent of the total of circulated sheets. The questionnaire form contained the following questions:

1. Age, sex, and marital status.
2. Level of educational achievement.
3. Occupation (same as SSCL).
4. Monthly earnings, including taxes (same as FIES).
5. Length of subscription.
6. Preferred time of concert opening.
7. Preferred day of concert.
8. Preferred length of subscription.
9. Reaction to price of subscription ticket.
10. Previous year's most impressive performance.
11. Favorite works.
12. Requests for selections.
13. Request for guest artists.
14. Frequency of attendance over the past year at concerts of the NHK Symphony Orchestra.
15. Musical activities (amateur or professional).

Apparently, no record or code is available to identify a specific individual responding to the questionnaire. It is also interesting to note that questions 1, 2, 3, 4, and 15 can be used as key variables to match the AUD Data File with the SSCL or the FIES.

The collected information is coded and stored in computers using the SPSS package program. A number of advantages in using the SPSS package program for our purposes are easily discerned. First, the package program is designed especially for statistical analysis in the social sciences where particular emphasis is placed on multivariate statistical analysis. Second, the package program is a powerful tool for the statistical analysis of cross-sectional data, which makes up the bulk

---

[13] There are more than 15 orchestras in Japan which give professional performances. The NHK Symphony Orchestra, which is financially sponsored by NHK (Japan Broadcasting Corporation), is the oldest and the best among them.

of the information stored in the AUD Data File. Third, the SPSS package program is no less advantageous than other computer programs in dealing with descriptional statistics. In particular, it can use its full potential to produce cross-tabulated tables according to any combination of characteristics. Some tables produced from the AUD Data File using the SPSS package program are displayed below. Before turning our attention to the cross-tabulations of Tables 3 – 5, it should be recalled that they could not be produced from those sets of statistical information which are compiled using the traditional method of vertical compilation in statistical surveys. One of the decided advantages of using a micro-data base for the statistical analysis of socioeconomic variables is clearly revealed in the illustrated tables.

The following tables are displayed here in summarized form:

(i) Table 3. The frequency of concert attendance (question 14) is cross-tabulated by the level of educational achievement (question 2).

(ii) Table 4. The frequency of concert attendance (question 14) is cross-tabulated by the class of monthly earnings (question 4).

(iii) Table 5. The frequency of concert attendance (question item 14) is cross-tabulated by the length of subscription (question item 5).

Table 3. Frequency of Attending Concerts Cross-tabulated by the Level of Educational Achievement (%)

	Middle school	High school	Junior college	College	Graduate school
(1)	22.4	20.6	15.9	18.5	18.7
(2)	59.5	50.2	52.0	50.7	51.5
(3)	5.2	20.5	21.4	21.8	21.2
(4)	2.6	2.7	2.5	4.7	5.0
(5)	10.3	6.0	8.2	4.3	3.6

Table 4. Frequency of Attending Concerts Cross-tabulated by the Class of Monthly Earnings (%)

	I	II	III	IV	V.I	V.II
(1)	15.8	10.6	17.6	20.5	20.6	21.2
(2)	49.9	59.9	50.3	52.4	50.9	51.1
(3)	24.6	19.4	22.0	17.4	20.9	19.5
(4)	3.6	4.2	5.6	3.7	3.9	4.0
(5)	6.1	5.9	4.5	6.0	3.7	3.2

[a] The classes of monthly earnings are formed on the basis of quintile income classes for urban workers; information is supplied from the Bureau of Statistics, Office of the Prime Minister. The highest income class (V) is further divided into the lower highest class (V.I) and the upper highest class (V.II).

Table 5. Frequency of Attending Concerts Cross-tabulated by the Length of Subscription (%)

	1 year or less	2–4 years	5–9 years	10 years or more
(1)	19.1	17.6	17.5	21.1
(2)	51.7	53.9	50.5	45.7
(3)	21.1	20.7	22.5	22.9
(4)	2.5	3.4	5.1	6.3
(5)	5.6	4.4	4.4	5.0

The figures in each table cell stand for the percentage distribution of samples to the column sum. The frequency of attending concerts is divided into five categories: (1) subscription concerts (10 times per year) only, (2) subscription concerts plus once or twice in 3 months, (3) subscription concerts plus once or twice per month, (4) subscription concerts plus once or twice per week, and (5) other. Although an exhaustive statistical analysis cannot be made here, the following brief comments will be offered.[14] In the illustrated tables, the frequency of concert attendance is chosen to represent the demand for concerts, one type of performing art. Generally speaking, quantitative measurement of the demand for the performing arts is not as easy as it may seem, for several reasons. First, data on expenditures for the performing arts by a household and its members are not easy to obtain, even though we have access to family budget information. Second, it is extremely difficult to obtain an appropriate deflator which transforms the expenditure for performing arts in current values into constant value terms. The difficulty is often caused by the existence of differential prices of tickets for performing arts events depending on seat locations. At present, little information is available on the extent of price differentiation. In this regard the information on the frequency of concert attendance supplied by the AUD Data File provides a relatively good measuring rod for gauging the demand for concerts because the growing frequency of attendance indicates a growing demand for this particular branch of the performing arts.

It is interesting to see from Table 4 that the level of income is not the definite variable in explaining the changes in demand because a higher frequency of attendance is not necessarily associated with a higher income. More precisely, it appears that the higher frequency of concert attendance is more closely correlated with the length of subscription

[14] Further results of detailed statistical analysis are reported in the joint work of Kurabayashi and Matsuda (1978), in which they are compared with the corresponding observations incorporated in the celebrated work of Baumol and Bowen (1967).

and the level of educational achievement. The observed high correlation between attendance and length of subscription should not come as a great surprise. The longer the duration of a subscription, the more awakened and persistent the taste for music will be. The growing demand for concerts naturally results in an intensified and persistent affection for music. It is also conceivable that the so-called "learning by doing" effect may strengthen the affection for music. But it must be stressed here that the "doing by learning" effect may be influenced by the higher level of educational achievement of those who show a higher frequency of concert attendance. Those who have higher educational backgrounds are more easily able to understand sophisticated music.

A large amount of statistical work still remains to be carried out. In particular, the statistical matching of the AUD Data File with the SSCL data and the FIES samples is a formidable task to be tackled in the future. Certainly a micro-data set adds a new dimension to quantitative treatment of the economic and social concerns that face industrialized countries.

References

Alter, H. "Creation of a Synthetic Data Set by Linking Records of the Canadian Survey of Consumer Finances with the Family Expenditure Survey 1970," *Annals of Economic and Social Measurement*, April 1974.

Aukrust, O., and Nordbotten, S. "Files of Individual Data and their Potential for Social Research," *Review of Income and Wealth*, June 1973.

Baumol, W. J., and Bowen, W. G. *Performing Arts: The Economic Dilemma*. Cambridge, Mass., 1966.

Benard, J. *Comptabilite nationale et models de politique economique*. Paris, 1972.

Dunn, E. S. Jr., *Social Information and Statistical Systems: Change and Reform*. New York, 1974.

Huizinga, J. *Homo Ludens: A Study of the Play-Element in Culture*. Boston, 1955.

Kurabayashi, Y., and Matsuda, Y. "Demand for and Supply of Performing Arts: The Case of a Japanese Orchestra," *Hitotsubashi Review*, January 1978.

Miller, A. R. *The Assault on Privacy: Computers, Data Banks and Dossiers*. Ann Arbor, 1971.

Moss, M. (ed.) *The Measurement of Economic and Social Performance*. New York, 1973.

Nordbotten, S. *Two Articles of Statistical Data Files and their Utilization in Sociodemographic Model Building*. Artikler fra Statistisk Sentralbyra, Nr. 40, Oslo, 1971.

Okner, B., "Data Matching and Merging: An Overview," *Annals of Economic and Social Measurement*, April 1974.

Ruggles, R., and Ruggles, N. *The Design of Economic Accounts*. New York, 1970.
———. "A Strategy for Merging and Matching Microdata Sets," *Annals of Economic and Social Measurement*, April 1974.
———. "The Role of Microdata in the National Economic and Social Accounts," *Review of Income and Wealth*, June 1975.

United Nations. *A System of National Accounts*. New York, 1968.

————. A Draft System of the Distribution of Income, Consumption and Accumulation, E/CN. 3/425, 1972.

————. *Towards a System of Social and Demographic Statistics.* New York, 1975.

Ura, S. *The Structure of Data Bases and Files.* Tokyo, 1973 (in Japanese).

Wolff, E. "Schooling and Occupational Earnings," *Review of Income and Wealth,* September 1977.

Social Statistics and Social Indicators: Selected Issues from the Indian Experience

M. Mukherjee and A. K. Ray

The general desire to improve social conditions is reflected in all Indian five-year plans.* Because the general process of social change encompasses so many elements, development efforts have to actually be directed to well-defined goals. Indian plans have incorporated, along with certain targets for economic development, a number of non-economic targets in the fields of health services, education, scientific research, and the welfare of workers and the underprivileged classes. The outlays needed to achieve both economic and non-economic targets have also been outlined. Further, a continuing concern has been expressed about the large body of the poor in the country.

Economic development targets, necessary outlays, and their finance are generally linked despite the fact that a large part of the economy remains unplanned and only indirectly influenced by public measures. It is possible, for example, to envisage a proximate pattern of economic development and to work out the necessary costs; it is also possible to check on what has happened in the past. All this is permitted because there is a conceptualization of the process of economic development. It is granted that, even here, the estimates we work with are based on inadequate information. It is further clear that the attainment of economic targets does not depend only on economic measures; it is frequently necessary to supplement these with social measures. Nevertheless, we have some general information and constructs enabling us to

* This paper presents some of the results of the Social Statistics and Social Indicators Project of the Indian Council of Social Science Research undertaken in collaboration with the Central Statistical Organisation, Government of India. The Project is under the direction of Professor M. Mukherjee of the Council with Mr. A. K. Ray attached as Assistant Director.

see possible alternative paths of economic development and then make reasonable choices. The information and constructs are generally provided by national accounting systems like SNA and MPB for non-socialist and socialist countries, respectively. These systems are based on a detailed study of the available economic information in many countries and its policy and research uses. The building up of a social statistical system for India would therefore entail a study of the available social information and its uses.

It has to be admitted that it is easier to conceive of a national accounting system than of a social statistical system. This is primarily because national accounts largely include variables expressed in value terms, and most variables correspond to concepts covered under economic theory. But not all research in economics is based on accepted theories. It often depends on empirical generalizations, and the need for such research is also catered to by national accounting systems. Since much social research (and, in consequence, much social policy) is, or could be, based on such generalizations and hypotheses, there is some justification in working towards a social statistical system.

In a poor country, care should be taken to present the information in a manner that will bring out the relative rates of progress of the poor, the general population, and the affluent. The central interest would be to ascertain to what extent social services are reaching the general population. But, in addition, it will be of interest to observe the distributional aspects and see to what extent the benefits are reaching the poor. The social services devised for the amelioration of the conditions of the poor should be carefully monitored. At the other extreme, a continuing study is necessary of the services that cater to the more affluent sections of the society.

The Program

It has been decided to cover the following aspects of social reality in India: (i) population, vital statistics, immigration, and emigration, (ii) labor conditions and employment, (iii) manpower, (iv) income and accumulation, (v) consumption, (vi) housing, (vii) health, and (viii) education. The subclassification to be adopted will take into account the suggestions made in the United Nations' *Towards a System of Social and Demographic Statistics* (UN, 1975) and in Chakravarty's report to the UN containing recommendations for developing countries (UNESCO, 1976). During the next five years, the work will be taken up by several research institutions and other agencies; the Indian Council of Social Science Research (ICSSR) and the Central Statistical Organization (CSO) will coordinate the studies. Apart from developing the system, there is a continuing aim of producing a volume on "social trends" annually, furnishing data and incorporating analytical studies in chosen fields of interest.

To begin with, the "social trends" will include statistics for only some parts of the fields enumerated earlier. There will, however, be a critical appraisal of data, timeliness, and validity including analytical studies in selected important problems; here the coverage will be smaller in the initial years. Gradually, the annual publication is expected to become an increasingly comprehensive compendium of social information.

But while this development is somewhat easy to plan and implement, it does not comprise the entirety of the ultimate task. The information system has to be arranged eventually according to well-defined social goals and human needs. Currently available information relates to government departments, and even social planning in different spheres of concern takes the form of planning for change and expansion in the activities of one ministry or another. In the process, social goals and human needs remain inadequately defined and frequently unattained. There is confusion between means and ends. In the Indian program, an attempt will be made, side by side with the preparation of the compendia, to work out the social goals and human needs in considerable detail and then to orient the information system to the statistics relevant to a goal or a need which may come from several government departments. The process is not easy and will involve a good deal of discussion and even experimentation. But after some time it is hoped that the information in the compendia will be arranged by social goals and human needs. Thus, it will no longer be a compendium of social statistics but a system of social indicators.

Developing Countries, Social Statistics, and Systems of Statistics

Since our ultimate concern is to obtain a social statistical system for India, a so-called developing country, it is desirable at the outset to set down our ideas about developing countries, social statistics, and systems of statistics. It is possible to elaborate on all these topics, but what we propose to do here is to give some indication of what we mean by these terms.

Advanced countries are in general highly industrialized and have high per-worker productivity not only in industry, but also in agriculture and in certain services. Social behavior in such countries is, to some extent, attuned to the production base. Nevertheless, industrial society has its stresses and strains; the high-productivity economy gives rise to disutilities such as urban congestion and environmental deterioration. Not all that goes under the name of production adds to human welfare. Further, in advanced societies, education and research are developed and can be used to combat purposefully the ill effects of the development of material resources on a huge scale. Of course, various advanced countries are at different stages of social development, and a few still have the problem of acclimatizing some segments of their population to the general mode of life of the society. Moreover, new stresses and strains arise in the process of development and affect families already acclimatized, particularly the younger generation. Finally, there appears to be an absence of goals, apart from a continuing improvement in the level of consumption.

In contrast, the developing societies exhibit a wider spectra of the stages of development, and it is more difficult to spell out their basic characteristics. In general, they are less industrialized and have lower per-worker productivity in industry, agriculture, and services. They have segments of modernized communities within a generally prevalent traditional atmosphere. These communities behave, to some extent, like advanced societies, though any expansion of the modern sector involves the problem of acclimatization. The demarcation between the modern and traditional areas is never very sharp, and there are small geographical areas in which both types of living go on side by side. The traditional areas lack modern educational facilities, and, in general, the levels of education and research in these countries remain low, resulting in a relative scarcity of purposeful domestic efforts at the formulation and solution of social problems that arise. The social and cultural atmosphere is based, by and large, on traditional rather than modern values. While the traditional values differ from one developing country to another, they are fairly strong in many countries. Such values are communicated from generation to generation through a process of education which has little resemblance to modern schooling. However, the traditional values are undergoing changes which vary according to social group. Consequently, the social behavior in a particular circumstance in a developing country is less predictable than that in a developed country; few variables can be considered as common parameters.

Social change in developing countries depends partly on the policy goals these countries are setting for themselves and partly on what they can realistically hope to achieve: the goals for which they are aiming may, in fact, be unrealizable. Improvement of material well-being remains one important aim, and in order to achieve it, rapid industrialization and improvement of agricultural technology seem to be necessary. In some countries egalitarianism is a conscious policy goal with emphasis on eradication of extreme poverty and improvement of living conditions for the weaker sections of the population. Some countries still work for communistic ideals, though at a moderate level of material output per man, and lay stress on non-material incentives. The achievement of all these transformations is sought in an orderly manner. The problem here remains teaching the population to live in a manner which is different from that of past generations. There is nothing sacrosanct about the modern way of life as we observe it in the advanced societies: this is essentially based on their traditions. Likewise, the modernism we seek for India and other developing countries has to be based on traditions. Its achievement requires that leadership be provided by political parties and by business, bureaucratic, cultural, and religious elites; very much depends on the behavior pattern of this relatively small elite group. We talk glibly about poverty and the population explosion as basic problems. But the solutions here, as experience has repeatedly shown, can wait. The major problem relates to these elites; it is necessary to work out what changes are necessary in their behavior pattern so that they can influence the general population so as to realize the achievement of desirable social objectives.

One may safely assert that for most developing countries it is utopian to work for a society akin to those observed in highly industrialized and affluent capitalist and socialist countries. Human society, in the future, is unlikely to become a vast United States of America or Soviet Union. This is partly because of the lack of necessary material inputs, partly because of the absence of any clear prescription for tackling the strains that are sure to arise in the process, and partly because of the absence of a clear view of the direction and goals of development in the affluent nations themselves. In view of this, many of the developing countries should probably try to achieve social goals at lower levels of output per man, which require only marginal change in their social values.

This process requires massive political and institutional experimentation. But this type of development will be hindered less by material requirements and should involve fewer social strains and consequent needs for adjustments. Ethnic, religious, cultural, and educational traditions have to be woven into future vision, and emphasis might be given only to such universal human social goals as require relatively fewer material inputs. This is desirable and also well within the realm of realistic possibility; one can think of numerous instances either in history or in the present-day world where the importance of a human community is much greater than the requirement of material inputs needed for its sustenance. In any case, developing countries need not traverse the exact path of development that the advanced countries followed from entirely different bases and in a quite different world historical situation; they can also take advantage of the example of the advanced countries and eschew the known mistakes that the advanced countries made during the process of their development. The above analysis puts in proper perspective the efforts at social development now being made in India.

It is difficult to define social statistics, and there is no general agreement about the connotation of the term. Let us agree to call all statistics pertaining to a society "societal statistics". Social statistics proper may then be regarded as societal statistics pertaining to social behavior. Social behavior is the abiding behavior among the members of groups and institutions as well as between groups and institutions, the society being conceived as an agglomeration of these groups and institutions. Some groups, for example families, may include almost the entire population while certain other groups, say trade unions, cover a much smaller part of the population. Government is an institution, and public measures to help families are an example of social action. We may include under "social statistics" all social statistics proper, all societal statistics other than economic statistics, and only such economic statistics as directly pertain to non-economic social behavior or are important aids to social policy-making. Certain environmental factors that influence social behavior should also be included. The social statistics covered should include relevant information about the individual members of the society as well, relevance being sought in the context of social behavior. While the above consideration of the nature of "social statistics" helps us to delineate a wide field, a manageable part of the information is directly related to fields where organized social action is taking place. In other words, a formulated social policy helps us to focus attention on a smaller well-defined body of social statistics. Finally, whenever a social process could be represented by a segmental theory or a model, some defined variables could be considered as descriptive indicators and some others as analytic indicators. Thus, before we name a social indicator, there should at least be an implicit model of a social process. Social indicators could be either just a subset of social statistics or constructs based on social statistics.

Social statistics (as well as statistics in many other fields) are collected, presented, and analyzed with two ends in view: (i) cognitive purposes—

that is, the improvement of the understanding of the society, the process of social change, and the factors affecting such changes; and (ii) operational purposes—furnishing a data base for concrete policy measures in order to bring about and monitor changes. After having considered the notions of developing societies and social statistics, one can focus attention on the statistical requirements of and possibly some system of social statistics for developing countries. A prognosis about the future will be of some help, and hence we have digressed a little about possible lines of development while considering the nature of developing countries. We shall consider, hereafter, what one should do about social statistics for developing countries in general and India in particular, both the cognitive and operational aspects.

A large volume of statistical information is collected, processed, and published in almost all countries. Some of this emerges in scientific investigations of all sorts, and we do not consider this material here. The rest of the information with which we are concerned forms roughly three classes: (i) the returns which individuals or groups of individuals have to file under the administrative legal setup of the country, supplemented sometimes by voluntary returns which the respondents can be persuaded to make, (ii) the records of the operations of public and private enterprises of all sorts which have to be kept for running enterprises, a part of which may be statutorially required; and (iii) the information collected through surveys, both repetitive and isolated, undertaken to meet specific needs, as well as more routine observations whose collection and study has a concrete use. The classes overlap to some extent, and they are justified only on the basis of their primary emphasis. The processing, summarization, and publication of this information is largely the responsibility of public authorities at several levels, though private institutions and research bodies, both public and private, play a significant role in some countries. The selected information meets some segmental needs which may be operational or cognitive-educative, though operational uses are frequently completed before the figures are in print. An organization must have some information about the environment within which it works apart from information about its own operations; such environmental information is conceived here to be included under cognitive information.

It is important to realize that most of this information is obtained in order to meet some social needs, both cognitive and operational, though there may be some information which does not cater to any current requirement. The social process of collection and dissemination of information has an inertia of its own: some data are undoubtedly collected and published because somebody or some agency in the past thought that it was a good thing to do so. On the other hand, there are large fields, particularly in developing countries, where there is no information despite a keenly felt need. But even when there are such difficulties, the available social statistical information in many countries provides a base from which one can take off. To make a beginning, it is necessary to observe the statistics that are being collected and processed in this field in order to cater to concrete policy and research needs. All of them have some relation with observable social action and social conditions or pertain to human environment; one can hope that a system may emerge eventually. In the present program we have deliberately selected certain items which have major policy implications, and we will be largely concerned with them. In other words, our concern is with a core of a system.

Weighting of Variables Depicting Social Change and Social Variability

The problems connected with the construction of index numbers of economic variables have been studied by economists and statisticians in a systematic way. When we come to the measurement of the composite effect of a set of variables representing changes in a chosen field of social concern—for example, health or educational services in a region over time, we are confronted with a difficult problem. Likewise, one may try to find out how a number of regions at a point in time can be ordinally arranged with respect to the provision of these services. But there are no straightforward means for constructing index numbers in such cases since, even when we get a set of measures representing the outputs of social services, there are no price counterparts that enable us to obtain objective weights.

Prior to construction of any index number, a suitable choice from the set of identified variables has to be made. There is a large body of literature on the relevant societal variables. The most important perhaps are those given in the United Nations' *Towards a System of Social and Demographic Statistics* (UN, 1975) suggested for all countries of the world or in Chakravarty's (UNESCO, 1976) system recommended for developing countries. Ganguli and Gupta (1976) selected a small number of variables in certain chosen fields for a study of social change in India in the recent past. Hellwig (a:69–90) presented a statistical model (regression analysis) on the choice of variables.

Index numbers are in general weighted combinations of relevant variables; the next problem is the choice of weights. As mentioned earlier, the weighting of social variables is a difficult task, and some amount of arbitrariness and subjectiveness play a part in almost all the methods suggested. Drewnowsky and Scott (1966) presented a (subjective) formula for index numbers of variables which has also been used by Ganguli and Gupta (1976) for India. More objective methods of weighting have been discussed by Hellwig (b:93–110). He examined critically the weights derived from

   i)   regression analysis (Gostkowski, 1967; Hellwig-b:93–98),

  ii)   capacity of information (Hellwig-b:99–101),

 iii)   factor analysis (Sovani and Subramanian, 1967),

 iv)   correlation matrix (Hellwig-b:106–108), and

  v)   coefficient of variation (Hellwig-b:109).

The methods available in the literature are not fully satisfactory. Some use subjective procedures while others, though objective, make use of notions that are not strictly relevant. In view of this, there appears to be room for devising a simple and straightforward weighting procedure. We turn to such a procedure in the next two sections, where we propose to use the method for weighting variables in the Indian social statistics and social indicators program.

Suggested Alternative Procedure for Weighting

While considering social change or social development in a country or region, it is customary to consider a large number of variables, x_1, x_2....x_M. When we are interested in change over time, these variables can be presented in a matrix $[x_{ij}]$ of order $MX(N+1)$ showing that we have the values of the variables at $N+1$ points of time (say years), the second subscript standing for time. The same setup can be used for studying the social change or social development in any major area of social concern, say health or educational services. Here the variables should reflect changes in different aspects of the particular area of social concern. For that matter, it will be desirable to classify the major areas of social concern, obtain variables relevant to each concern, work out series depicting social changes or development for the individual areas, and then combine these series so as to obtain a series for overall social change or development.

It is obvious that before we can talk about a change between two points of time, the variables have to be chosen and combined. Whether we are concerned with the overall social change or with the change in a particular area of social concern, the choice of variables remains to some extent arbitrary, depending on the available data or data that could be collected at reasonable cost. While variables depicting outputs would be desirable, they have to be replaced frequently by variables depicting inputs. Next, it would be desirable to avoid retrogressive variables. In other words, we take as a variable only a positive *prima facie* change which indicates social development. This stipulation does not militate against generality because available retrogressive variables can be replaced, say, by their reciprocals or some other suitable functions. Third, when a large number of variables are used for the analysis and their annual percentage changes do not widely differ from one another, any linear combination of these percentage changes with positive weights adding up to unity would obviously lie between the highest and the lowest of the percentage changes. Even taking an unweighted simple average would not be an unsatisfactory way of combining the variables. And this average would not materially change when some variables are randomly left out because of our postulation of a large number of variables each having an annual percentage change not widely different from the others. Finally, while choosing variables, care should be taken not to give more weight to certain aspects of the change by choosing more variables to depict that particular aspect. Subject to these remarks, we would for the present leave the choice of variables to some extent open and hence subject to the bias of the investigator.

In the process of combination of variables, however, we should try to avoid arbitrary procedures. Here assignment of subjective weights to different variables would be extremely risky because the investigator may deliberately choose his weights to satisfy some of his preconceived notions about social development. Thus, the permissible weighting systems should be value-free and entirely objective. In our review of the available weighting systems given earlier, we have seen that some are subjective while others are objective but based on assumptions which do not appear satisfactory to us.

To present a method which appears somewhat more satisfactory, we replace matrix $[x_{ij}]$ by the annual percentage changes $[y_{ij}]$ of order $M \times N$, where $y_{ij} = x_{i,\,j+1}/x_{ij}$. These are all positive numbers, mostly ranging between, say, 0.5 to 1.5 or even smaller limits. Since overall development is consistent with annual ups and downs, some of the ratios will be above and some below unity. Also, the arithmetic mean of the numbers in a column (*i.e.*, the unweighted combination of variables) would be between the largest and smallest figures in the column. We cannot take this unweighted combination because there is no compelling reason why each variable should have equal weight. Consequently, we have to seek some weighted combination:

$$Y_j = w_1 y_{1j} + w_2 y_{2j} + . - . + w_M y_{Mj} \qquad (1)$$

$$(j = 1, 2 \ldots N)$$

where $\displaystyle\sum_{i=1}^{M} w_i = 1$.

We then set up a quadratic function depicting the overall variability within rows. Such a convenient function is

$$\frac{1}{2} \sum_j \sum_k (Y_j - Y_k)^2 ; j,k = 1, 2, \ldots, N.$$

We then set up a function

$$L = \frac{1}{2} \sum_j \sum_k (Y_j - Y_k)^2 + \lambda \left(1 - \sum_{i=1}^{M} w_i\right). \qquad (2)$$

Minimizing this function with respect to w_i and λ, we get M equations to solve for λ and w's with the stipulation that $\sum_i w_i = 1$. The process is one x of minimization because the second derivatives $\dfrac{\partial^2 L}{\partial w_i^2}$ and $\dfrac{\partial^2 L}{\partial \lambda^2}$ are all positive. The solution of the system of equations $\dfrac{\partial L}{\partial wi} = 0$ for all $i = 1, 2, \ldots M$ comes out as

$$D'Dw = \frac{\lambda}{2} e \qquad (3)$$

where $D' = [D^{(1)'} | D^{(2)'} | \ldots | D^{(j)'} | \ldots | D^{(N-1)'}]$ and $D^{(j)}$ is a $(N-j) \times M$ — matrix with a typical element $d_{rs}^{(j)} = y_{s,j} - y_{s,r+j}$; $1 \leq s \leq M$, $1 \leq r \leq N - j$.

Thus, e is the column vector of $M \times 1$, and w is the vector of weights, $w_1, w_2, \ldots w_M$. On applying $\dfrac{\partial L}{\partial \lambda} = 1 - \sum w_i = 0$ Over Eq. (3), one may obtain the weight vector w as

$$w = \frac{(D'D)^{-1} e}{e'(D'D)^{-1} e} ; \qquad (4)$$

assuming that the inverse of $(D'D)$ exists.

An alternative formula for w may be given in the following manner. Observe that Eq. (1) may be alternatively written as

$$Y = w'y;$$

$$\text{where, } Y' = (Y_1, Y_2, \ldots\ldots, Y_N)$$

$$w' = (w_1, w_2, \ldots\ldots w_M).$$

and $y = [yij]$ as defined earlier; and the total variability,

$$\frac{1}{2} \sum_{j=1}^{N} \sum_{k=1}^{N} (Y_j - Y_k)^2 = N^2 w' sw,$$

where S is the variance-covariance matrix of rows of y. As before, the problem is to minimize the total variability $N^2 w' sw$ subject to $w'e = 1$. Applying the usual Lagrange multiplier technique, one obtains the solution as

$$w = \frac{s^{-1}e}{e's^{-1}e}. \tag{5}$$

Note that for independent variables, where the variance-covariance matrix S is a diagonal matrix of variances, Eq. (5) suggests that the weights are inversely proportional to the respective variances. One important corollary is that the independent standardized variables have equal weights.

As a general rule, weights should all be non-negative, *i.e.*, $w_i \geq 0$ for all i. The solution in (5) does not ensure the non-negativity of all w_i's. However, preliminary selection of variables should be such that they are, to the extent possible, not correlated among themselves, and one may get all positive weights in this case. Further, addition of some highly correlated variables does not bring adequate additional information. In other cases, where such selection is not possible, there is a likelihood of getting negative weights. To avoid this, the non-negativity constraints of weights should be incorporated in the minimization problem. That is, we should in general minimize the total variability $N^2 w' sw$ subject to two constraints:

$$w_i \geq 0 \quad \text{for all } i \text{ and } \sum_i wi = 1.$$

This problem can be solved by quadratic programming.

In the next section we have presented an illustrative example and obtained weights using both the Lagrangian multiplier (without non-negativity constraints) and quadratic programming (with non-negativity constraints) and compared the results.

Table 1. Original Ratios from Divatia – Bhatt Paper and Their Averages*

Year	54-55 to 55-56	55-56 to 56-57	56-57 to 57-58	57-58 to 58-59	58-59 to 59-60	59-60 to 60-61	60-61 to 61-62	61-62 to 62-63	62-63 to 63-64	Weights using Eq. (4)	Obtained by quadratic programming
1	2	3	4	5	6	7	8	9	10	11	12
1. Entrepreneurship	1.05	1.02	1.01	1.05	1.06	1.01	1.05	1.07	1.01	0.387	0.351
2. Capital	1.07	1.14	1.10	0.96	1.11	1.13	1.06	1.08	1.08	0.243	0.168
3. Skills	1.12	1.12	1.13	1.16	1.09	1.10	1.11	1.05	1.08	0.303	0.310
4. Factory employment	1.02	10.9	1.02	0.98	1.06	1.04	1.04	1.05	1.06	0.145	0.000
5. Technical change	1.12	1.17	1.12	1.16	1.09	1.12	1.12	1.19	1.21	0.211	0.171
6. Unweighted average	1.076	1.108	1.076	1.062	1.082	1.080	1.076	1.088	1.088		
7. Growth based on factor scores	1.075	1.088	1.068	1.024	1.096	1.075	1.068	1.094	1.071		
8. Growth based on our weighting given in											
(a) col. (11)	1.094	1.100	1.089	1.090	1.078	1.084	1.086	1.094	1.082		
(b) col. (12)	1.087	1.097	1.081	1.088	1.083	1.077	1.082	1.086	1.078		

(Divatia & Bhatt, 1969: 14–15)

An Example

The example is taken from a paper by Divatia and Bhatt (1969: 14–15). The data relate to the period 1954–55 to 1963–64. We have used only five series representing (i) entrepreneurship, (ii) capital, (iii) skills, (iv) factory employment, and (v) technical change. The five series, based on 21 series, are as given by the authors in the above-mentioned paper. The ratios depicting annual changes are given in Table 1. Rows 6 and 7 are also based on figures given in the paper. The weights obtained by us are given in cols. 11 and 12. The annual percentage changes obtained by using these weights are given in the last two rows of the table, 8 (a) and 8 (b). It is clear that the proposed methods give series which exhibit lower variability than the unweighted averages. The series based on factor scores, on the other hand, shows a higher variability than the unweighted averages.

The example shows that the procedure is a feasible one, and we do not intend to claim anything else for the method at this stage. All we want to convey is that there is scope for further discussion and thinking about the method. When a real-life problem is taken, the number of series used will be larger, and we can perhaps afford to drop a few variables carrying zero weight in the quadratic programming setup.

The above method is presented mainly to indicate that, along with considering more substantial aspects of a social indicators program, attention is also being paid to some of the perennial theoretical problems which have not yet been solved in a satisfactory manner. In addition to trying to evolve an objective weighting procedure, we are also trying to use the concepts of distance and clustering both for intertemporal and interregional comparisons. While a lot of work has been done in this field, none appears to be fully satisfactory in the context of our social indicators program.

References

Divatia, V. V., and Bhatt, V. V. "On Measuring the Pace of Development," *Banca Nazionale del Lavoro Quarterly Review*, No. 89, Rome, June 1969.

Drewnowsky, J. and Scott, W. *The Level of Living Index,* Report No. 4, UNRISD, Geneva, 1966.

Ganguli, B. N., and Gupta, D. B. *Levels of Living in India,* 1976.

Gostkowsky, Z. Suggested in a meeting of experts on methodology of human resources indicators, Warsaw, December 1967.

Hellwig, Z. (a). "On The Optional Choice of Predictors," in Gostkowsky, Z. (ed.), *Towards a System of Human Resources Indicators for Less Developed Countries.* Institute of Philosophy and Sociology, Polish Academy of Sciences, undated.

Hellwig, Z. (b) "On the Problem of Weighting in International Comparisons," in Gostkowsky, Z. (ed.), *Towards a System of Human Resources Indicators for Less Developed Countries.* Institute of Philosophy and Sociology, Polish Academy of Sciences, undated.

Sovani, N. V., and Subramanian, A. M. *An Index of Socio-Economic Development of Nations.* UNRISD, Geneva, 1967.

United Nations. *Towards a System of Social and Demographic Statistics*, ST/ESA/ STAT/SERF/18. New York, 1975.

United Nations Economic and Social Council. *Framework for the Integration of Social and Demographic Statistics in Developing Countries*, E/CN. 3/490, April 1976.

Social Indicators for the Philippines

Mahar Mangahas

Why Measure Welfare?

As one appraises a national development effort, the initial impression of general progress is often marred by an undeniable perception of old problems still holding sway.* There is a serious need to more fully quantify specific goals of national development for the sake of an honest measurement of progress, as part of a scientific determination of the solutions to development problems. Most governments, of course, do have some sort of statistical system. But what the social indicators movement represents, in the Philippines as in other countries, is the feeling that the present system is particularly inadequate with respect to the measurement of final well-being, or welfare.

Sincerity is an important issue. When a goal is not quantified, there is a tendency for plans to degenerate into lip service. Since Philippine development programs, for example, do not set clear numerical goals for improved nutrition or poverty eradication or pollution control, the implicit implication is that there is a low priority for these concerns. Thus one may be less surprised to find that the measures taken against poverty are either half-hearted or directionless. A quantified target is one convincing sign of sincere commitment to a program.

Next, one needs to be able to tell, at least *ex post facto*, which policies promote development and which do not. Of course, if some indicator shows a deficiency in well-being, this does not by itself provide the

* The current paper draws on work undertaken by the Development Academy of the Philippines for the Social Indicators Project, of which Professor Mangahas was Director. For numerical illustrations of points raised here see (DAP, 1975) and (Mangahas, 1976).

precise solution to the problem; but given the solutions which are in fact being tried, the measurement of the final results would help indicate, beyond wishful thinking, whether the policies are effective. There should be a willingness to learn from failures as well as from successes. The habit of thinking about national well-being as having many dimensions also reminds us to check on possible side effects of policies, sometimes positive but at other times negative.

A system of measuring national well-being would help the citizenry rate their government objectively. The people deserve to know the extent to which government pledges for development are being fulfilled, and government is duty-bound to inform its citizenry about the accomplishments of its national development programs in the most balanced and concrete way possible.

Thus the "social indicators movement" is not merely a drive to collect and publish a large array of statistics, but is an insistence on the application, in the efforts to promote national development, of a common-sense scientific principle: observing the results of one's experiments. It contends that for many problems of development the solutions are only very vaguely defined and that many government policies are essentially experiments—hopeful of success, but nevertheless experiments. It is the duty of government, both technicians and politicians, to strive to learn the best solutions. Where the monitoring system is active, as in exports, or food production, or national security, or manufacturing, or even population, the process of learning-by-doing tends to be dynamic, corrective of discovered errors, abundant with new ideas. But where surveillance is irregular, often postponed, fragmentary, and, indeed, sometimes altogether refused, it is little wonder that problems persist over decades while conflicts of ideas amount to little more than interchanges of rhetoric.

The DAP Social Indicators Project

At the Development Academy of the Philippines, a Social Indicators Project was instituted for the purpose of studying a means of quantifying the national well-being (or welfare) and measuring it over time. Work on the project took place between October 1973 and January 1975. It did not seek to produce either glowing or disparaging reports of the New Society.[1] Its aim was solely a system of measurement capable of depicting objectively and concretely the changes, whether positive

[1] The martial law government dates from September 21, 1972.

or negative, in national development. The research project came to be guided by certain working principles:

1. There are basic social concerns—health, education, employment, peace and order—which comprise the widely accepted and more or less permanent goals of Philippine society. National well-being is, then, a composite of concrete achievements in these basic areas of social concern.

2. Present national well-being consists of the general well-being of Filipinos today and the present provision for the well-being of future generations.

3. Success in any social concern must include an equitable sharing within society of the welfare which results from success: an equitable sharing of health services and of educational opportunities; equality before the law; equality of freedom of political dissent; and so on.

4. Social or welfare indicators are specific and measurable elements of each area of social concern. They reflect both the degree of improvement in each area and the degree of sharing in that improvement among present-day Filipinos and between the living and those yet unborn.

5. The weights or priorities for any social group, social concern, or social indicator are best left to the users of social indicators. But whenever value judgments are involved, they should be explicitly stated and clarified.

Some Ethical Considerations

National welfare, though indeed an abstraction, has identifiable and measurable components in terms of various aspects of the major social concerns. The DAP research effort focused on these components rather than on the nature of their relationship to national welfare since, from the outset, it was not our intention to set weights or priorities among the social concerns in order to construct some grand variable called Philippine Welfare. Every citizen has the right to hold and express his preference for some component, say, "economic freedom", over some other, say, "political freedom". Those who, through the political process, are the leaders and representatives of groups of citizens have the duty to discern and to set the priorities. In addition, the priorities of those who make the welfare decisions will change with circumstances, and in the long run, the decision-makers themselves will give way to a new generation. Thus, the pertinent priorities cannot in any case be established once and for all, but will change with circumstances.

Our national priorities need not bear any resemblance to those of any other country. Japan, for example, has made a policy shift towards "realization of a vigorous welfare society". Its economic plan envisions the "creation of a rich environment" and "ensuring a stable, comfortable life", *i.e.*, better social security, better housing, and improvement of facilities for leisure.[2] The Philippine situation, being entirely different, requires a different set of priorities.

Our proposed set of social indicators cannot, but also need not, be entirely free from ethical judgment. As I.M.D. Little puts it, "the welfare terminology is a value terminology...for the reason that we take a moral interest in welfare and happiness.... Getting rid of value judgments would be throwing the baby away with the bathwater" (Little, 1957: 79–80).

Some ethical judgment is implicit, first of all, in the exclusion of some indicators. The Social Indicators Project could not avoid making some exclusions, even though it emphasized breadth (completeness of concepts measured) rather than depth (sophistication) of measurement. A system of social indicators would be made much more useful by stressing completeness of coverage even at the expense of some refinement of measurement in certain individual components.

A degree of ethical judgment also enters into the formation of variables by combination. There would probably be no serious objection if all food, or even food and non-food consumption, were combined, according to peso value.[3] One could go even further and place money imputations on gains and losses from education, crime, sickness, pollution, and even life expectancy.[4] On the assumption that every peso's worth in one category equals that in another, one could then combine disparate variables. But, very likely, many would find this a questionable ethical assumption. Thus, some combinations need not be attempted, while others are unavoidable for practical reasons; one should recognize the ethical judgment implicit in any combination of welfare components.

The choice of social groups whose shares in total welfare are to be measured also involves an element of ethical judgment. We have, for instance, excluded the physically handicapped and the ethnic minori-

---

[2] See (Osborne, 1973) and (Government of Japan, 1973).

[3] When consumer aggregation is done, a problem arises. Samuelson (1969) has shown that one cannot infer an increase in consumer welfare from an increase in the total value of goods consumed by all consumers unless some essentially ethical assumption is made regarding the welfare derived by individual consumers. This objection is met by presenting data broken down according to social group (say, income class), allowing users to apply their own ethical standards.

[4] See (Juster, 1973) and (Usher, 1973).

ties[5] on the assumption that such social groupings are of small significance to national welfare. We have also focused on differences between
groups, thereby ignoring possible differences among individuals in any
one group, on the assumption that what primarily concern society are
the differences between the groups. Technicians should, of course,
avoid measurement techniques which favor any particular group.
Nevertheless, it is obvious that social decisions are made by those in
responsible positions on the basis of implicit priorities for the welfare of
various groups.[6]

Finally, the very labels which we apply to our indicators have, in
themselves, an ethical content. The terms welfare, development, social,
national, all have emotive force. Indeed, the very first ethical premise
is that well-being ought to be increased. One should also be aware that
definitions can be persuasive, that descriptions which are in effect rec-
ommendatory contain a measure of value judgment.

Social Concerns

Social concerns are clearly universal in nature and not unique to the
Philippines. But, by considering the most important problems confronting the nation, the DAP Social Indicators Project listed the following as basic Philippine social concerns[7]:

1. Health and Nutrition. Our people desire freedom from hunger,
malnutrition, and disease, a lower infant mortality, and a longer life
expectancy.

2. Learning. Our people desire greater and more equal opportunity
and better quality in training and education toward more productive
roles in society.

---

[5] The Muslim population is an exception. Certain provinces can be considered as
a proxy for the Muslim sector, so that social conditions for this group can be revealed
by appropriate regional disaggregation.

[6] President Marcos, for instance, has recently declared that "an ideology for the
new society must, therefore, base itself on one ruling principle: that the interests,
objectives, and needs of the poorest of the working people must take precedence over
those of the rest" (Marcos, 1973: 52).

[7] The most useful guide to a statement of Philippine social concerns is, naturally,
the Philippine Constitution, in particular Article II, "Declaration of Principles and
State Policies", and Article IV, "The Bill of Rights". The development plans and
programs of the national government and the structure of its administrative machinery point up the multi-dimensionality of national welfare. Previous research on social
concerns and on social indicators in other countries also provides useful guidelines in
drawing up the list of basic Philippine social concerns; see (Aidenoff and Johnston,
1974), (Bauer, 1966), (Christian, 1974), (Kendall, 1972), (Moss, 1973), (U.S. Office
of Management and Budget, 1973), (Sheldon and Moore, 1968), (Stanford Research
Institute, 1969), and (United Nations Statistical Office, 1974).

3. Income and Consumption. Our people desire freedom from poverty, sufficiency of income for basic needs, and protection against inflation.

4. Employment. Our people expect full protection of the right to work and desire employment that fits their qualifications and fulfills them as human persons.

5. Non-human Productive Resources. Our people expect their natural resources to be fruitfully exploited for the benefit of all and conserved for future generations, and those who till the land desire to own it by right.

6. Housing, Utilities, and the Environment. Our people desire proper housing with adequate provision for water, sanitation, and electricity, and expect that the physical environment will be kept free from pollution.

7. Public Safety and Justice. Our people desire equality before the law, speedy justice, and peace and order.

8. Political Values. Our people desire representation, participation, and freedom of political dissent in a truly democratic government.

9. Social Mobility. Our people desire freedom to change occupations and rise to better positions in a truly open society.

Certainly, these social concerns are not fixed and complete once and for all. The pattern is liable to change with development. People who are relatively poor, for instance, may be more concerned with their own personal welfare than with the welfare of the nation as a whole,[8] or more concerned with their income than with conditions of work or job placement (Strumpel, 1972). Certain aspects of life are not as yet too significant at this stage of our national development. Leisure, for example, or cultural heritage are more meaningful in an affluent society. Alienation from schooling among the young or monotony of work among the employed are not serious problems today in comparison with unemployment or housing inadequacy. Similarly, family instability, which tends to become a serious social problem in a rapidly developing economy, is not a relevant concern in the face of more pressing problems like poverty and malnutrition.

Lack of data forced the exclusion of some social concerns that might have been included: national security, working conditions (with special reference to fringe benefits and worker safety), protection against economic hazards, and inequity in the distribution of wealth. National

---

[8] In Cantril's study (1965: 148–49 & 373), richer Filipinos in 1959 gave themselves higher welfare ratings than poorer Filipinos; the richer group gave national welfare a lower rating than the poorer group.

security is a special case since it is maintained precisely by secrecy over vital information.

On the other hand, the Social Indicators Project included two general areas not commonly found in lists of social concerns: non-human productive resources and political values. Ever since the oil crisis of 1974, the issue of sufficiency of natural resources for the future has been impossible to ignore. The issue of political well-being in the Philippines, under martial law since September 1972, is perhaps even more vital. No one can deny that, in the past five years, the question of whether martial law has been good for the Filipinos has been a great controversy. Precisely because it is part of the spirit of the social indicators movement to be conscious of social problems, it would have been most improper, if not hypocritical, for the DAP Social Indicators Project to claim to measure Philippine well-being in the round with political welfare excluded from the research agenda. In retrospect, the Project only managed to suggest several experimental, perception-type indicators of political well-being based on their operability in a pilot survey conducted in 1974. There do not as yet exist sufficient data for these indicators to give a "before-vs.-after-martial law" representation.

The DAP List of Indicators of Philippine Well-being

The Social Indicators Project recommended the use of a set (Table 1) of thirty major indicators and nineteen sub-indicators, not counting decompositions.[9] Sixteen of the indicators are listed as "experimental" since they are not ordinarily measured or computed within the present Philippine statistical system.[10]

The disaggregation of the indicators should also follow criteria which are *per se* relevant to national welfare. One set of modes of disaggrega-

[9] Judgments vary on the necessary minimum number of indicators. According to Seers (1972), there is no development, regardless of the state of per-capita income, unless there is a lessening of (1) poverty, (2) unemployment, and (3) inequality. Kendall (1972) suggests the following ten principal indicators of "social development": (1) the population growth rate; (2) the expectation of life at birth; (3) the percentage of households, in urban and rural areas, in "permanent" and "semi-permanent" dwellings; (4) calories available per capita for domestic consumption; (5) the first schooling level entry rate at the normal age; (6) the second schooling level entry rate at the normal age; (7) the literacy rate; (8) the percentage of the population at working age who are gainfully employed, by sex, in urban and rural areas; (9) the percentage of the economically active population who are covered by social security schemes; and (10) the crime rate. Other useful references are (Taylor and Hudson, 1972), (Asian Development Bank, 1973), and (Adelman and Morris, 1967).

[10] A summary of the discussion involving proposed social indicators techniques of measurement is presented in (Mangahas, 1976).

tion consists of the classifications found in the table of recommended social indicators. Disability due to illness, for example, is classified according to participation in the labor force and according to family headship. Given the number of days lost due to illness, society is obviously worse off when the persons afflicted are workers than when they are non-workers, and worse off when they are family heads (who have more responsibilities) than when they are family dependents. The proportion who are ill is classified by disease because the seriousness of diseases varies, and by occupation because the importance to society of occupations varies. It is presumed to be worse for college graduates to be unemployed than for unschooled persons, for example, since college graduates are supposed to be more productive members of society.

A second set of modes of disaggregation pertains to the social groups which share in national welfare. In general, we recommend that the social indicators be disaggregated according to (a) urban vs. rural, (b) region, (c) sex, (d) age, and (e) family income. It is by means of these social groupings that the issue of equity or the matter of sharing in the enhancement of social welfare can be reflected. These groups are chosen on the principle that society is keenly interested in reducing disparities between the various groups or classes that constitute it. The disparities among individuals or families belonging to any one group are of secondary importance.

For the new, experimental indicators, time series data will obviously not be ready until they have been adapted by the statistical system. However, many of the recommended indicators either are already being collected or can be constructed from basic available series. The Project made an analysis of the trends in well-being, wherever possible, and found a complex picture. In some areas, the improvements have been substantial, particularly in education, peace and order, and (recently) justice. In other areas progress has been modest, as in net beneficial product, employment, capital formation, and basic utilities. In still other areas the situation is critical, particularly in price inflation, forest depletion, and continued worsening of poverty.

These complex findings were felt to justify the working assumptions of the Project. With some aspects of life getting better, but others worse, one can make a summary evaluation of Philippine welfare only by frankly expressing one's priorities and values among the different social concerns. Persons having different value orientations may, and indeed have the right to, disagree. To compel them to accept some grand Index of Development—a notion which the Project rejected—may be as bad as, if not worse than, offering them an incomplete set of indicators on which to base their judgment. The inevitable individual differences of opinion are resolvable, not by the statistical system, but by the political system.

Table 1. Philippine Social Indicators Recommended by the Development Academy of
the Philippines

Recommended indicators	Recommended frequency of evaluation
Health and nutrition	
1. Infant mortality rate	annual
2. Expectation of life at birth	quinquennial
3. Days disabled due to illness per capita per year in disability days equivalent by membership in the labor force and by family status (experimental)	annual
3.1 Proportion of persons who are ill (prevalence) by degree of disability and by occupation	semestral
3.2 Proportion of persons who became ill during the period (incidence) by type of disease and by occupation	semestral
4. Available supply of calories per capita per day	annual
4.1 Proportion of children under 7 who are underweight by degree of undernourishment	annual
5. Available supply of proteins per capita per day by origin (animal or vegetable)	annual
Learning	
6. School enrollment ratio per level of schooling (primary, secondary, tertiary)	annual
7. Value of human capital stock created by schooling (experimental)	annual
7.1 Ratio of mean educational quintile to mean educational capital in the least educated quintile	annual
Income and consumption	
8. Net beneficial product per capita (experimental)	annual
9. Proportion and number of families below the food poverty threshold (experimental)	annual
9.1 Proportion and number of families below the total poverty threshold (experimental)	annual
10. Ratio of mean income of richest quintile to mean income of poorest quintile	annual
11. Rate of inflation of consumer prices	monthly
Employment	
12. Unemployment rate of the totally unemployed by occupation and by educational attainment	quarterly
12.1 Underemployment rate in totally unemployed equivalent by occupation and by educational attainment	quarterly
13. Real wage rate index, skilled vs. unskilled workers, by occupation	monthly
Non-human productive resources	
14. Reproducible capital stock	annual

Recommended indicators	Recommended frequency of evaluation
15. Arable land	annual
15.1 Concentration ratio of cultivable land ownership	annual
16. Forested land	annual
17. Mineral reserves by type of mineral	annual
Housing, utilities, and the environment	
18. Proportion of occupied dwelling units adequately served with water	biennial
18.1 Proportion of the population served by electricity at home	annual
19. Index of housing adequacy (experimental)	annual
19.1 Proportion of households with 1.5 persons or less per room	annual
19.2 Proportion of occupied dwelling units made of strong materials	annual
19.3 Proportion of occupied dwelling units with toilets	annual
20. Air pollution index for Greater Manila (experimental)	quarterly
20.1 Pollution concentration levels by type of pollutant and by station	quarterly
21. Proportion of river-lengths polluted by river/by degree of pollution and	biennial
Public safety and justice	
22. Crime incidence rate by type of crime	
22.1 Index of citizens' perception of public safety and justice (experimental)	annual
23. Backlog of judicial cases	
23.1 Ratio of judicial cases disposed to total cases needing disposition by court of jurisdiction	annual
24. Number admitted to penal institutions	
24.1 Number confined in penal institutions	annual
Political values	
25. Ratio of votes cast to registered voters	every election
25.1 Ratio of registered voters to population aged 21 and over	every election
26. Index of political mobility (experimental)	biennial
27. Index of political participation (experimental)	biennial
27.1 Index of political awareness (experimental)	biennial
27.2 Index of freedom of political dissent (experimental)	biennial
28. Index of political efficacy (experimental)	biennial
Social mobility	
29. Index of occupational mobility (gross mobility) (experimental)	quinquennial
29.1 Coefficient of openness of occupations (circulation mobility) (experimental)	quinquennial
30. Index of perceived social mobility (experimental)	quinquennial

The Use of Social Indicators: Problems and Issues

Many intervening factors come between the design and the use of a set of indicators. Only part of the responsibility for overcoming these difficulties can be accepted by the researchers who design the indices. The final responsibility must be assumed by the decision-makers in government who control the resources, human and otherwise, by which statistical series can be produced on a wide geographic scale and on a continuing basis. This division of labor and of responsibility must be clearly understood.

It is the researchers' function, in the first place, to demonstrate the feasibility of constructing indicators with certain desirable properties. These properties should pertain not only to the adequacy of the measurements, as approximations of reality, but also to the costs and difficulties of obtaining them. There is no point in designing a measurement technology dependent on an abundance of highly trained statisticians, programmers, and computer hardware. The constraints on the supply of statistical resources in the country have to be fully appreciated.

Secondly, the researchers can also accept the task of communicating their findings and recommendations in a fashion convenient to decision-makers. There is no question that the messages should be in understandable language, attractively presented, presented to the proper audiences with proper regard for protocol, and patiently presented over and over again, if necessary. Specialists in the science and art of communications can be set to work on the important problem of ensuring an adequate comprehension of the indicators by prospective users.

It is sometimes suggested that the dichotomy between researchers and decision-makers can be directly resolved by merging people from both parties into some sort of task force. To a limited extent it is possible to draw personnel from the government implementation agencies into the research project itself. But it would be unrealistic to expect that these persons can come from the important decision-making levels of government. Moreover, it would be rather unfortunate if social science research could not be undertaken except by such government directive. Scientists and research administrators should and do take the initiative to try to discern priority problems and initiate the research needed in order to solve them.

With respect to social indicators research in particular, conscious emphasis is placed on identifying society's main areas of concern. The national constitution, the official economic and social development plans, the writings and other statements of the highest leaders in government, among other sources, are all consulted. Unless these statements are merely rhetoric, one might therefore expect that, if any research topic has a close connection with national government priorities, social indicators should be a strong candidate. The thesis might even be advanced that, when an officially declared objective is not accompanied by government efforts to measure its achievements along objective lines, then government has revealed that the objective is not really a high priority.

Another issue pertains to the direct applicability of social indicators to the rating of government performance. The welfare indicators by themselves do not indicate how lines of responsibility or credit need to be drawn. They are independent of the structure of governmental organization and authority. Yet these relationships need to be established in order that the rating procedure may be rational. The performance indicators which are appropriate to a government agency may be one or more steps removed from the indicators of national welfare. Furthermore, the performance of a government agency needs to be related to the resources at its disposal.

An ideal social indicators system cannot be quite neutral, either in its attitude to history or in its effects on present-day socio-political competition. When successes are unfailingly achieved in an area of social concern, the expense of frequent quantitative monitoring loses its justification. A monitoring system should be concentrated in the problem areas, where things always seem to go wrong, when everyone seems to be at a loss as to how to cope with the problems, when present programs are, in effect, only experiments, hopeful yet unsure of success.

Social problems are so complex, so country- and culture-specific, that it is very rare for theoretical models to do more than suggest broad guidelines for policy. The science of development has great need for the elementary task of recording, precisely and frequently, the conditions of the problem areas in the social laboratory. It is from the small changes, the little failures and successes detectable by a monitoring system, that the managers of development can learn the most, can correct errors early before the social costs get too large, and can arrive at new ideas. But where surveillance is irregular or fragmentary or, sometimes, even deliberately avoided, it is little wonder that solutions to social problems are difficult to discover.

In its selective attitude to social phenomena, the social indicators movement eschews as merely archaeological the expectation that it should provide background data for a "balanced" social history, diplomatically reviewing national achievements as well as problems. With its problem orientation, but without the shelter of one or two generations' distance enjoyed by traditional historians, it should not expect to be widely popular, and, indeed, it requires the means to remain viable even when unpopular.

Obviously, it is possible that a set of social indicators, being problem-oriented, can become another data source for governmental critics to exploit. Yet, it adds a good deal to the credibility of government intentions when problem areas are regularly and frequently investigated. One may not overlook the alternative that a private interest group, either domestic or foreign, may feel free to develop its own statistics on what it considers a neglected but socially important area. Of course the option of keeping information confidential, when other socially important reasons require it, always remains open to the proper authorities.

The primary duty of social indicators is to face the problem areas and, obviously, to depict them not propagandistically but objectively and scientifically. For some people, at some times, they may be inconvenient, irritating, or embarrassing. Their purpose, however, is to serve the nation as a whole, and assist in bringing about improvements in the quality of life, looking towards the time when the statistics will no longer be really needed.

References

Adelman, I., and Morris, C. T. *Society, Politics and Economic Development: A Quantative Approach.* Baltimore and London: The Johns Hopkins Press, 1967.

Aidenoff, A., and Johnston, R. "International Work on Social Indicators." United Nations Statistical Office, unpublished paper, 1974.

Arrow, K, J., and Scitovsky, T. (eds.) *Readings in Welfare Economics.* Homewood, Illinois: Richard D. Irwin, Inc., for the American Economic Association, 1969.

Asian Development Bank. *Key Indicators of 23 Developing Member Countries,* 1973.

Bauer, R. A. (ed.) *Social Indicators.* Cambridge, Mass., and London: The Massachusetts Institute of Technology Press, 1966.

Cantril, H. *The Pattern of Human Concerns.* New Brunswick, N. J.: Rutgers University Press, 1965.

Christian, D. E. "International Social Indicators: The OECD Experience." Paper prepared for the Annual Convention of the International Studies Association, St. Louis, March 1974.

Development Academy of the Philippines. *Measuring the Quality of Life: Philippine Social Indicators,* 1975.

Government of Japan, Economic Planning Agency. *Basic Economic and Social Plans—Toward a Vigorous Welfare Society—* 1973–1977, February 1973.

Little, I.M.D. *A Critique of Welfare Economics.* London: Oxford University Press, 1957.

Mangahas, M. (ed.) *Measuring Philippine Development,* Development Academy of the Philippines, 1976.

Marcos, F. E. "Notes on the New Society of the Philippines." Marcos Foundation, Inc., 1973.

Moss, M. (ed.) *The Measurement of Economic and Social Performance.* New York: National Bureau of Economic Research, 1973.

Osborne, M. "Development in Southeast Asia: Goals in the 1970's." Paper presented at the SEADAG Tenth Panel Seminar on Southeast Asian Development Goals–1980, New York, June 1973.

Seers, D. "What are We Trying to Measure," *Journal of Development Studies,* 8:3 (April 1972).

Stanford Research Institute. *Toward Master Social Indicators,* Research Memorandum EPRC-6747–2. Menlo Park, California, February 1969.

Sheldon, E. B., and Moore, W. E. *Indicators of Social Exchange: Concepts and Measurement.* New York: Russel Sage Foundation, 1968.

Strumpel, B. "Economic Stress as a Source of Societal Discontent," Survey Research Center, Institute for Social Research, The University of Michigan. Paper presented at the Annual Meeting of the American Sociological Association, New Orleans, August 1972.

Taylor, C. L., and Hudson, M. C. *World Handbook of Political and Social Indicators,* 1972.

United Nations Statistical Office. "System of Social and Demographic Statistics (SSDS)/Draft Guidelines on Social Indicators," E/CN. 3/450, 26 April 1974.

U. S. Office of Management and Budget. *Social Indicators 1973.* Washington, D.C.: U. S. Government Printing Office, 1973.

PART III

Income Distribution

Economic Growth, Employment Expansion, and Reduction in Income Inequality: The Singapore Experience, 1966–75*

V. V. Bhanoji Rao and M. K. Ramakrishnan

Ever since Simon Kuznets enunciated in the early 1950s the possibility of an increase in the degree of income inequality in the early stages of modern economic growth and a reduction in inequality in the later stages of growth, much research has been done on the important theme of the relationship between economic growth, structural change, and income inequality.* On the same general theme, the objective of the present paper is to ascertain the trends in income inequality in Singapore over the 1966–75 decade, a decade characterized by all-around economic expansion. A brief summary of the 1966–75 economic record of Singapore and a short statement concerning the objective of this paper are presented below. In Section II, methodology and data are reviewed. The empirical results and discussion are contained in Section III. The final section is devoted to a summary and concluding remarks.

Singapore's economic record, 1966–75 [1]

Singapore, with a population of 2.2 million in mid-1975, had a per-capita gross national product amounting to $5880[2] in that year. Until recently Singapore's principal economic activity was *entrepot* trade. During the early 1960s the economy diversified into export-oriented

---

* We are thankful to the Council for Asian Manpower Studies, Ltd., Manila, for research support. Professors You Poh Seng and Harry Oshima gave valuable comments throughout the various stages of research. While thanking them, we note that any remaining errors are our responsibility.
[1] For more detailed tables and discussion see (Bhanoji Rao and Ramakrishnan, 1976: 93–95).
[2] Unless otherwise stated, $ refers to the Singapore dollar. Per-capita GNP in US$ was approximately $2450 in 1975.

manufacturing, banking, and financial services and tourism. Gross domestic product (GDP) at constant prices grew at an average annual rate of 13 percent during 1966–73. The growth rate was less during 1974 and 1975, at 7 percent and 4 percent, respectively. Inflationary pressures were virtually unknown before 1972, but Singapore had its share of the world inflation in 1973 and 1974. The GDP deflator increased by 15 percent in 1973 and 17 percent in 1974, compared to the average annual increase of less than 3 percent during the 1966–72 period and a 5 percent increase in 1975.

As for the sectoral composition of GDP, the share of manufacturing and construction increased from about 22 percent in 1966 to over 30 percent in 1975. The share of commerce was about the same in both years at around 39 percent. The share of services (government, professional, personal, and domestic) declined from 22 percent in 1966 to 15 percent in 1975. The primary sector (agriculture, fishing, and quarrying) is insignificant in terms of its share in GDP.

Considerable gains have accrued on the employment front. Unemployment declined from 8.9 percent in 1966 to 4.5 percent in 1973. The year 1974 was characterized by a tight labor market, with an unemployment rate of 4 percent. The cumulative effect of the low GDP growth rates in 1974 and 1975 (with no growth in the first half of 1975) was the slight increase in the unemployment rate from 4 percent in 1974 to 4.5 percent in 1975. The 1966–73 progress on the employment front has had considerable impact on female participation in the working force. The percentage of females in the working population increased from 20 percent in 1966 to 29 percent in 1973 and 31 percent in 1974, but showed a slight decline in 1975.

As for the changes in sectoral composition of total employment, manufacturing absorbed 24 percent of the working population by 1973, compared to 19 percent in 1966. The boom conditions of 1973 encouraged even more absorption by the manufacturing sector, whereas the 1974–75 recession slightly reduced the 1975 employment share of manufacturing. The share of commerce in employment increased from 23 percent in 1966 to 27 percent in 1973, while the share of services declined from 37 to 26 percent.

In the decade 1966–75 the outstanding features of the economic record were the phenomenal increase in per-capita output, the structural changes that have brought about and accompanied the rapid economic growth, the achievement of full employment, and the increasing participation of women in the labor force. To these must be added the achievements of the public housing program. The Housing and Development Board (HDB) was established in 1960, when less than 10 percent of the population was housed in public sector dwelling units. By the end of 1975 over half the population was housed in the public sector dwelling units, mostly flats in high-rise housing estates.

The scope of this paper

Against the background of the 1966–75 record of economic growth, structural changes, employment expansion, and public housing development, the general objective of this paper is to ascertain and explain the trends in the Gini ratios of personal income distribution during the period. The study covers aggregative as well as sectoral income distributions, nominal as well as real income distributions, and pre-tax as well as post-tax distributions. The effect of subsidized public housing on the income distribution is also discussed. The statistical evidence is used basically to point out that economic growth *per se* need not lead to an increase or a reduction in the degree of inequality; the pattern of development, the changes in the rate and structure of employment, and social policies such as housing development are to be treated as the principal determinants of the degree of income inequality.

Methodology and Data

Methodology

In this paper we use the Gini ratio (G) as the measure of inequality of income.[3] For analytical purposes, we require a method of decomposing the G into components. One example would be the income distribution by sex. Since the overall income distribution is the aggregate of the income distributions by sex, it is natural to ask how the overall Gini ratio and the ratios for each sex are related.

Let X and Y be the income variables for two populations (*e.g.* male population and female population). Then for the combined population, the distribution function of the income variable Z is given by

$$F(z) = p_1F_1(z) + p_2F_2(z)$$

where F_1 and F_2 are the distribution functions of X and Y respectively, and p_1 and p_2 are the respective proportions of people belonging to the

---

[3] By and large, the trends in income distribution portrayed by G and other measures of inequality were about the same in the Singapore context. For more details see (Bhanoji Rao and Ramakrishnan, 1977: 39).

first and the second populations in the combined population. Let G, G_1, and G_2 be the respective Gini ratios for Z, X, and Y. We have

$$G = W_1G_1 + W_2G_2 + \frac{p_1p_2}{\mu} D_{12} \qquad (2)$$

where $\mu = E(Z)$,
$W_1 = $ share of the first population in total income,
$W_2 = $ share of the second population in total income,

and

$$D_{12} = \int_0^\infty [F_1(x) - F_2(x)]^2 \, dx.$$

The interpretation of relation (2) is straightforward. The first term indicates the contribution of the inequality in the first population to total inequality. Similarly, the second term indicates the contribution of the inequality in the second population. In the third term, the factor D_{12}, in a suitably standardized form, may be called an index of distributional disparity. The third term as a whole indicates the contribution of the disparity between the income distributions of the two populations to the inequality of the combined or total population. Where the two populations have identical income distributions, D_{12} becomes zero.

Relation (2) can be generalized for more than two populations. Thus, if the overall income distribution is the aggregate of the distributions of k sectors, we have

$$G = \sum_{i=1}^{k} W_iG_i + \frac{1}{\mu} \sum_{i<j=1}^{k} p_ip_jD_{ij} \qquad (3)$$

with an interpretation analogous to that for relation (2).[4]

In most of our practical work, we found that the second term of (3) is rather insignificant, partly because the values of D_{ij}/μ are small in several instances (but not always) and more importantly because $0 \le p_i, p_j \le 1$ implies invariably extremely low values for the product of p_i and p_j. If we now consider only the first part of relation (3) and assume

[4] Relation (3) is identical to a formulation given in (Mangahas, 1975: 286–344) for discrete income distributions. Recently we came across another decomposition formula in (Pyatt, 1976: 243–255). We feel that Pyatt's decomposition of the Gini ratio does not allow a simplistic understanding of the links between structural change and income inequality. For other references to decomposition formula close to relation (3), see (Pyatt, 1976: 251).

$$G' = \sum_{i=1}^{k} W_i G_i \qquad (4)$$

and utilize time subscripts 'o' and t, we have

$$(G'_t - G'_o) = \sum_{i=1}^{k} W_{io}(G_{it} - G_{io})$$

$$+ \sum_{i=1}^{k} G_{io}(W_{it} - W_{io})$$

$$+ \sum_{i=1}^{k} (W_{it} - W_{io})(G_{it} - G_{io}). \qquad (5)$$

Relation (5) is useful for the purpose of analyzing the change in the Gini ratio over time or across countries. Without loss of generality we may refer to the first term in (5) as the contribution of the change in intra-sectoral inequality to the change in the overall degree of inequality, to the second term as the contribution of structural change to the change in the degree of inequality, and to the third term as the contribution of the interaction between structural change and changing intra-sectoral inequalities.

Data

The basic data on income distribution were obtained from the reports of different sample surveys. In the Appendix to this paper, a brief discussion of the sources of data is provided. In all, personal income distribution data were available for five time periods: 1966, 1972, 1973, 1974, and 1975. The income covered was generally limited to employee and proprietary incomes, thus omitting rents, interests, and dividends. The data on aggregate (employee and proprietary) income distributions are given in Tables 1 and 2. For the various income brackets in these tables, the assumed mean income levels are indicated. These were arrived at as follows.[5] For the lower open-ended income groups, instead of taking the minimum income earned as zero, different minimum levels for different years were assumed; the mid-points of the class intervals were then taken. For the other income groups below $250 in the 1966 distribution and below $400 in the distributions for other years, the mid-points of the income class intervals were taken. For the closed income groups above $250 in the 1966 distribution and above $400 in the distributions for other years, the geometric means of the

[5] The explanation that follows is considered necessary since the computed Gini ratios are very sensitive to assumed mean income levels.

Table 1. Personal Income Distribution, 1966

Monthly income group ($)	Mean income ($)	Percent of persons
Less than $100	60	22.7
100 – 150	125	20.8
150 – 200	175	19.1
200 – 250	225	12.5
250 – 500	353	16.0
500 – 750	612	4.4
750+	1850	4.5
Total (%)		100.0
(No.)		491,977

a Data sources are given in the Appendix.

Table 2. Personal Income Distributions, 1972–75

Monthly income groups ($)	Mean income($)	Percent of persons			
		1972	1973	1974	1975
Less than $200	b	55.4	47.1	38.8	29.4
200 – 400	300	29.5	34.6	38.1	44.1
400 – 600	490	7.6	9.5	12.3	13.6
600 – 800	693	3.2	3.3	4.3	4.8
800 – 1000	894	1.3	1.6	2.0	2.3
1000 – 1500	1225	1.6	2.0	2.9	3.1
1500+	c	1.4	1.6	1.9	2.7
Total (%)		100.0	100.0	100.0	100.0
(No.)		709,397	777,607	800,794	807,766

a Data sources are given in the Appendix.
b The means assumed for the low income group are $120 for 1972 and $125 for 1973, 1974, and 1975.
c For the upper income group the assumed means are $3300 for 1972 and $3500 for 1973, 1974, and 1975.

income class bounds were taken since these means, rather than the class mid-points, appear to be closer to the actual means.[6] For the upper open-ended group, the mean income levels were fixed after an examination of the estimated means based on two alternative approaches. The first approach is to fit a Pareto curve for the last two income groups (a perfect fit since there are only two points) and then estimate the mean income of the last group. The second approach is to take the mean income close to the mean assessed income of the appropriate income groups from the income tax assessment data.

[6] The Singapore Inland Revenue Department publishes data on taxpayers' assessed income distributions. The data contain the actual mean assessed incomes for the various assessed income groups. It was found that the geometric means of the class bounds were close to the actual means in respect of various years.

The two approaches may be illustrated with reference to the 1966 income distribution. Based on fitting a Pareto curve to the last two income groups, the mean income of the "$750 and over" group is estimated to be $1,850. On the other hand, from the assessed income distribution of taxpayers it was found that the mean income was about $1,625 for the taxpayers above the monthly assessed income level of $833. The two estimates ($1,850 and $1,625) are not very close. We prefer to take the higher value of $1,850 since in 1966 (one year after the separation of Singapore from the Malaysian Federation) it is likely that there was some undercoverage in income tax data.

For 1972 the two estimates are quite close and for 1973 they are almost equal. Assessed income distribution data for 1972 and 1973 (assessment years 1973 and 1974) are obtained from the annual reports for 1973 and 1974 of the Singapore Inland Revenue Department. The total assessed income above the annual income level of $20,000 was considered along with the number of resident individual taxpayers to estimate the mean income of the "$1,500 and over" income group for each of the years 1972 and 1973. The estimated mean incomes were $3,300 and $3,500, respectively. Based on a Pareto fit for the last two income groups for each year, the estimates were $3,200 and $3,500. For the years 1974 and 1975 (*i.e.*, tax assessment years 1975 and 1976) the annual reports of the Inland Revenue Department were not yet available at the time of this writing. The 1973 figure of $3,500 was also used as the estimate of mean income of the upper open-ended group for the years 1974 and 1975. Based on a Pareto fit to the last two income groups, the estimated means for 1974 and 1975 for the upper income group were $2,500 and $3,100, respectively. The first was extremely low, but the second was close to $3,500.

The assumed mean income levels for the various income brackets and

Table 3. Comparison of Annual Income Estimates with GDP Estimates*

Year	Annual employee and proprietary income estimates ($ Million)	Estimate of GDP at factor cost ($ Million)	Ratio of column (2) to column (3)
(1)	(2)	(3)	(4)
1966	1581	3037	0.52
1972	2484	7524	0.33
1973	3149	9438	0.33
1974	3481	11738	0.30
1975	4091	12608	0.32

* Data for employee and proprietary incomes from Tables 1 and 2. Data for GDP from (Department of Statistics, 1975) and (Ministry of Finance, 1976).

the proportion of persons in the income brackets may be used to estimate the annual total income figures. These may be compared with GDP at factor cost for each year, as shown in Table 3. The ratios in column (4) are indicators of the extent of undercoverage of the income distribution data used in this study, although GDP at factor cost is not entirely available for distribution to individuals. Apart from the undercoverage due to nonresponse and understatement of income by respondents, the most important limitation is the fact that only employee and proprietary incomes are covered in the data.[7]

Results and Discussion

Mean incomes and Gini ratios, 1966–75

The income distributions and the assumed mean incomes in Tables 1 and 2 are used to obtain the data in Table 4. During the period 1966–72, the estimated mean income per worker increased by 8.5 percent. This rate of growth is insignificant compared to the growth of GDP per worker during the period.[8] It is possible that since employment increased by 44 percent during 1966–72, the cost of this increase has been in depressing the mean incomes throughout the period, for government policies also have favored wage restraints to generate employment opportunities. During the years 1973–75, the mean income

Table 4. Gini Ratios of Personal Income Distributions and Related Data, 1966–75*

Year	Gini ratio*	Mean monthly income per worker[a] ($)*	Percentage change in Gini ratio	Mean income
1966	0.4983	268		
1972	0.4428	291	−11.1	8.6
1973	0.4570	338	3.2	16.1
1974	0.4342	363	− 5.0	7.4
1975	0.4484	422	3.3	16.2

* Computed on the basis of the data in Tables 1 and 2.
[a] The term "worker" includes both employees and proprietors.

[7] The decline in the ratio in column (4) of Table 3 from the 1966 level of 0.52 to 0.30 - 0.33 during 1972–75 may not be interpreted as indicative of an increase in under-enumeration of employee and proprietary income. Instead, the high rates of growth of GDP that occurred during the period could well be associated with a reduction in the proportion of GDP set aside for distribution after deductions for net factor payments to abroad, depreciation, corporate reserve funds, and provident funds.

[8] GDP at current factor cost per worker increased by 72 percent during 1966–72.

changes were affected by inflationary conditions in 1973, by inflation and recession in 1974, and by the relatively larger wage increases recommended for low-income and middle-incomes groups by the National Wages Council in 1975.[9]

The Gini ratios in Table 4 portray a reduction in the degree of income inequality during 1972–75 compared to 1966. The period 1966–72 was one of rapid economic growth for Singapore without any inflationary pressures. Employment expanded considerably. Even though mean personal incomes did not increase much during the period, the addition of more and more workers led to reduction in income inequality. The Singapore experience might be summarized in either of two ways. First, it might be noted that GDP per worker increased by 72 percent during 1966–72 and that the Gini ratio was 11 percent lower in 1972 than in 1966. Hence, one might conclude that a high rate of economic growth need not stand in the way of inequality reduction. A second and alternative interpretation considers the growth of monthly income per worker. Since mean income per worker did not increase significantly during 1966–72, and since this apparent restraint on incomes aided the expansion of employment opportunities, one could conclude that the achievement of full employment and not the high rate of economic growth *per se* was responsible for bringing about the reduction in the Gini ratio. Clearly, the second interpretation is more appropriate in the empirical context of Singapore.

Within the sub-period 1972–75, the levels of the Gini ratio are about the same in 1972 and 1975. The years 1973 and 1974 may be considered years of temporary adjustment, since both years were subject to a high rate of inflation. Thus, in 1973, when inflation first hit Singapore, the Gini ratio increased, presumably due to the adverse effect of the inflation on wage and salary incomes and the beneficial

---

[9] In 1973, as noted above, Singapore had an inflation rate of 15 percent (in terms of the GDP deflator), but economic growth continued to be high (11.2 percent of GDP growth at constant prices). In 1974, the inflation rate was 17 percent and the economic growth slackened to 7 percent. The National Wage Council (NWC), a body set up by the Government in 1972 to promote orderly wage increases, recommended flat 8 percent and 9 percent wage increases for July 1972-June 1973 and July 1973- June 1974, respectively. Thus, the 1973 increase of 16 perc nt in the mean income per worker was brought about by the favorable effect of inflation on proprietary incomes. The low growth rate of the mean income per worker in 1974 was due to the slackening of the economic growth rate and its unfavorable effect on proprietary incomes. In 1975, the inflation rate and the growth rate were 5 percent and 4 percent, respectively. However, the NWC recommended wage increases of $40 plus 6 percent of wages and salaries for the July 1974 to June 1975 period. Thus, the majority of lower and middle income groups could have obtained higher percentage increases in wages and salaries compared to the upper income groups. It must be this factor that has brought about the high growth rate of the mean income per worker in 1975.

impact on proprietary incomes.[10] In 1974, wages and salaries adjusted to the inflation, proprietary incomes were adversely affected by the low rate of economic growth, and the Gini ratio declined before regaining the 1972 level in 1975.

Whether one considers the 1966–72 experience or the 1966–75 experience, the reduction in the Gini ratio in 1972-75 compared to 1966 can be confirmed, subject of course to the annual fluctuating due to inflationary effects and adjustments.

Gini ratios by sector of economic activity, 1966 and 1975

In Table 5 the Gini ratios for eight sectors of economic activity are given for 1966 and 1975. For the economy as a whole the weighted sums of sector Gini ratios are given along with the overall Gini ratios obtained from Table 4. It is notable that the weighted sums of sector Gini ratios are very close to the overall ratios.

For the nation as a whole the Gini ratio was lower in 1975 than in

Table 5. Gini Concentration Ratios by Sector of Economic Activity, 1966 and 1975

Sector of activity	Gini ratios	
	1966	1975
Agriculture and fishing	0.4471	0.4364
Quarrying	0.5210	0.5436
Manufacturing	0.4816	0.4462
Construction	0.3512	0.3724
Utilities	0.3150	0.4862
Commerce	0.5230	0.4614
Transport and communication	0.3994	0.3407
Services	0.5213	0.4694
All sectors: Weighted total[a]	0.4914	0.4421
Overall ratios: Table 4	0.4983	0.4484

[a] Defined as $\Sigma\, W_i\, G_i$

[10] The Gini ratios for employee and proprietary incomes are as follows:

	Employees	Proprietors
1966	0.4744	0.5741
1975	0.4171	0.4751

As may be expected, the Gini ratio is higher for proprietary incomes than for employee incomes in both years. The reduction in the employees' Gini ratio can be explained on the basis of expanding employment opportunities. The reduction in the proprietary Gini ratio, however, can be explained only on the basis of increasing competition among proprietors (assuming that the degree of under-reporting of incomes in 1975 is not significantly different from that in 1966 and the reduction in the Gini ratio noted is not due to errors of observation).

1966. This pattern of change in the Gini ratio is exhibited by the following sectors which, taken together, constitute the mainstay of the Singapore economy: agriculture and fishing, manufacturing, commerce, transport, and communications and services. The Gini ratios increased during 1966–75 in the quarrying, construction, and utilities sectors.

To explain the trends in sectoral Gini ratios, we consider three characteristics of the working population: age, sex, and employment status. The hypotheses are that an increase in the proportion of young people in the working force will depress the Gini ratio of an income distribution by increasing the numbers in the lower income groups and that an increase in the proportion of females has a similar effect. An increase in the proportion of employees may tend to increase the share of employee income in total income and thus contribute to a lowering of the degree of income inequality. Alternatively, if the increase in the proportion of employees coincides with a nation's efforts to increase total employment through restrictions on wage increases, then the reduction in employee income inequality will itself contribute to the reduction in overall inequality.

In Table 6 these three characteristics of the working population are shown for the years 1966 and 1975. For the nation as a whole during 1966–75 increases are shown in the proportion of workers below 30 years of age, the proportion of females in the working population, and the proportion of employees. The major sectors (namely, manufacturing, commerce, transport, and communications and services) broadly conform to the expected trends in the three characteristics of the working population.

In agriculture and fishing, the proportion of employees in the working population has declined and the proportion of young people has increased marginally. The proportion of females has declined substantially. Thus, the decline in the Gini ratio during 1966–75 could be mainly due to the decline in inequality of proprietary incomes. In the quarrying sector, the proportion of young people declined, the proportion of females increased substantially, and the proportion of employees also increased. The slightly higher 1975 Gini ratio (compared to 1966) was probably due to the strong effect of the decline in the proportion of young people. In the construction sector, the major factor behind the increased Gini was the decline in the proportion of employees.

In the utilities sector the major change during 1966–75 was the increase in the proportion of young people. Yet, the Gini ratio increased during the period. Disproportionate salary increases during the period could have caused a widening of employee income inequality in this sector. We should note, however, that sampling errors can be sub-

Table 6. Selected Characteristics of the Working Population, 1966–75*

Sector of activity	Year	Percentage aged 10–29	Percentage of females	Percentage of employees
Agriculture and fishing	1966	34.6	16.9	31.1
	1975	38.3	11.3	20.6
Quarrying	1966	38.2	5.4	98.2
	1975	36.2	8.6	100.0
Manufacturing	1966	50.8	22.2	86.1
	1975	63.1	39.3	90.3
Construction	1966	45.2	7.8	95.8
	1975	49.2	7.8	89.9
Utilities	1966	33.4	4.8	100.0
	1975	49.1	8.5	100.0
Commerce	1966	39.8	13.3	67.1
	1975	47.5	28.7	70.7
Transport and communications	1966	27.2	4.9	72.5
	1975	39.1	11.5	86.5
Services	1966	40.0	32.6	86.6
	1975	55.4	32.5	94.4
All sectors	1966	40.9	20.5	79.8
	1975	52.5	28.8	84.6

* Data from (Daroesman, 1971) and (Ministry of Labor and National Statistical Commission, 1975).

stantial in these minor sectors; hence, the Gini ratios, as well as the data in Table 6, may be affected.

By and large, the entry of females into the working force in large numbers and the increase in the proportion of young people have affected most of the economic activities in Singapore. The reduction in income inequality during 1966–75 was broadly in consonance with the expected effects on income inequality of these changes in the characteristics of the work force.

Structural change and its effect on income inequality

Incomes accrue to individuals in the process of producing various types of goods and services. Each activity is characterized by its own peculiar income distribution, as the Gini ratios in Table 5 show. For instance, for 1966 the Gini ratios are high in quarrying, commerce, and services and low in the construction, utilities, and transport sectors. Between these extremes are the Gini ratios of the agricultural and manufacturing sectors. The important question here is the subsequent effect of production structure changes on the national Gini ratio.

In Table 7 are presented the income shares by sector and the Gini ratios for 1966 and 1975. As far as the structure of income is concerned, a significant change is the increase in the income share of manufacturing and the decline in the income share of commerce and services. If the income distributions had remained unaltered over the period and only the structure of income had changed, the weighted Gini ratio would have been 0.4864. In this case, the Gini ratio would have declined by only 1.1 percent. Thus, a change in the structure of income, other things remaining equal, has only a negligible effect on the overall Gini ratio.

Table 7. Income Shares and Gini Ratios by Sector, 1966 and 1975

Sector	Income shares (W_i)		Gini ratios (G_i)	
	1966	1975	1966	1975
Primary	2.0	2.4	0.4619	0.5222
Manufacturing	15.9	23.7	0.4816	0.4462
Construction	4.4	4.2	0.3512	0.3724
Utilities, transport, communications	11.5	13.4	0.3892	0.3555
Commerce and services	66.2	56.3	0.5226	0.4673
All sectors: Weighted total[a]			0.4920	0.4446
Overall ratios: Table 4	100.0	100.0	0.4983	0.4484

[a] Defined as * $\Sigma W_i G_i$.

The change in the Gini ratio over the 1966–75 period may be decomposed as follows in line with the formula given above and on the basis of the data given in Table 7:

Change in the overall (weighted sum) Gini ratio   = –0.0474

(i)   Change attributable to variation in intra-sectoral
                                             Gini ratios   = –0.0440

(ii) Change attributable to variation in sectoral
                                             income ratios   = –0.0056

(iii) Change attributable to the interaction of the
      two sets of variation mentioned in (i) and (ii)   =   0.0022

In relative terms, the major factor contributing to the decline in the Gini ratio was the change in intra-sectoral inequality. Thus, if one were to view structural change in the narrow sense of the changing sectoral composition of income, its effect on inequality is rather insignificant.

However, if one were to take a broad view of structural change and include in it reduction of unemployment, the changing sex composition of the working force, and the changes in various other characteristics of income recipients, then, naturally, whatever happens to income inequality is the result of "structural change" only. The same applies to the view one takes of economic growth. If one considers simply the growth of GDP as "economic growth", then (depending on the direction in which all other factors change) one may or may not find a reduction in income inequality over a period of GDP growth.

Inequality of real income

So far reference has been made only to money-income inequality. The consumer price index shot up from 100 in November 1972 to over 140 in 1975. In view of this extraordinary increase in consumer prices, one naturally doubts the wisdom of considering only money-income changes and money-income distributions. The solution, of course, is not the deflation of the income accruing to various income groups by an overall price index, since this will not alter the Gini ratio. An attempt is therefore made to apply different price indices to different income groups. The indices are based on the consumption patterns given in the 1972–73 household expenditure survey for different expenditure groups as well as the individual commodity price indices used in the revised consumer price index compiled by the Department of Statistics taking November 1972 as the base. These indices[11] refer to various family expenditure groups. It is possible that family expenditure patterns and price indices based on these patterns may differ significantly from those of individual income earners in similar expenditure or income groups. In the hope that this discrepancy may not be a significant factor, the price indices are applied to the personal income distributions of 1966 and 1975.

In terms of 1972 consumer prices, mean personal income in 1966 amounted to $295 and to $293 in 1975. Average purchasing power (average real income) has thus changed little. It was suggested earlier that in the process of achieving full employment, relatively more people were added at the lower income levels. Fortunately, this very achievement had a favorable impact on household and family incomes, since the average number of workers per household increased from 1.5 in 1966 to 2.1 in 1975. Thus, in terms of 1972 consumer prices, average household income increased from $442 in 1966 to $615 in 1975, an

---

[11] For the actual values of the indices see (Bhanoji Rao and Ramakrishnan, 1976: 114).

increase of nearly 40 percent over a period of nine years. This is a reasonable way of looking at the record of performance of the employment-oriented growth strategy adopted by Singapore. As for the degree of inequality, the 1966 income distribution at 1972 prices gave a Gini ratio of 0.4964 as against the money income inequality of 0.4983. For 1975, the two ratios are, respectively, 0.4616 and 0.4484. Thus, in 1975 real income was less equally distributed than money income when "real income" was defined in terms of a 1972 consumption goods basket. The extent of decline in the real-income Gini ratio of real income was only 7 percent over 1966–75 compared to the 10 percent decline in the money-income Gini ratio.

Inequality: Pre-tax and post-tax

In the above income distribution analysis we have used pre-tax incomes. Since income taxation is progressive, it is of interest to see its effect on the Gini ratio. For this purpose the actual tax rates for each income group were computed, and the equivalent amount of real income for each income group was subtracted in the real income distributions. The post-tax Gini ratios for 1966 and 1973 were, respectively, 0.4803 and 0.4339 as against the pre-tax ratios of 0.4964 and 0.4616. The post-tax real income Gini ratio has declined by 10 percent compared to the 7 percent decline in the pre-tax Gini ratio. The income tax structure did perform one of its tasks—that is, the mopping up of excess purchasing power in the hands of the upper income groups.

Subsidized public housing and income inequality

One important aspect of life in Singapore is the availability of decent living accommodations. Over half the population live in flats in high-rise buildings constructed by the Housing and Development Board (HDB). This public sector construction activity has been a great benefit. For example, a one- or two-person household with a monthly income of $260 in 1975 paid a monthly rent and service charge of $26. Thus, some 90 percent of income was available for other consumption. If there were no public sector flats, the household under consideration would probably have ended up paying more for rent and also probably had lower-quality accommodation. This indirect effect on real income and its distribution is of some importance when we are comparing the degree of inequality in 1966 and 1975.

Our basic data refer to the income distributions of individuals. To impute a rental benefit to the individuals staying in HDB accommodation we need data on the number of earners in the HDB estates, their income distributions in 1966 and 1975, the types of flats (*e.g.* number of rooms) they occupy, and the types of households to which they belong (*e.g.* number of earners) as well as rental differentials between HDB and private flats in the two years under consideration. Published data on these various aspects are not available, and we have to depend on some other sources.

Two sample surveys were conducted by the Research and Statistics Department of HDB, one in October 1968 and the other in early 1973.[12] The following data are taken from these two surveys:

Type of flat	Mean household income per month ($)		Monthly rent and service charge ($)[13]
	1968	1973	
1 room	180	267	26
2 room	294	400	46
3 room	447	605	66
4 or 5 rooms	677	900	86

In 1968, rent constituted 14 percent, 16 percent, 15 percent, and 13 percent of household income, respectively, for the four types of accommodation. In 1973 the respective percentages were 10, 11, 11, and 10. A direct implication of these percentages would be that in the years of inflation, such as 1973, the residents of HDB flats benefited through savings in purchasing power.

But a more important aspect is the rental differential between the public and private sectors. In 1966, the average monthly rentals paid by households in public and private flats were as follows[14]:

Type of flat	Average monthly rental ($)	
	for HDB flat	for private flat
1 room	22	45
2 room	48	160
3 room	69	170
4 or more rooms	80	252

[12] (Yeh, 1972) contains the data and report of the 1968 survey of HDB households. There is no published report for the 1973 survey, but the results are summarized in (Lee and Lim, 1974: 99–114).

[13] Data refer to 1973 standard flats. There were no significant changes in the charges between 1966 and June 1975, the period of concern in our study.

[14] In the published report of the *1966 Sample Household Survey* various tables are

Even in a year of low inflation such as 1966, the private-sector rentals were at least twice the public-sector rentals. In 1975, consumer prices were about 55 percent higher than in 1966. The most reasonable assumption one can make about private flat rents in 1975 is that they were at least triple the HDB sector rents. Thus, an average household living in a HDB flat in 1966 paid about 15 percent of its income as rent whereas in the private sector it would have paid at least 30 percent. In 1975, the HDB rent as a proportion of average household income was about 10 percent as against the possible minimum of 30 percent in the private sector. Applying the same percentages to individuals, the imputed benefit to an individual of living in a HDB flat amounted to a minimum of 15 percent of his income in 1966 and 20 percent in 1975.

In 1968, the number of income earners living in HDB flats was around 122,000, or 22.4 percent of an estimated 545,000 workers (excluding unpaid family workers) in the total economy. Assuming that in 1966 20 percent of a total of 492,000 workers lived in HDB flats and that they were distributed in the personal income range of $0 to $500 in the same way as all the other individuals of the economy, it was found that in the said income range (in 1966) there were a total of 448,000 persons, of which 98,400 or 22 percent were in HDB flats. Thus, in the various income groups up to $500, a total of 22 percent had real income (purchasing power) enhanced by 15 percent. Alternatively, the real income of each income group as a whole was enhanced by 3.3 ($=15 \times .22$) percent. With this adjustment in the purchasing power of the income groups up to $500, the real income Gini ratio works out to 0.4903, which is slightly less than the ratio of 0.4964 for the distribution of real income not including the imputed HDB rental benefits.

In 1973, there were 271,000 workers residing in the HDB flats. They constituted about 35 percent of the total number of workers in the economy. Let us assume that in 1975 40 percent of the workers in the economy lived in HDB flats and belonged to the various income groups up to a monthly income level of $800; further, assume that the income distributions of all workers and HDB workers were alike. In each income group up to $800 a total of 43.6 percent of the workers were living in HDB flats, and, as noted earlier, the imputed extra income these HDB residents derived was 20 percent of their income. Alternatively, the real income of each income group as a whole was enhanced by 8.7 percent. The real-income distribution suitably ad-

available on the distribution of households by monthly rental group, number of rooms, type of house (bungalow, HDB flat, private flat, etc.) and other criteria. Note that the average HDB rentals for 1966 given above from the 1966 survey are very close to the rentals of standard flats for 1973.

justed for the accrual of imputed benefits of HDB accommodation resulted in a Gini ratio of 0.4494 for 1975, lower than the unadjusted real-income Gini ratio of 0.4616 by about 2.6 percent.

The provision of accommodation by HDB to nearly half the population of Singapore had the desirable effect of reducing real income inequality. The extent of reduction was greater in 1975 than in 1966 because, on the one hand, prices were high in 1975, but HDB rentals did not change, thus making available more purchasing power to HDB residents; and, on the other hand, in 1975 there was a much larger number of people staying in HDB flats. It should be made clear, however, that the imputations of benefits to HDB residents and the Gini ratios that we have computed based on the adjusted real-income distributions are only crude indicators involving a large number of assumptions.

Summary and Concluding Remarks

The following is a summary of the Gini ratios for 1966 and 1975 in regard to the income distributions based on different income concepts:

Income concept	Gini ratios		Percentage decline
	1966	1975	
1. Money income	0.4983	0.4484	10.0
2. Pre-tax real income	0.4964	0.4616	7.0
3. Post-tax real income	0.4803	0.4339	9.7
4. Pre-tax real income adjusted for imputed benefits of HDB accomodation	0.4903	0.4494	8.3
5. Post-tax real income adjusted for imputed benefits of HDB accomodation	0.4742	0.4223	10.9

The main conclusion of this paper has been that a high rate of employment expansion within an environment of rapid economic growth has facilitated the reduction in money-income as well as real-income inequality in Singapore during 1966–75. Public housing development for the lower and middle income groups has also contributed towards a reduction of inequalities. Progressive income taxation has performed its designated role of reducing the purchasing power of the upper income groups.

Developing countries in Asia and elsewhere suffering from high rates of unemployment may well be informed that full employment, when achieved, will have its own contribution to make towards reducing income disparities, and the objective of full employment should thus take precedence over policies aimed at redistributing income among the currently employed. Economic growth does not necessarily lead to growth in employment, but employment-oriented economic growth can be planned and fostered within the framework of appropriate policies. Whether or not steps are taken to reduce the incidence of poverty or to reduce income disparities, employment opportunities must keep pace with labor force growth rates in the developing countries. Reduction in income inequality can be a happy by-product of employment growth.

Appendix: Sources of Data

In Table I of this Appendix, a summary of the sources of data is provided. The methodology, coverage, concepts, and available tabulations in the different sample surveys are briefly described below.

Table I. Income Distribution Data Sources, 1966–75

Date of survey	Title of survey	Sampling fraction (%)	Comments on income data collected	Place of publication
Sept. to Nov. 1966	Singapore Sample Household Survey, 1966	4.0	Separate data on employee and proprietary income were collected. Data were available in unpublished computer printouts. Income relates to "last month".	(You Poh Seng & Associates, 1967) and (Daroesman, 1971)
March 1972	Preparatory Survey for the Household Expenditure Survey, 1972/73	1.3	"Principal monthly income" of each member of household was collected. Mostly employee and proprietary incomes could have been covered.	(Dept. of Statistics, 1974 and 1975)
June 1973	Labor Force Survey, June 1973	1.0	"Income last month" was obtained for each	(Dept. of Statistics, 1974 and 1975)

Date of survey	Title of survey	Sampling fraction (%)	Comments on income data collected	Place of publication
			member of household. The published report does not explain the income concept, but most probably it is the same as in the 1972 Survey.	
May-June 1974	Labor Force Survey of Singapore, 1974	2.06	"Gross monthly income last month" was obtained for each member of household. The income concept distinguishes employee income and business income.	(Ministry of Labor & National Statistical Commission, 1974 and 1975)
May-June 1975	Labor Force Survey of Singapore, 1975	1.85	—same—	(Ministry of Labor & National Statistical Commission, 1975 and 1975)

1966 sample household survey[15]

In 1966, the Economic Research Centre of the University of Singapore and the Ministry of National Development organized a household sample survey as part of which data was obtained on individual incomes. The survey covered 4 percent of the Singapore population. The data on personal incomes did not form part of the published reports on the survey. The authors had access to the computer printouts of the 1966 survey, from which elaborate tabulations were scrutinized and the data on personal income distribution were obtained by sex, ethnic group, industry, occupation, and education. The overall undercoverage due to non-response to the income question may be in the region of 4 to 5 percent. This, however, is the undercoverage of income recipients. In addition, there is the significant problem of inadequate income coverage. Only employee and proprietary incomes were covered.

[15] Two reports were published relating to the survey: (You Poh Seng and Associates, 1967) and (Daroesman, 1971).

1972 and 1973 surveys[16]

The two surveys which provide income distribution data for 1972 and 1973 were conducted by the Singapore Department of Statistics. The first, conducted during March 1972, was a preliminary survey undertaken as a part of the household expenditure survey of 1972–73. The preliminary survey covered 1.3 percent of the Singapore population and collected information on the average monthly "principal income" of the members of the sampled households. Based on the explanation in the Survey Report, it would appear that the principal income of the households was income from employment, business, or from property. We feel, however, that in the majority of cases the principal income will be either employee income or proprietary income.

The labor force survey conducted in June 1973 covered 1 percent of the Singapore population. Data on "income last month" were collected for each household member. The income concept was not explained in the published report. Presumably, the concept was comparable to that of the household expenditure survey of 1972–73.

1974 and 1975 labor force surveys[17]

The two labor force surveys were conducted by the Ministry of Labor and the National Statistical Commission. The 1974 survey covered 2.06 percent of the population. The questionnaire consisted of a household schedule and an individual schedule for persons aged 10 years or over. As part of the individual schedule, the income question was asked thus: "What was your gross income last month?" Seven income groups were used on the questionnaire itself to record the response for the income question. As for the income concept, the published report states that gross monthly income refers to the total amount of income earned during the calendar month preceding the data of interview. For employees the information supplied relates to wages or salaries inclusive of allowances and overtime for all jobs, commissions, tips, and bonuses. For employers and own account workers, however, the information supplied relates to the total receipt from sales or services performed less the business expenses incurred. It is apparent that property incomes were not covered in the income distribution data for

[16] Published by the Department of Statistics in 1974 and 1975; see (Department of Statistics, 1974 and 1975).
[17] Published by the Ministry of Labor and National Statistical Commission in 1974 and 1975; see (Ministry of Labor and National Statistical Commission, 1974 and 1975).

1975. The 1975 survey followed closely the pattern set by the 1974 survey in terms of the questionnaire and the income concept. The tabulations are also equivalent to those of the 1974 survey.

Notes on data comparability

None of the sample surveys described above were single-purpose income distribution surveys. Collection of data on income was a somewhat tail-end affair as far as the questionnaire goes, and the sampling schemes are designed mainly to get a representative collection of different ethnic groups and different geographical parts of Singapore. Such schemes need not necessarily provide a representative sample from the income distribution population. Under such circumstances, a larger rather than a smaller sample size is more likely to cover the various income groups in the population. On this score, we should think that the 1966 sample survey provides relatively better income distribution data than the other surveys. As for comparability based on the size of the sampling fraction, comparing data from the 1966 survey with the data from the 1974 and 1975 surveys may be more justifiable than comparing the data from the 1966 survey with the data from the 1972 and 1973 surveys.

In the 1966, 1973, 1974, and 1975 surveys the income data refer to individual incomes. In the 1972 survey both individual and household incomes are collected. The 1966 tabulations on individual income distributions exclude unpaid family workers. For the other surveys, even though the unpaid family workers are included in the tabulations, eliminating them from the tabulations is not a problem. Thus, comparability of the income recipients can be achieved.

Next we have the problem of comparability of the income concept and its measurement. Broadly speaking, the income concepts of the 1966, 1974, and 1975 surveys appear to be comparable. But the income concept of these surveys is not comparable with the concepts used in the other two surveys. In the 1972 survey average monthly income was collected, and the concept of principal income used in the survey was apparently more comprehensive than simply employment income and business income. The 1973 survey income concept was probably the same as that of the 1972 survey. In 1973, however, the income data collected were for "income last month", not average monthly income.

From the standpoint of sample size, income concepts, and related aspects, we feel that the data for 1966, 1974, and 1975 are broadly comparable; the data for 1972 and 1973 are used as supplementary information.

References

Bhanoji Rao, V. V., and Ramakrishnan, M. K. "Economic Growth, Structural Change and Income Inequality, Singapore, 1966–1975," *The Malayan Economic Review*, October 1976.

Bhanoji Rao, V. V., and Ramakrishnan, M. K. *Economic Growth, Structural Changes and Income Inequality, Singapore, 1966–1975* (mimeo), September 1977.

Daroesman, Ruth. *Singapore Sample Household Survey, 1966, Report No. 2, Administrative Report*. Singapore: Economic Research Center, University of Singapore, October 1971.

Department of Statistics. *Singapore National Accounts, 1960–73*, Singapore, 1975.

————. *Report on the Household Expenditure Survey, 1972/1973*. Singapore, December 1974.

————. *Labour Force Survey, June 1973*. Singapore, January 1975.

Lee, T. S., and Lim, S.W.H. "Housing and Development Board Household Survey, 1972," *Singapore Statistical Bulletin*, December 1974.

Mangahas, Mahar, "Income Inequality in the Philippines: A Decomposition Analysis," in *Income Distribution, Employment and Economic Development in Southeast and East Asia, Volume I*. Tokyo: Japan Economic Research Centre and Manila: Council for Asian Manpower Studies, July 1975.

Ministry of Finance. *Economic Survey of Singapore*, Singapore, 1976.

Ministry of Labor and National Statistical Commission. *Report on the Labor Force Survey of Singapore, 1974*. Singapore, December 1974.

————. *Report on the Labor Force Survey of Singapore, 1975*. Singapore, December 1975.

Pyatt, Graham, "On the Interpretation and Disaggregation of Gini Coefficients," *The Economic Journal*, June 1976.

Yeh, Stephen H. K. (ed.) *Public Housing in Singapore*. Singapore University Press, 1975.

You Poh Seng and Associates. *Singapore Sample Household Survey, 1966, Report No. 1, Tables Relating to Population and Housing*. Singapore: Ministry of National Development and University of Singapore, September 1967.

Economic Growth and Income Inequality in Hong Kong

L. C. Chau

The experience of Hong Kong during the decade and a half since 1961 provides a most useful case study of the impact of economic growth on income distribution.* The combination of conditions prevailing in Hong Kong is rarely found in other developing economies: an uninterrupted process of growth stretching for over two decades,[1] complete economic freedom, lack of price distortions,[2] and a high degree

---

* The findings presented here are from a study completed under the auspices of the Council for Asian Manpower Studies. The author is indebted to Professor Oshima for valuable comments on an earlier draft of this paper presented at the Second Asian Regional Conference of the International Association for Research in Income and Wealth.

[1]For Hong Kong the decade of the 1960s was a period of sustained prosperity and rapid growth which can be dated back to the mid-1950s (Chou, 1966: 81). Over the period 1961–71, gross domestic product was growing at 9 percent per annum in real terms and per-capita real income at 7 percent. The backbone of this growth was the export-oriented manufacturing industry. The value of domestic exports (re-exports remain an important source of income), of which 95 percent was manufactured goods, expanded at a compound rate of 17 percent, and employment at registered manufacturing establishments at 8.8 percent (Riedel, 1974: 8, 17). In 1971, the manufacturing sector employed 48 percent of the labor force, up from 43 percent a decade earlier. And from 80 to 90 percent of its output, mostly light, labor-intensive consumer goods, was sold overseas.

The pace of economic growth slowed markedly around the turn of the decade. Both internal and external forces had contributed to this. With its rapidly rising wages and skyrocketing land rents, Hong Kong gradually lost its competitive edge in the export markets to such newcomers as Taiwan and South Korea. The pace of export growth dropped noticeably during 1970–72. This was followed by the world recession in 1974 and 1975. All told, over the 1971–75 period, the real growth in gross domestic product was down to 5.8 percent per year and per-capita product to 3.8 percent. Furthermore, there were only minimal increases in manufacturing employment.

[2]A number of circumstances that characterized Hong Kong's economic growth are of particular relevance for analyzing the impact of growth on income inequality. For the period considered, the government of Hong Kong was justly renowned for

of entrepreneurship and economic motivation among people of all economic classes. Finally, because of Hong Kong's sealed border the resulting inelastic labor supply greatly accelerated the process of labor force absorption.[3] Over one to two decades in Hong Kong we can observe structural change in, for example, employment and wage rates, which may take generations to complete in other countries. As a result, the effects that we want to observe are not obscured by long-term factors such as population growth, technological progress, and political change. In sum, we may say that development in Hong Kong during this period provides a laboratory case for observing the economics of the impact of growth on income distribution.[4]

The objectives of this study are to assess the impact of rapid economic growth in Hong Kong on inequality in the size distribution of income, to identify and evaluate various sources of change in inequality, and to generalize on the pattern of change and its surrounding circumstances.[5]

---

its strict *laissez-faire* policy. Allocation and distribution were left entirely to market forces. Intervention in the price mechanism was carefully avoided. There were no controls on foreign exchange, the interest rate, or wages. There were no tariff or import controls. Regulations on labor and capital markets were kept to a minimum. Competition was further enhanced by a proliferation of small firms, a high degree of economic motivation, and a general lack of social or cultural obstacles to mobility. In particular, unionism has not developed in Hong Kong. As a result, there has emerged a highly competitive labor market with a high rate of labor mobility.

Characteristically, land was sold at auction. The government of Hong Kong steadfastly resisted the demand from industrialists for making industrial land available to selected pioneering industries at preferential prices. The belief was explicit that market allocation alone would lead to the most efficient allocation of resources. This policy was modified in 1972 (Jao, 1976: 287–288).

[3]Immigration into Hong Kong was, after the mid-1950s, strictly and effectively controlled by governments on both sides of the border. By 1961, the rapidly expanding manufacturing sector had largely absorbed the substantial labor surplus of earlier years which resulted from the large refugee influx from China during 1949–51. The 1961 Census showed that the rate of open unemployment was only 1.7 percent. Therefore, industrialization in subsequent years resulted in an increasingly tight labor market. Specifically, as employment in manufacturing increased at a considerably higher rate than the overall supply of the working population, labor relocation was necessary. As already noted, this was achieved through the price mechanism with a far-reaching impact on income distribution.

[4]Unfortunately, data for evaluating income distribution change over this period are most unsatisfactory. Information hardly exists for the period before 1966. Household income data were collected in the by-census of 1966, but the sampling fraction was only about 1 percent, and only 64 percent of those asked volunteered an answer to the income question. Because of this last fact, the income information might not be from a random sample of households. Comprehensive information on household income became available in 1971, as all households were required to provide income information to the 1971 population and housing census. The 1976 by-census also collected information on both household and personal income. But only preliminary results are now available.

[5]Opinions differ widely about the trend of inequality during the 1960s. Information from the 1966 by-census and the 1971 census shows a substantial fall in the con-

In evaluating the effects of a given structural change[6] on income distribution, general criteria for decomposition can prove to be highly useful. Classifying households by the structural variable concerned,[7] the overall income dispersion can be expressed in terms of three components which are associated with different aspects of the income distribution curves of the various identifiable sectors.[8] The first component relates to the shares of the various classes of households and may be referred to as the share effect. The second component relates to the location of different income distribution curves and may be referred to as the within-group effect. The third component relates to

centration ratio—from 0.487 to 0.439—between the two dates. Working with fragmentary data pertaining to the industrial sector, Owen (1971: 204) and Riedel (1974: 103) suggested that the income share of labor in manufacturing fell during the 1960s. Chau and Hsia examined changes in various determinants of income distribution reported in the census data of 1961, 1966, and 1971, as well as changes in wage structure, and concluded that there was a narrowing of income dispersion among households between 1961 and 1971 (Chau and Hsia, 1975: 628–9). However, there also exist other well-documented views. For example, from the fact that the growth rate of the average wage was below that of national income, Walker concluded that growth did not benefit the workers (Walker, 1972: 53).

[6]Rapid industrialization under limited labor supply conditions will be accompanied by extensive structural changes. The existing labor force is employed more intensively. The labor force participation rate of the more "marginal" members of the working age population rises, altering the sex–age structure of the labor force. Rapidly expanding industries attract workers away from industries with a less elastic demand for labor. The improving employment situation reduces the supply of unskilled workers, contributing to an upward shift in the general occupational level. In a free-enterprise economy all these adjustments will be effected through rising wages and a changing wage structure. The changing economic situation will also affect a number of socio-demographic factors related to income distribution such as the size of household, the age of marriage, and education. To assess the trend effect on household income distribution, we need to evaluate the net balance of these forces.

[7]Relying on information collected in the 1971 census, we have analyzed the relationship between the distribution of household income and some of the factors mentioned above and found that income distribution is significantly related to the following variables: industrial affiliation, occupation, employment status, education, household size, and number of earners. These cross-section results are reported in (Chau and Hsia, 1975: 608–621). These relationships observed in 1971 will be used as the basis for evaluating the impact of changes in these factors over 1961–71. In addition, we will analyze changes in the following relevant variables: wages, national income by industrial origin, and distribution of household expenditure.

[8]In general, the effects of a given change on the overall equality of income distribution can be assessed from an analysis of these three sources of inequality. For example, any change which enlarges the relative size of a class with a narrow income dispersion would contribute to overall equality. Similarly, a change which reduces the differential of the mean incomes of the various classes would bring about the same effect. The same result would also follow from any change that narrows the intrasectoral distribution of one or more of the household classes. A decomposition along this line was used by Kuznets to analyze the effect of growth on income distribution (Kuznets, 1955: 12–18). Oshima also derived a formula to decompose the total absolute deviation in terms of these three components (Oshima, 1970: 17–19).

the income dispersion for individual sectors and may be referred to as the between-group effect.[9]

The Share Effect

A change in the distribution of the labor force among various groups would affect the overall income distribution through the share effect, inasmuch as the income dispersion differs between these groups. In this section we will examine changes for those groups for which information is available: industry, occupation, and employment status.

Change in industrial structure and income distribution

Rapid industrialization in Hong Kong has resulted in notable changes in the deployment of labor force among different industrial sectors. Such changes are presented in Table 1 by one-digit ISIC classification. Though the period spans only 15 years, significant structural changes have taken place and a clear trend can be identified. Among the major sectors, the primary sector, including agriculture, fishing, and mining, is the big loser: its employment share fell from 8 percent in 1961 to less than 3 percent in 1976. The trade and finance sectors are the big gainers: their employment share rose steadily over the entire period. Manufacturing, the largest employer, followed a checkered course. After rising from 43 to 48 percent during the first decade, its employment share fell back to 45.3 percent in 1976. Textiles accounted for all the relative growth of manufactures during the first period and continued to grow in relative importance during the second period. The employment share of the service sector fell sharply at first, but the trend has

[9]Algebraically, the relationship can be expressed as follows. For a population of N households which are classified by some criterion into K groups, the total variation of household income can be decomposed as

$$\sum_k \sum_i (y_{ik} - \bar{y}..)^2 = \sum_k \sum_i (y_{ik} - \bar{y}._k)^2 + \sum_k N_k (\bar{y}._k - \bar{y}..)^2$$

where y_{ik} is the income of the ith household in the kth group, $\bar{y}$. denotes the mean income for the entire population, $\bar{y}._k$ denotes the mean income for the kth group, and N_k is the number of households in group k. Dividing both sides by the total number of observations, the relationship can be written as

$$\frac{\sum_k \sum_i (y_{ik} - \bar{y}..)^2}{N} = \sum_k \frac{N_k}{N} \sum_i \frac{(y_{ik} - \bar{y}._k)^2}{N_k} + \sum_k \frac{N_k}{N} (\bar{y}._k - \bar{y}..)^2.$$

The left-hand side now represents the overall variance of income. On the right-hand side, N_k/N represents the share effect, $\sum_i (y_{ik} - \bar{y}._k)^2/N_k$ is the within-group effect (of group k), and $\sum_k (\bar{y}._k - \bar{y}..)^2$ is the mean effect.

Table 1. Industrial Structure of Employment and Concentration Ratio of Earnings*

Industry	Percentage share in total working population			Percentage change		Gini ratio of earnings (1976)		
	1961	1971	1976	1961–71	1971–76	Male	Female	Total
Agriculture, hunting, forestry, and fishing	7.3	4.0	2.6	−28.1	−23.0	0.541	0.268	0.518
Mining and quarrying	0.7	0.4	0.1	−49.1	−77.4	0.391	—	0.391
Manufacturing (textiles)	16.4	21.2	21.8	71.2	21.5	0.307	0.245	0.307
Manufacturing (others)	26.6	26.5	23.5	35.2	2.5	0.340	0.261	0.351
Electricity, gas, and water	1.1	0.6	0.5	−29.7	9.5	0.377	—	0.373
Construction	4.9	5.3	5.6	42.9	25.1	0.345	0.315	0.346
Wholesale and retail trade and restaurants and hotels	14.4	16.0	19.4	48.3	42.4	0.409	0.334	0.407
Transport, storage, and communication	7.3	7.2	7.3	32.3	18.7	0.336	0.320	0.335
Financing, insurance, real estate, and business service	1.6	2.6	3.3	114.3	51.2	0.588	0.327	0.522
Community, social, and personal services	18.3	14.7	15.3	7.2	22.1	0.452	0.406	0.441
Activities not adequately defined	1.4	1.6	0.7	48.6	−45.9	—	—	0.491
Total working population	100.0	100.0	100.0	32.9	18.0	0.402	0.356	0.409

* Data from (Census and Statistics Department, 1973: 76) and (Census and Statistics Department, 1977: 37–39).

been reversed since 1971. The employment shares of other sectors were quite stable.

Considering the share effect alone—that is, abstracting from changes in dispersion within industry and relative income between industries—the observed changes in the industry-mix of employment between 1961 and 1971 should lead to greater equality. Textiles, by far the most rapidly expanding sector, was characterized by the smallest concentration ratio. The two major contracting sectors, agriculture and services, on the other hand, were characterized by relatively high concentration ratios. While this tendency to greater equality would be offset to some extent by the expansion of trade and finance, both with relatively high Gini ratios, it is likely, from the magnitude of the changes, that the net effect would be a reduction in inequality.

The impact of changes between 1971 and 1976 is more difficult to judge. The continuous decline of agriculture works for greater equality, but the decline in relative importance of manufacturing had the opposite effect. The expansion of business services and finance should also work to increase inequality, but its impact was modified by the fact that such expansion primarily affected secondary earners.[10] The net result of the share effect between 1971 and 1976 is likely to be a small increase in inequality.

Deduction on the basis of one-digit classification is of limited value. Clearly, the change in industry mix within these large sectors should be taken into consideration. Information on employment changes for such an analysis is available only for 1961 and 1971, and only for the major sectors of manufacturing, commerce and finance, transportation, and services. Accordingly, industry groups (two-digit classification) within each of these sectors are separated into three categories: (1) rapidly growing industries—those with an employment growth rate at least 10 percent higher than the overall growth rate (32 percent); (2) slow-growing industries—those with an employment rate at least 10 percent lower than the overall growth rate; and (3) the rest.

The income distribution for the first two categories has been calculated on the basis of 1971 data, and the results are presented in Table 2. In each and every case, households belonging to sub-sectors with above-average growth in employment are characterized by a lower concentration ratio than those belonging to sub-sectors with below-average growth in employment. When all households are taken together, including sectors for which information on employment changes by sub-

---

[10]The increase in the relative share of household heads in the financial sector between 1971 and 1976 was negligible.

Table 2. Income Distribution in Hong Kong by Industry and by Employment Growth, 1961–71*

Industry	Employment growth 1961–1971	Shares of ordinal groups (percent)						Concentration ratio
		0–20 20	21– 40	41– 60	61– 80	81– 100	Top 5%	
Manufacturing	above average	7.2	12.0	15.8	21.2	43.8	20.1	0.36
	below average	6.9	11.4	15.0	20.7	46.0	22.2	0.38
Commerce and	above average	5.0	8.6	12.3	17.8	56.3	32.9	0.49
finance	below average	4.0	6.9	9.7	15.1	64.3	32.7	0.57
Transportation,	above average	7.5	11.3	14.3	19.1	47.9	26.3	0.39
storage, and	below average	6.5	10.2	13.3	18.6	51.3	27.3	0.43
communication								
services	above average	5.1	8.3	11.9	19.3	55.5	32.0	0.48
	below average	5.3	9.0	12.3	17.6	55.8	33.3	0.49
All industries	above average[a]	5.9	9.9	13.4	18.9	51.8	27.8	0.44
	below average[b]	5.6	9.7	13.1	18.5	53.2	30.3	0.46

* Data from (Census and Statistics Department, 1973: 128–32; 180–95) and (Census Commissioner, 1962: 25).
[a]. Including construction and "unclassified".
[b]. Including farming, fishing, mining, and utilities.

sectors is not obtainable, those households belonging to fast-growing industries are again characterized by lower income concentration, but the difference is marginal. Thus, the evidence is clear that, with respect to the share effect, changes in the industrial structure of employment between 1961 and 1971 contributed to a reduction of income inequality.

Change in occupational structure and income distribution

The distribution of the working population by occupation for the three census years of 1961, 1971, and 1976 is presented in Table 3. Between 1961 and 1971 the sharpest change occurred in the proportion of farmers and fishermen, which fell by more than half. The share of sales workers and managerial workers also declined substantially. The gainers were clerical workers and workers in the industrial sectors (manufacturing, construction, and transportation). On the basis of Gini ratios observed in 1971, this pattern of change should lower overall inequality. The three sectors with relatively high concentration ratios fell in relative importance.

For most occupations, the trend observed in 1961–71 did not repeat itself for 1971–76. A notable exception here is the trend for clerical workers, which continued upward at about the same rate. The per-

Table 3. Concentration Ratio, Distribution of Working Population, and Household Income by Occupation*

| Occupation | Dist. of working population (%) | | | Gini ratio |
	1961	1971	1976	(1971 household income)
Professional, technical, and related workers	5.1	5.0	5.4	0.507
Administrative and managerial workers	3.1	2.4	2.1	0.568
Clerical and related workers	5.8	8.1	9.5	0.363
Sales workers	13.7	10.4	11.3	0.353
Service workers	15.1	14.7	14.8	0.349
Farmers and fishermen	7.3	3.9	2.6	0.560
Workers in production, transport, and communication	49.8	52.8	52.4	0.311
Armed forces, unclassifiable, jobseekers, and economically inactive	1.1	2.7	1.9	0.423
Total	100.0	100.0	100.0	0.442

* Data from (Census Commissioner, 1962), (Census and Statistics Dept., 1973) and (Census and Statistics Dept., 1977).

centage share of farmers and fishermen continued to drop, but at a much lower pace. For other occupations, the earlier trend leveled off or reversed itself. The share effects of these changes work in different directions; the net effect cannot be judged *a priori*.

As in the case of industrial classification, the impact of changes in occupational structure by two-digit classification between 1961 and 1971 can be assessed using the same computational procedure. Households belonging to each one-digit occupational classification were divided into three groups according to the growth performance of their two-digit occupation groups. Distribution statistics were then calculated for each of the two extreme groups from 1971 income data and are presented here in Table 4. For the economy as a whole, the concentration ratio of households belonging to fast-growing occupations is only 0.33, compared with 0.49 for slow-growing occupations. If individual occupations are considered, this inverse correlation between the concentration ratio and the growth rate is pronounced for transportation workers and service workers, but negligible for the two remaining groups in Table 4.

Change in employment status and income distribution

The distributions for the working population and household heads are

Table 4. Income Distribution in Hong Kong by Occupation and by Employment Growth, 1961–1971*

Occupation	Relative employment growth 1961–1971	Number of households	Shares of ordinal groups (percent)						Concentration ratio
			0– 20	21– 40	41– 60	61– 80	81– 100	Top 5 %	
Craftsmen,	above average	199,489	7.9	13.0	16.9	22.3	39.9	15.8	0.309
production	below average	71,563	8.0	13.2	16.9	22.1	39.7	15.8	0.304
workers and									
laborers									
Transport and	above average	36,334	9.2	13.2	16.3	21.1	40.2	17.6	0.299
communica-	below average	9,893	4.6	8.3	11.0	15.4	60.7	40.3	0.537
tions workers									
Clerical and	above average	35,657	7.4	11.6	15.6	21.3	44.0	19.3	0.355
sales workers	below average	83,352	7.1	11.9	15.9	21.8	43.4	18.9	0.353
Service	above average	23,760	9.0	13.4	16.5	21.2	39.9	16.5	0.296
workers	below average	79,869	6.9	12.0	15.8	21.3	44.1	20.2	0.359
All oc-	above average	295,240	7.7	12.5	16.3	21.8	41.8	17.7	0.330
cupations[a]	below average	324,891	5.2	9.0	12.3	17.6	55.9	33.0	0.489

* Data from (Census Commissioner, 1962: 7–19, 54–55, 72–73) and (Census and Statistics Dept., 1973: 110–13, 196–203).
a. In addition to the occupational groups in the table, the following occupations are also included: 1) workers and proprietors in agriculture, fishing, mining, and quarrying; 2) directors, managers, and working proprietors.

shown in Table 5. For household heads, the change can be calculated only between 1961 and 1971. For that period, both the working population and household heads followed essentially the same trend: except for unpaid family workers, the proportion of permanent employees went up sharply.[11] All the rest (i.e., employers, self-employed, and casual workers) lost in relative importance.

In the context of the labor market situation in developing countries, most of the self-employed, casual and seasonal workers, out-workers, and unpaid family workers belong to the informal sector. Employment in such a market is often "supply-determined" (Bhalla, 1970: 521), harboring substantial underemployment and disguised unemployment. The sharp reduction in the proportion of these categories of workers in Hong Kong between 1961 and 1971 suggests that rapid industrialization had mobilized much of the underemployed, resulting in a much tighter labor market. The sharp reduction in the percentage of employers reflects the rise in the average size of enterprises, an expected concomitant of modernization. As such involuntary unemployment or

[11]Excluded here are unpaid family workers who are not significant as household heads.

underemployment was eliminated by 1971, the trend could not continue beyond that point into 1976.

Other changes in activity status between 1961 and 1971 resulted in a reduction of the inequality of income distribution through the share effect. For example, relying on the 1971 Gini ratios of Table 5, we note that the largest gain was registered by permanent employees, paid at daily rates, who had the lowest Gini ratio. On the other hand, the share of employers, with the highest concentration ratio, dropped substantially. There may have been some offsetting trends working to increase inequality, but these were smaller than the equalizing movements. We do not have information to enable us to determine the change in inequality between 1971 and 1976 resulting from changes in employment status. But such an effect is likely to be small in view of the relatively small change in the mix of working population classified by employment status.[12]

Table 5. Concentration, Distribution of Working Population, and Household by Income Activity Status*

Activity status	Distribution of working population (percentage)			Distribution of household heads		Gini ratio
	1961	1971	1976	1961	1971	1971
Employers	4.8	2.6	2.9	8.8	5.1	0.511
Self-employed	10.4	8.3	8.9	17.4	13.1	0.411
Employees	78.7	86.2	81.6			
Permanent, monthly rate				49.7	55.6	0.443
Permanent, daily, piece rate				10.3	18.1	0.288
Casual or seasonal workers				11.8	6.9	0.308
Out-workers, commission workers, and trainees	0.9	0.3	3.7	1.9	1.0	0.405
Unpaid family workers	4.4	2.2	2.8	0.0	0.2	—
Total	100.0	100.0	100.0	100.0	100.0	0.443
Total	1,191,099	1,582,849	1,814,190	560,121	650,597	

* Data from (Census Commissioner, 1962: 14), (Census and Statistics Dept., 1973), (Census and Statistics Dept., unpublished) and (Census and Statistics Dept.,1977: 20–21).

[12]A seeming reversal of the trend since 1971 may be suggested by changes in the distribution of the working population, such as the sharp increase which occurred in the proportion of out-workers in 1976. This may be explained, at least partly, by differences in coverage. For example, to be included in the 1971 count an out-worker

Magnitudes of share effects: Simulated results

Taken together, the observed changes in the industrial structure, occupational composition, and employment status of the labor force were likely to contribute to greater income distribution equality, at least for 1961–71. The size of these share effects can be numerically specified, though we do not have information on 1961 income distribution. In talking about the share effects of, say, industrial changes, we abstract from income distribution changes within any industry and from relative income changes between industries. This being the case, we can assign the 1961 household population of any given industry to various income classes according to the distribution observed for that industry in 1971. Taken by industry, the entire 1961 population can be assigned to the 11 income classes, after which distribution statistics can be computed.

The calculations were made for each of the following three determinants: industry, occupation, and employment status. The results are shown in Table 6, along with comparable indexes for 1971. Of the various changes being examined, industrial structure change had only a marginal share effect on the overall inequality. Changes in employment status and occupational structure, on the other hand, have significantly affected the degree of equality. Both changes, as expected, have contributed to a narrowing of income inequality.

Table 6. Observed and Simulated Income Distribution in Hong Kong, 1961 and 1971

Year	Basis for simulation	Shares of ordinal groups (percent)						Concentration ratio
		0–20	21–40	41–60	61–80	81–100	Top 5%	
1971	Observed data	5.6	10.1	13.6	19.3	51.4	27.4	0.443
1961	Employment status	5.4	9.7	13.3	19.0	52.5	28.4	0.455
1961	Industrial structure of employment	5.5	9.9	13.5	19.1	51.9	27.9	0.448
1961	Occupational structure of employment	5.2	9.4	12.8	18.3	54.3	30.7	0.473

Each of the improvements shown in Table 6 represents a partial effect. While the three changes are not independent, their effects are nevertheless partially additive. Thus, the resulting overall change should be larger than any single effect. The largest single improvement was the

had to work 15 hours or more during the 7 days prior to remuneration. However, this criterion was waived for out-workers in 1976, and the increase suggested in Table 5 may be due to changes in coverage which occurred between 1971 and 1976.

6 percent that accrued to occupational change between 1961 and 1971. Thus, the overall improvement should be higher, say about 8 percent. More important, changes in within-group inequality or in between-group inequality (relative income) have yet to be considered.

The Within-group Effect

In this section we shall consider changes in income dispersion within industrial as well as occupational groups.

Inequality within industrial groups

Both structural changes within industrial sectors and data on wage rates and earnings point to a narrowing of income dispersion within major industrial sectors.

The general pattern of changing employment status has already been noted. For the economy as a whole, there was a sharp reduction in the proportion of employers, the self-employed, out-workers and workers on commission, and family workers, while the proportion of casual workers also fell substantially. On the other hand, the gain has accrued to permanent in-workers. As expected, a similar pattern of change is found within most industrial sectors, but to different degrees. As shown in Table 7, these changes appear quite sharply for manufacturing and construction, transportation, and services and undoubtedly contribute to greater equality. A reduction in number of employers trims the upper tail of the income distribution move, while a reduction in number of casual workers has the same effect on the lower tail.[13] Replacing casual workers by regular workers also reduces variations in the employment level and thus improves the equality of income distribution.

Occupational structure within major industrial sectors also underwent significant change during the decade. In general, there was a marked increase in the share of the dominant occupational group of a given industrial sector. For example, the proportion of craftsmen and production workers in manufacturing increased from 75 to 85 percent, while the proportion of managerial, clerical, and sales workers fell sharply. The change may be caused by the disappearance of a large number of handicraft workshops catering largely to domestic markets as well as to a general increase in the average size of enterprise. As the change results in a more homogeneous labor force and as the dominant

---

[13] Our earlier results show that employers have a mean income at least twice as high as that of any other group, whereas casual and seasonal workers as a rule have the lowest incomes (Chau and Hsia, 1975: 42).

Table 7. Distribution of Working Population by Industry and Employment Status, 1961 and 1971*

Unit: %

Industry Employment status	Farming & fishing		Manufacturing & construction		Commerce		Transport & communications		Services		Total	
	1961	1971	1961	1971	1961	1971	1961	1971	1961	1971	1961	1971
Employer	4.57	1.26	4.79	1.81	10.95	8.16	2.60	1.34	2.89	1.85	4.82	2.58
Self-employed	38.65	48.47	6.84	3.53	22.64	25.19	7.47	5.84	3.95	2.73	10.40	8.26
Permanent in-workers	11.50	11.79	65.08	77.76	59.84	59.88	71.81	81.36	87.95	90.06	66.20	74.95
Causual in-workers*	1.65	3.37	18.85	12.67	1.26	2.43	12.52	9.08	3.30	3.29	11.53	9.12
On commission & out-worker	0.96	0.07	1.91	0.67	2.56	1.55	1.99	0.12	0.83	0.23	1.68	0.65
Unpaid family workers	42.67	34.35	0.94	0.59	2.52	2.21	3.36	1.80	1.02	0.34	4.43	2.25
Other workers	—	0.10	1.59	2.96	0.23	0.58	0.25	0.45	0.32	1.49	0.94	2.19

* Data from (Census Commissioner, 1962: 29) and (Census and Statistics Dept., 1973: 114–127). In 1971 these included homemakers and retired persons working part-time. In the 1961 tabulation part-time workers are not reported separately.

group is itself characterized by low income concentration, the result is likely to be a more equal distribution of income within the manufacturing sector. A change of similar nature and consequence was found also in construction, transportation, and services. In commerce, however, the occupational diversification widened.

For the industrial sectors under the supervision of the Labor Department we have more direct evidence of an equalizing trend. Most notably, within manufacturing relative wage differentials between different levels of skill narrowed considerably during the period. As shown in Table 8, between 1961 and 1971 the wage rates of unskilled and semiskilled workers grew much faster than those of skilled labor, thereby narrowing the wage dispersion of workers in the manufacturing sector. Apparently this trend had run its course by 1971 so that the relative wage level between broad skill classes of manual workers changed very little between 1971 and 1976.

Table 8. Daily Wages in Manufacturing Industries

Year (March except where indicated)	Index of real wages in all manufacturing industries	Average daily wages in manufacturing industries (HK$)		
		Un-skilled	Semi-skilled	Skilled
1961	82	5.00	6.75	14.50
1964	100	7.15	11.05	17.30
1966	113	8.20	13.25	17.75
1971	148	11.85	17.76	23.95
1976 (Sept.)	157	22.75	30.65	45.50
1971/61	1.78	2.37	2.61	1.65
1976/71	1.06	1.92	1.73	1.90

* Data from (Reidel, 1974: 97, 99), (Commission of Labor, 1976: 8) and (Government of Hong Kong, 1977: 40).

This finding is consistent with results from two other sources of data. First, the Labor Department regularly collects wage rate data by major job (10 or more for each industry) for a selected number of manufacturing and other industries. We considered the structure of these wage rates in six manufacturing industries as well as for communications, motor repairs, and godowns for the years 1961, 1966, 1971, and 1976. Without exception, there had been a significant and persistent narrowing of wage dispersion, as measured by the coefficient of variation, over the entire period of 1961–76. Specifically, for the three key industries of cotton spinning, garments, and electronics, the coefficient of variation of wage rates fell by more than one-half. Second, between 1967 and 1975, a number of manpower surveys were conducted for ten major

industries which provide data on the distribution of earnings of production workers (excluding managerial, clerical, and technological
workers). By and large, the concentration ratio fell during this period.

This narrowing wage dispersion was the result of the growing labor
shortage which emerged clearly during the period under consideration.
The changing structure of employment status can be interpreted in this
light. Specifically, there was a marked increase in the labor force participation rate of females, including the very young as well as those over 55.
In general, this tightening of the labor market produces relatively
greater wage increases for unskilled workers because of their high
mobility. A positive correlation between the concentration ratio and
the unemployment rate has been reported for developed countries such
as the United States and Norway (Reder, 1969: 238-39). For developing
countries the relation is likely to be even stronger. With an excess supply
of labor, wages for unskilled workers are very low, and employers can
afford to keep redundant workers on the payroll precisely because their
wages are so low (Lewis, 1966: 76). Their wages are determined not so
much by their marginal productivity, which is often negligible, but
according to the cost of subsistence. The wages of unskilled workers will
increase substantially once they can be employed in productive jobs.
Therefore, as labor force absorption increases, the income of unskilled
workers can rise sharply.

The narrowing of wage differentials in the industrial sector was not
due to institutional factors but was the result of changing supply-
demand conditions in the labor market. Therefore, one would expect the
same kind of changes to have taken place in the commerce and service
sectors as well. Though formal data are not available, impressions gained
from casual observations, as well as sporadic information, do corroborate such expectations. For example, in 1961 the starting salary
of a primary school teacher was about 4 times higher than the average
wage of a housemaid. By 1971, the ratio was less than 2 to 1.

Inequality within occupational groups

The dispersion of earnings within an occupational group reflects
closely, in a competitive labor market such as that existing in Hong
Kong, variations in productivity and in the degree of employment. As
such, it is related to employment status, educational attainment, age,
sex, and the degree of dualism. Unfortunately, because of data limitations not all of these factors can be taken into consideration here.

The trend in the structure of employment status within major occupational groups during the 1960s closely parallels those changes

observed for industry groups described earlier. Broadly speaking, there was a sharp drop in the share of employers and self-employed, a sizeable increase in the share of regular employees, and a decline in the share of casual and other workers. This pattern of change, as pointed out earlier, tends to reduce income dispersion within occupational groups. While these changes apply to all occupational groups, they are more extensive for professional, technical, clerical, and sales workers. Since these occupations are characterized by relatively high degrees of income inequality, equalization within these occupations should have a large impact on overall equality.

The educational attainment of workers in major occupational groups for the three census years of 1961, 1971, and 1976 is presented in Table 9. The rise in the general level of education of the working population

Table 9. Distribution of Economically Active Population by Occupation and Education, 1961, 1971, and 1976

| Occupation | | Unit: % Educational attainment | | | | | |
		No school-ing	Primary	Secon-dary	Post-secon-dary	Univer-sity	Years of school attended[a]
Professional &	1961	0.52	3.30	57.39	10.76	28.03	11.57
technical	1971	1.67	3.18	50.74	21.06	23.35	11.65
	1976	0.41	5.83	54.36	12.91	26.48	11.43
Administrative	1961	0.93	9.16	61.90	8.03	19.97	10.47
& managerial	1971	19.54	27.49	34.45	5.49	13.03	7.33
	1976	2.16	16.10	45.67	10.68	25.32	10.56
Clerical &	1961	17.64	38.71	39.27	1.80	2.58	5.91
sales	1971	14.63	27.29	51.79	3.46	2.83	6.83
	1976	9.40	29.53	52.12	5.49	3.46	7.23
Transportation	1961	22.01	47.77	28.19	0.93	1.09	4.88
& communication	1971	21.11	50.08	27.24	1.05	0.52	4.81
workers	1976	16.95	52.93	28.99	0.79	0.34	4.89
Production & re-	1961	24.30	61.85	12.99	0.27	0.58	3.92
lated workers,	1971	19.91	59.86	19.38	0.55	0.30	4.37
laborers	1976	11.83	57.14	29.62	0.78	0.64	5.17
Service	1961	39.17	43.33	16.62	0.38	0.50	3.49
workers	1971	32.14	45.06	21.47	0.82	0.51	4.08
	1976	23.88	48.00	26.26	1.28	0.58	4.56
All workers	1961	23.10	47.97	24.36	1.49	3.08	4.97
	1971	21.67	45.91	27.55	2.37	2.50	5.18
	1976	13.89	45.39	34.87	2.74	3.12	5.87

* Data from (Census Commissioner, 1962: 24), (Census and Statistics Dept., 1973: 98–100) and (1977; 26–27).

[a]. In calculating the mean of years of education, the year equilvalent for each level of education is assigned as follows: no schooling and kindergarten = 0, primary = 4, secondary = 9, post-secondary = 14, and university = 17.

is clearly discernible, particularly so during the period of 1971–76. A narrowing in the disparity of educational attainment between workers is evident in three occupational groups: clerical and sales, transportation workers, and service workers. As the level of educational attainment is highly correlated with income, this trend should work for greater income equality. For production workers, the education class already accounting for the largest share (*i.e.,* primary education) did not further increase in relative importance as was true for the three occupations mentioned above. For production workers the change consisted mainly of an increase in the proportion of those with secondary education at the expense of those with no schooling. While the impact of this change on income distribution is equivocal, it should be noted that the increase in the manufacturing work force with secondary education consisted primarily of younger workers. Their higher level of education might compensate for their lack of training, experience, and seniority. If so, the result may well be a leveling off of earnings, in the short run at least.

Only in the case of administrative and managerial workers did the education level changes contribute to widening income disparity. Here we can identify a large increase at both ends of the educational spectrum. But this group was also the smallest group, accounting for only 2 percent of the working population and 3 percent of households in 1976 (see Table 3).

The Between Effect

Given the income classification, concentration can be reduced through a narrowing of the income differentials between homogenous groups. Time series information for analyzing this change is most inadequate as very little wage and income data were collected in Hong Kong during off-census years for the non-industrial sectors. In this section we will examine the available time series for income dispersion trends between industrial and occupational groups.

Relative income between industries

Income data by sector are not available for the 1960s. However, average wage figures for manual workers in a number of industrial sectors were regularly collected by the Labor Department. The general trend over the period 1958–74 is presented in Table 10, where we can see a strong equalizing trend between 1958 and 1971. During this period earnings in different industries tended to regress toward the overall

Table 10. Index of Nominal Average Daily Wages for Industrial Workers
(including fringe benefits)*

Industry	1958	1961	1965	1966	1971	1974
1. Overall	100	124	170	180	304	416
2. Manufacturing	93	121	168	178	303	412
3. Textiles	103	128	171	182	309	410
4. Dockyard	128	142	180	193	316	411
5. Electricity supply	169	182	228	229	341	522
6. Tramway operators	170	184	231	243	235	565
7. Communications	150	172	208	224	330	506
8. Motor repairing	135	163	183	209	309	511
Ratio of highest to lowest observation	1.61	1.52	1.38	1.37	1.13	1.38
Coefficient of variation (items 2–8)	0.222	0.165	0.136	0.119	0.043	0.135

* Data from (Census and Statistics Dept., 1968: 66; 1971: 10; 1975: 6).
a. Index figures are compiled by using the 1958 overall average wage as the common base throughout the industrial sector, so that comparison can be made directly between any industry at any time.
b. Industry data are for the month of March in the year indicated.

mean. The coefficient of variation of mean income was halved between 1958 and 1966 and halved again between 1966 and 1971. However, the trend reversed itself after 1971, and wage disparity rose sharply between 1971 and 1974, the last year for which comparable data are available.

A useful proxy for the average income of a large group of households is average consumption expenditure. Using information from household expenditure surveys, we computed the average expenditure for household groups classified by the industry of employment of the household head for two benchmark periods, 1963–64 and 1973–74.[14] Our results show that the inter-industry variation in expenditure decreased substantially between the two periods. The coefficient of variation fell from 0.103 in 1963–64 to 0.061 in 1973–74. In the absence of any drastic variation in the relative consumption propensity of household groups among industries, this sharp reduction in the disparity of consumption should reflect a narrowing of income inequality.

[14] The periods used here refer to September 1963 to August 1964 and July 1973 to June 1974, respectively. For each period information was collected from about 2,800 households using the bookkeeping method. The following industrial classification was used: textiles and garments, other manufacturing, construction, utilities, commerce, transportation, and services.

Income disparity among occupations

Our earlier results showed that the variability of income within occupational groups was much larger than that within industrial groups, or indeed within groups classified by any other attribute considered so far. This is to be expected, as remuneration scales are usually defined in terms of occupation which refers to the task a worker performs and is most closely correlated with such factors as education, responsibility, and working conditions. It is particularly unfortunate that data on income by occupation are so scanty.

Information on non-industrial wages is only sporadically available. For earlier years, data are available only for government employees. Two series pertaining, respectively, to the public and the commerce sectors are presented in Table 11. They cover a wide range of skills, mostly white-collar occupations, and span the entire period under consideration. In both series there can be seen a very distinct trend of narrowing income differentials between occupations. While the reduction in the general spread of wages, as measured by the coefficient of variation, appears to be moderate, the contraction of the range is remarkable. For example, in 1962 a senior medical officer earned 23 times as much as an unskilled worker; by 1971 the ratio was down to 13 times. Similarly, in commerce, the ratio fell from 15 to 9 between 1967 and 1975. While the information pertains to only two sectors, it is fairly

Table 11. Household Expenditure by Occupation of Household Head, 1963/64 and 1973/74*

Occupation	1963/64 survey			1973/74 survey	
	Number of households	Average size of households	Average household expendit.	Number of households	Average household expendit.
Professional, technical, adminstrative and related workers	186	5.8	897	296	1,950
Clerical workers	345	5.9	774	321	1,650
Sales workers	564	6.3	690	348	1,663
Production workers, transport equipment operators and laborers	1,006	5.5	494	1,148	1,426
Service workers	692	5.7	496	347	1,491
Mean expenditure (unweighted)			670		1,636
Coef. of variation of expenditure			0.262		0.124

* Data from (Commerce and Industry Dept., 1965: 46–7, 65–67) and (Census and Statistics Dept., 1975: 95–97).

safe to expect that a similar trend would prevail for workers in comparable occupations working in other sectors since the skills concerned are not tied to any specific industry.

A comparison of Table 10 and Table 11 reveals that the wage gap between white-collar workers and blue-collar workers was also narrowing. Table 11 shows that the average income of clerical workers in commerce (typists, clerks, and secretaries) went up by 57 percent (from $1,806 to $2,837) between 1967 and 1975. From the first row of Table 10, we see that the wages of manual workers in the industrial sector more than doubled over the comparable period 1966–74.

To obtain a wider cross-section of occupations, we consider again the change in the variation of household expenditure across occupational groups between 1963–64 and 1973–74. Between the two periods we see a sharp reduction in the disparity of average household expenditure where households are classified by occupation of head; the coefficient of variation fell from 0.262 to 0.124.[15] It is interesting to note that the trend here is even sharper than that shown using the industrial classification.

Finally, results from census data also show a discernible narrowing of income dispersion across levels of educational attainment between 1971 and 1976. In particular, the income disparity between university graduates and those with no schooling fell from 5.8 to 4.6. As occupation is closely correlated with the level of educational attainment, the trend in income differentials between education levels should be a reliable indicator of the trend in inter-occupational differences.

Summary

In this paper we have assessed the impact on income distribution of the rapid industrialization of Hong Kong over the period 1961–76. The effects of changes in employment and wage structure, education, and labor force participation are evaluated mainly on the basis of their relationship to income distribution observed in 1971.

In spite of the short time span covered, there was a substantive change in employment structure in accordance with the trend generally observed during the development process: the employment share of manufacturing went up by 12 percent while the share of agriculture almost halved. On the basis of 1971 industry income distribution data

---

[15] Households were classified into the following five occupations: professional, technical and administrative, clerical, sales, production workers in manufacturing and transport, and service workers.

we find that industries with above-average growth rates during the 1961–71 period show a lower degree of inequality than industries with below-average growth rates. Thus, the observed changes in the industrial structure of employment should contribute to greater equality.

Using the same approach to evaluate the impact of occupational structure changes, we have identified an even stronger tendency towards equality. The distribution of workers by employment status changed as might be expected: the proportion of regular employees went up while the proportion of self-employed, out-workers, and unpaid family workers fell. When the effect of these three employment status changes was calculated, it was found that the impact of industrial change was small. However, the change in occupational structure produced an estimated 6 percent reduction in the concentration ratio, and the change in employment status, a 3 percent reduction. These effects are partially additive, but the overall share effect could have been an 8 percent reduction in the concentration ratio.

A number of forces were at work over the decade reducing income dispersion within industrial as well as occupational groups. The occupational structure of major industries became more homogeneous with the percentage of wage earners rising. Growing labor shortages led to a sharp reduction in wage differentials by skill level. The spread of education reduced the dispersion of educational attainment as well as related income differentials. This deduction is corroborated by wage rate data and the results of manpower surveys, both of which show a strong trend of equalization in wage rates or employment income for production workers within major manufacturing industries, as well for workers in transportation.

There was a strong tendency over the 1961–71 period for wages of manual workers belonging to different manufacturing industries, utilities, and transportation to regress toward the overall mean. Similarly, available evidence points to a narrowing of income differentials between different non-industrial occupations, between blue-collar and white-collar workers, between public and private employees, and between workers with different levels of educational attainment. Analyses of consumption expenditures also show a drastic reduction of dispersion, between 1963 and 1973, in mean expenditure for households belonging to different occupations, and a substantial reduction of mean expenditure dispersion when households are classified according to the industry of employment of the household head.

For the first half of the 1970s information for evaluating overall inequality changes is only sporadically available. However, the results drawn from this data are equivocal, with different indicators producing conflicting conclusions regarding the direction of change. For example, the effects of structural changes in industry tend to be offsetting. From 1971 we can identify a leveling off or trend reversal in the relative growth of most occupations. Changes in within-group and between-group inequality are equally confusing. The rising trend in the relative wage rates of the unskilled and semi-skilled leveled off, but wage dispersion within the major divisions of the manufacturing sector continued to narrow. Wage disparity between industries rose sharply between 1971 and 1976, reversing a 13-year trend. But wage disparity by occupation in commerce and services fell between 1967 and 1976; there was also a mild reduction in the disparity of earnings by educational level. Earnings data from manpower surveys convey the same general picture: falling inequality during the second half of the 1960s and a mixed trend over the period 1970–1975.

References

Bhalla, A. S. "The Role of Services in Employment Creation," *Int. Labor Rev.*, May 1970, 101.

Census Commissioner. *Report of the Census 1961, 3 vols.* Hong Kong, 1962.

Commerce and Industry Department. *The Household Expenditure Survey, 1963–64, and the Consumer Price Index.* Hong Kong, 1965.

Census and Statistics Department. *Hong Kong Statistics 1947–67.* Hong Kong, 1969.

————. *1971 Census*, unpublished tabulations.

————. *Hong Kong Monthly Digest of Statistics*, August 1971 and January 1975.

————. *Hong Kong Population and Housing Census, 1971 Main Report.* Hong Kong, 1973.

————. *The Household Expenditure Survey 1973–74 and the Consumer Price Indexes.* Hong Kong, 1975.

————. *Hong Kong By-Census 1976, Basic Tables.* Hong Kong, 1977.

Commissioner of Labor. *Annual Department Report.* Hong Kong, 1976.

Government of Hong Kong. *The 1977–78 Budget: Economic Background.* Hong Kong, 1977.

Chau, L. C., and Hsia, R. "An Anatomy of Income Distribution in Hong Kong, 1971," in *Seminar on Income Distribution, Employment and Economic Development in Southeast and East Asia, papers and proceedings*, 2 vols. Tokyo: Japan Economic Research Center, 1975.

Chou, K. R. *The Hong Kong Economy, A Miracle of Growth*, Hong Kong: Academic Publications, 1966.

Jao, Y. C. "Land Use Policy and Land Taxation in Hong Kong," in Wong, J. (ed.), *The Cities of Asia.* Singapore: University of Singapore Press, 1976.

Kravis, I. B. *The Structure of Income.* Philadelphia: University of Pennsylvania Press, 1962.

Kuznets, S. "Economic Growth and Income Inequality," *Amer. Econ. Rev.*, March 1955, p. 45.

————. *Modern Economic Growth.* New Haven: Yale University Press, 1966.

Lewis, W. A. *Development Planning.* London: George Allen & Unwin, 1966.

Oshima, H. T. "Income Inequality and Economic Growth; The Postwar Experiences of Asian Countries," *Malayan Economic Review*, October 1970, 15(2).

Owen, N. C. "Economic Policy in Hong Kong," in Hopkins, K. (ed.), *Hong Kong: the Industrial Colony*. Hong Kong: Oxford University Press, 1971.

Reder, M. W. "A Partial Survey of the Theory of Income Distribution," in Soltow, L. (ed.), *Six Papers on the Size Distribution of Income*. New York: National Bureau of Economic Research, 1969.

Riedel, J. *The Industrialization of Hong Kong*. Tubingen: J.C.B. Mohr (Paul Siebeck), 1974.

Walker, J. *Under the White Wash*. Hong Kong, 1972.

Economic Growth and Income Disparity in Taiwan

Han-yu Chang

Students of income distribution usually focus their attention on the size distribution of personal income and its change over time, namely the tendency toward greater or lesser equality in the distribution of family income.* Changes in family income distribution are greatly affected by, among other factors, structural changes in the economy, the demand-supply-reward relationship for the factors of production, and the relative income between sectoral economic units. Drawing on basic information presented in the national income accounts and family income and expenditure surveys, I will, in this paper, attempt to examine Taiwan's income distribution and identify its over-time pattern of change during the postwar period of rapid growth. Furthermore, I will seek to relate this pattern to the key factors mentioned above as well as offer a brief comparison of Taiwan's size distribution of income with that of other countries.

Structural Change in the Distribution of National Income

The national income (Y) of the Republic of China can be divided broadly into three categories: (1) income from property and enterprises,

* This paper is a condensed English version of a more detailed paper "Changes in Income Distribution and Economic Growth: Taiwan's Case" presented in Chinese at the Annual Conference of the Chinese Economic Association held in Taipei in 1975. I would like to extend my thanks to Professor Albert R. O'Hara for his help in preparing the condensed English version and to the members of the Organizing Committee of the Second Asian Regional Conference of the International Association for Research in Income and Wealth for the opportunity to participate in the Manila Conference.

whether public or private; (2) compensation of employees, whether public or private; and (3) mixed income including farm income, the income of other unincorporated enterprises, and professional income. Taken together, categories (1) and (2) represent the labor-employing (that is, the so-called capitalist or modern) sector (Y_1), and category (3) represents the traditional sector (Y_2) (that is, income from family labor and self-employed businesses, including agriculture as well as other small enterprises).

During the period 1953–74, the growth rate of income from public property and entrepreneurship, private property and incorporated enterprise, and employee compensation was much higher than that from farm and other mixed income. As can be seen in Table 1, the percentage share of the modern sector in national income (Y_1/Y) increased from 73 percent to about 87 percent while that of the traditional sector (Y_2/Y) decreased from 27 percent to about 13 percent. Further, farm income, which accounts for by far the largest part of traditional sector income, decreased from 26 percent to 11 percent. Thus, the distribution of Taiwan's national income, reflecting this change in industrial structure, has been modernized and industrialized or de-agriculturized. This structural change in income distribution provides the basic context in which to observe and explain changes in the other dimensions of income distribution to be discussed here.

Table 1. Structural Change in National Income Distribution: Selected Subperiods, 1953–74*

Unit: %, six-year average

Year	Modern sector		Traditional sector	
	Employees' compensation	Income from property & incorporated enterprise	Mixed income	Farm only
1953–58	45.10	27.60	27.31	25.86
1958–63	45.98	29.07	24.95	23.52
1963–68	47.96	30.47	21.61	20.14
1968–74	57.07	30.03	12.88	11.29

* Data from (DGBAS, 1972 & 1975).
a. Calculated from 1966 price data.

Factor Shares: Capital and Labor

Turning our attention to the modern sector, we will want to examine the income distribution between the relevant factors of production. Modern sector income (Y_1) will broadly be divided into the labor share

(W_1), *i.e.*, the compensation of employees, and the capital share (R_1), the income from property and enterprises, public and private. The labor share consists of wages and salaries, the pay and allowances of government and military personnel, and employers' contributions to social security. The capital share includes the income from property received by households and non-profit institutions (*e.g.* rent, interest and dividends), the savings of corporations (private and public), the direct taxes and charges on private corporations, the general government income from property and enterpreneurship, and the interest on the public debt.

As can be seen in Table 2, over the period 1953–74 the labor share in modern sector income (W_1/Y_1) shifted between 61.97 percent and 61.80 percent while the capital share (R_1/Y_1) moved between 38.03 percent and 38.69 percent. Therefore, the ratio of distribution appears to be quite stable on the whole. However, if the entire period is divided into the four equal subperiods as indicated in Table 2, the percentage share of labor in each subperiod was, respectively, 62.0 percent, 61.3 percent, 61.3 percent, and 61.8 percent. In other words, labor's factor share decreased after the first subperiod and did not show a clear increase until the last subperiod.

Table 2. Modern Sector Factor Shares: Labor and Capital for Selected Subperiods, 1952–74*

Year	(1) Labor's income	(2) Capital's income	(3) = (1)/(2) Labor share
	Modern sec. income $\left(\dfrac{W_1}{Y_1}\right)$	Modern sec. income $\left(\dfrac{R_1}{Y_1}\right)$	Capital share $\left(\dfrac{W_1}{Y_1}\Big/\dfrac{R_1}{Y_1}\right)$
'53–'58 (52/54–57/59)	61.97	38.03	163.04 (100.00)
'58–'63 (57/59–62/64)	61.31	38.69	158.47 (97.20)
'63–'68 (62/64–67/69)	61.32	38.69	158.45 (97.24)
'68–'73 (67/69–72/74)	61.80	38.19	161.96 (99.34)

*W_1, R_1, and Y_1 data from (DGBAS, 1972 and 1975). Percentage shares are calculated for six-year periods using three-year averages to determine the beginning and end points for each subperiod.
a. Figures in ( ) under share ratios are index numbers with 1952/54–57/59 = 100.
b. The percentage share for each of the six-year periods is calculated as the average share for the period using the three-year moving average figure for annual percentage shares.

In order to first corroborate and then explain the trend observed above, we shall investigate further the factors that affect the labor-capital share. The key elements and their relationship which determine the ratio of labor-capital shares are formulated in the following equation:

$$\frac{W}{R} = \frac{L \cdot w}{K \cdot r} = \frac{L}{K} \cdot \frac{w}{r} \qquad (1)^1$$

In Eq. (1), W denotes the total reward to labor, R the total reward to capital, L the number of laborers employed, w the per capita compensation of labor, K the total capital stock, and r the rate of return on capital, namely R/K.

Taking the time differential, we can derive Eq. (2) to illustrate the dynamic state:

$$\dot{W} - \dot{R} = (\dot{L} + \dot{w}) - (\dot{K} + \dot{r})$$
$$= (\dot{L} - \dot{K}) + (\dot{w} - \dot{r}). \qquad (2)$$

In (2), $\dot{W}$ represents the rate of change in labor's total reward, $\dot{L}$ that of employment, $\dot{w}$ that of per-head labor compensation, $\dot{R}$ that of total return on capital, $\dot{K}$ that of capital stock, and $\dot{r}$ that of the rate of return on capital.

Equation (2) tells us that the relative size of the growth rate of the total return to labor ($\dot{W}$ or $\dot{L} + \dot{w}$) in comparison with that of the total return to capital ($\dot{R}$ or $\dot{K} + \dot{r}$) is determined by adding the difference between the growth rates of employment and capital ($\dot{L} - \dot{K}$) and the difference between the growth rates of per-capita labor compensation and the rate of return to capital ($\dot{w} - \dot{r}$). In short, ($\dot{W} - \dot{R}$) will change with the sum total of ($\dot{L} - \dot{K}$) + ($\dot{w} - \dot{r}$).[2]

Therefore, if $(\dot{L} - \dot{K}) + (\dot{w} - \dot{r}) \gtreqqless 0$

or $(\dot{L} + \dot{w}) - (\dot{K} + \dot{r}) \gtreqqless 0$

Then $\dot{W} \gtreqqless \dot{R}$, and so $Wt/Rt \gtreqqless Wo/Wo$. (3)

In other words, as can be seen in Eq. (3), when the sum of the growth rates of employment and the per-capita return to labor is larger than the sum of the growth rates of capital and the rate of return to capital, the growth rate of total employee compensation is higher than the growth rate of total return to capital. Therefore, the current labor-capital share ratio (Wt/Rt) is larger than the ratio of the initial period (Wo/Ro), and we may conclude that labor's share will improve.

Calculations for the labor-capital share ratio are presented in Table 3 by selected subperiods over 1953–75 together with data for the rel-

---

[1] Adapted from Kravis's equation $R/W = Q_k/Q_L \times P_k/P_L$ (Kravis, 1968: 140).
[2] The derivation of Eq. (2) owes much to Ohkawa's analysis of changes in factor prices and factor quantities (Ohkawa, 1969: 360).

Table 3. The Labor-capital Share Ratio: Selected Subperiods, 1953–74*

$\dot{L}$	$\dot{K}$	$\dot{L}$-$\dot{K}$	$\dot{w}$	$\dot{r}$	$\dot{w}$-$\dot{r}$	$(\dot{L}-\dot{K})+$ $(\dot{w}-\dot{r})=$ $=\dot{W}-\dot{R}$	$\frac{W_1}{R_1}\left(\frac{W_1}{Y_1}\Big/\frac{R_1}{Y_1}\right)$
1953 3.0 –58	1.6	1.4	5.0	5.0	0.0	1.4	163.04 (100.0) 52/54–57/59
1958 3.2 –63	2.7	0.5	3.4	5.5	—2.1	—1.6	158.47 (97.2) 57/59–62/64
1963 4.9 –68	5.6	—0.7	4.6	2.7	1.9	1.2	158.54 (97.2) 62/64–67/69
1968 7.1 –74	9.8	—2.7	3.1	—2.4	5.5	2.8	161.96 (99.3) 67/69–72/74

* Data from Tables 4 and 5.
a. Figures in ( ) under share ratios are index numbers with 1952/54–57/59 = 100.

evant series from which these calculations were made. From these results the following conclusions can be drawn:

1. In the first subperiod (1953–58) the growth rate of labor employed was larger than that of capital by 1.4% ($\dot{L} - \dot{K} = 3.0\% - 1.6\% = 1.4\%$), and the growth rate of the per-capita return to labor was almost equal to that of the rate of return to capital ($\dot{w} - \dot{r} = 5.0\% - 0.0\%$). As a result of these changes in supply-demand conditions, the growth rate of total labor compensation proved to be larger than that of the total return to capital by 1.4 percent ($\dot{W} - \dot{R} = 1.4\%$). The labor-capital share ratio (W_1/R_1) amounted to 163.04 percent, the highest figure recorded over the 1953–75 period.

2. In the second subperiod (1958–63) the growth rate of employment was somewhat larger than that of capital ($\dot{L} - \dot{K} = 0.5\%$) while the growth rate of the per-capita return to labor was smaller than that of the rate of return to capital ($\dot{w} - \dot{r} = 3.4\% - 5.5\% = - 2.1\%$). Consequently, $\dot{W} - \dot{R} = -1.6$ percent, and W_1/R_1 declined to 158.47 percent.

3. In the third subperiod (1963–68) the growth rate of labor employed became somewhat smaller than that of capital ($\dot{L} - \dot{K} = -0.7\%$); accordingly, the growth rate of the per-capita return to labor became somewhat larger than the growth rate of the return to capital ($\dot{w} - \dot{r} = 4.6\% - 2.7\% = 1.9\%$). Therefore, we can see that the growth rate of the total return to labor was larger than that of the total return to capital ($\dot{W} - \dot{R} = 1.2\%$). Nevertheless, the labor share ratio had not significantly improved ($W_1/R_1 = 158.54\%$) and remained virtually stationary from the second to third subperiod.

4. In the last subperiod (1968–74) the growth rate of employment lagged behind that of capital ($\dot{L} - \dot{K} = - 2.7\%$), and the growth rate

of the per-capita return to labor was remarkably larger than that of the rate of return to capital ($\dot{w} - \dot{r} = 5.5\%$). Consequently, the growth rate of the total return to labor was higher than that of the total return to capital ($\dot{W} - \dot{R} = 2.8\%$) and caused the labor share ratio (W_1/R_1) to rise to 161.96 percent, almost recovering the level of the initial subperiod (1953–58).

The above analysis provides the basis for a quantitative explanation of the changes in Taiwan's labor-capital share ratio during the postwar period of rapid growth. Of particular interest are the changes taking place during the last subperiod where labor has come to be in short supply, thus providing the basis for a rise in the labor share.[3]

Table 4. Rates of growth of total return to capital, capital stock, and the rate of return to capital: Selected subperiods, 1953–74*

Unit: %

Growth rate / Year	1953–63	1963–73	1953–58	1958–63	1963–68	1968–74
a. Capital total reward ($\dot{R}_1$)	8.22	10.34	6.67	8.35	8.39	7.15
b. Capital stock ($\dot{K}_1$)	2.35	8.21	1.59	2.72	5.58	9.83
c. Capital reward rate ($\dot{r}$)	5.74	1.97	5.01	5.49	2.65	−2.43

* R_1 data from (DGBAS, 1972 & 1975). K_1 data from (CIED, 1951–73 & 1964) and (DGBAS, 1952–74).
a. R_1 includes property income received by households and non-profit institutions, savings of corporations, income from general government property and entrepreneurship, and interest on the public debt, all at 1966 prices.
b. Let GFCF = Gross Domestic Fixed Capital Formation, CC = the provision for Domestic Capital Consumption, NFCF = Net Domestic Fixed Capital Formation, and the suffixes a & na refer to agriculture and non-agriculture, respectively. Then, GFCF−CC = NFCF; GFCFa−CCa = NFCFa. Thus, Kna in year t plus NFCFna for year t + 1 = Kna for year t + 1; conversely Kna for year t + 1 minus NFCFna for year t + 1 equals Kna for year t. Thereby, using 1964 as the starting point, we can obtain capital stock data for every succeeding and preceeding year for the period under study. For 1964 Kna is calculated by subtracting the fixed capital stock of primary industry from total capital stock.
c. r = R/K.

Relative Income: Farm and Non-farm

During the years of rapid postwar growth income in the traditional sector (represented by agriculture) has risen at a slower rate than the income in the modern sector (represented by returns to labor and property and entrepreneurship). Behind this lagging growth of farm

[3] Similar quantitative evidence has been provided in the Lewis model (Lewis, 1954; Lewis, 1963: 431 & 449).

Table 5. Rates of Growth of Employee Compensation, Numbers Employed, and Per-capita Employee Compensation: Selected Sub-periods 1953-74*

Year		1953-63	1963-73	1953-58	1958-63	1963-68	1968-74	1964-74
a. Employees' compensation	($\dot{W}$)	8.15	11.71	8.22	6.67	9.78	9.89	10.11
b. Numbers employed	($\dot{L}$)	3.37	6.58	3.02	3.16	4.91	6.63	6.61
c. Employee's compensation per head	($\dot{w}$)	4.62	4.81	5.05	3.40	4.64	3.05	3.29
d. Wages per head		4.52	4.49	5.16	3.11	5.03		4.65
e. Household revenue								5.39

NT$ (1966 value)

Year	1953	1954	1955	1956	1957	1958	1959	1960	1961	1962	1963
a. Employees' compensation	12,723	15,199	16,057	17,059	16,678	17,103	16,693	17,565	18,455	19,826	20,903
d. Wages per head	8,712	9,863	10,503	11,064	11,598	11,784	11,445	11,381	13,293	13,876	14,163
c. Household revenue											

Year	1964	1965	1966	1967	1968	1969	1970	1971	1972	1973	1974
a. Employees' compensation	23,734	25,764	27,193	26,186	27,441	30,181	32,073	32,398	31,807	35,059	33,875
d. Wages per head	14,568	15,632	16,445	17,933	19,008	18,812	19,874	22,265	22,088	22,951	21,221
e. Household revenue	15,797	17,439	17,797	19,799	19,799	19,417	19,524	22,477	22,477	24,386	24,103

* W data from (DGBAS, 1972 & 1975). L data from (EPC, 1975). Per-capita wage data from (Dept. of Construction, 1957-73) and (LFSRI, 1973-74). Household revenue data from (Dept. of Budget, 1964, 66, 68, 70-74).
a. $\dot{w}$ indicates the growth rate of W/L.

income, the following factors appear to be important: (1) the un-favorable terms of trade between the products of the small farmer and those of the modern business enterprise; (2) the official rice fertilizer barter system, in force until a few years ago; (3) the decreasing share of food expenditure in most family budgets which has greatly affected the relative importance (in average household income) of farmers' income

Table 6. The Ratio of Farm to Non-farm Disposable Income, 1961–75*

Unit: 1966 NT$ and %

	1. Per capita			2. Per capita			3. Per household		
	Non-farm income[b]	No-minal ratio[c]	Ad-justed ratio[e]	Non-farm income[b]	No-minal ratio[d]	Ad-justed ratio[e]	Non-farm income[b]	No-minal ratio[d]	Ad-justed ratio[e]
1961	5,491	0.75	0.77						
1962	5,903	0.72	0.75						
1963	6,367	0.73	0.76						
1964	7,656	0.63	0.64						
1965	8,042	0.65	0.65						
1966	8,620	0.65	0.65	6,206	0.68	0.68	32,718	0.93	0.93
1967	9,674	0.63	0.63	—	—	—	—	—	—
1968	10,778	0.61	0.61	7,807	0.57	0.58	42,365	0.71	0.72
1969	11,975	0.48	0.50	—	—	—	—	—	—
1970	13,444	0.48	0.50	8,454	0.59	0.62	46,660	0.71	0.74
1971	15,057	0.49	0.52	9,209	0.63	0.67	49,252	0.78	0.83
1972	16,174	0.58	0.62	10,776	0.66	0.70	57,022	0.81	0.86
1973	20.920	0.58	0.57	13,472	0.61	0.61	70,318	0.74	0.74
1974	25,948	0.67	0.63	18,275	0.69	0.65	93,204	0.85	0.80
1975	29,547	0.65	0.60	21,277	0.67	0.62	108,086	0.80	0.74

* Non-farm income data for household receipts and taxes (DGBAS-NIROC, 1974 & '76) and (EPC-TSDB, 1976). Nominal ratio for per-capita #2 and per-household also from (TCG-FIEPID, 1971–75). Population data from (EPC-TSDB, 1976).
a. Farm household per-capita income calculated from DAF by dividing exclusively farm earnings by the number of family members.
b. Non-farm per-capita income was calculated according to the following equation:
$$\frac{Yh - Th - YfNf}{N - Nf}$$
where Yh = household receipts
Th = direct taxes
Yf = per-capita farm income
N = total population
Nf = farm population.
Non-farm income treated as an index = 1.
c. The nominal ratio here is obtained by dividing the farm income (DA data) by the non-farm income.
d. Per-capita #2 and per-household figures for 1971–75 are weighted household averages of SFIE and FIEPID data. Since 1971, separate surveys have been conduct-ed by the TPG and the TCG; Taipei City, as a special municipality, is not included under the jurisdiction of the TPG.
e. Adjustments made using consumer price index numbers as well as index numbers for prices paid by farmers.

from food product sales in recent years; and (4) the heavier dependent-labor ratio of farm households relative to that of the non-farm household.[4]

In order to make up for the resulting shortage of farm income in comparison with rising living expenses, an ever larger number of farmers have taken non-farm jobs. Accordingly, non-agricultural income has been accounting for a more important part of farm income. In 1975, the share of non-agricultural income reached 70 percent for small landowners (less than 0.5 hectares) and was no less than 25 percent for "larger" landowning farmers (more than 2 hectares).

Notwithstanding the absolute increase in farm household income and the changes in its composition, its tendency to decline relative to non-

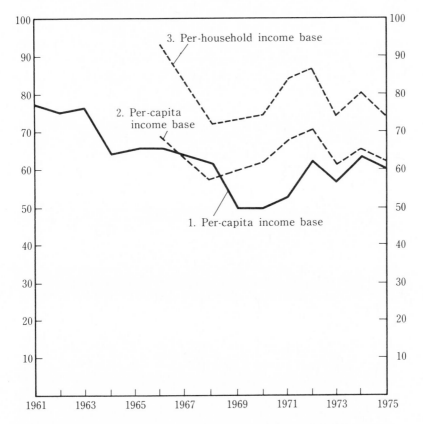

Figure 1. The ratio of farm to non-farm disposable income, 1961–75*

* Data from Table 6, adjusted ratios.   Unit: Non-farm income = 100

[4] For a more detailed treatment of this subject see (Chang, 1972; 1973).

farm income has continued until the last few years. As shown in Table 6 and Figure 1, the ratio of farm to non-farm per-capita disposable income was about 0.75 in the early 1960s, decreased to between 0.65 and 0.61 in the middle 1960s, then sank to 0.50 in about 1970. This decline, it would appear, has been checked in recent years, though a trend toward improvement cannot as yet be firmly identified. We will next want to turn our attention to how the relative income inequality between farm and non-farm income has affected the nationwide income distribution.

Size Distribution of Income

Here we will want to examine the size distribution of income within families, first for the nation as a whole and then separately for the non-farm as well as the farm family. For our measure of inequality over the period 1964–75, we have chosen the Gini coefficient as the "classical and most popular method" (Mizoguchi *et al.*, 1976: 263). Calculations have been made for the quintile as well as decile household groups mentioned previously—that is, nationwide as well as farm and non-farm families. The results are shown here, respectively, in summary form in Tables 7, 8, and 9. A graphic summary of the Gini coefficient curves is presented in Figure 2.

Table 7. Nationwide Family Income Distribution*

Quintile	Percentage share								
household groups	1964	1966	1968	1970	1971	1972	1973	1974	1975
Q_1	7.7	7.9	7.9	8.5	8.8	8.9	8.7	9.0	9.2
Q^2	12.6	12.5	12.2	13.2	13.3	13.5	13.3	13.4	13.7
Q^3	16.6	16.2	16.3	17.2	17.4	17.2	17.0	17.0	17.4
Q^4	22.0	22.0	22.3	22.4	22.6	22.7	22.4	22.1	22.3
Q^5	41.1	41.5	41.4	38.7	37.9	37.8	38.5	38.4	37.4
Top fifth percentile (96–100%)	16.3	16.2	17.3	14.6	13.6	13.1	14.7	14.5	12.2
g.c.q.[a]	.381	.383	.386	.348	.338	.335	.344	.338	.325
g.c.d.[b]	.357	.359	.362	.321	.315	.313	.320	.316	.304

* Data from (SFLE, 1964, '66, '68, '70–75) and (FIEPID, 1971–75).
[a] g.c.q. = Gini coefficient quintile.
[b] g.c.d. = Gini coefficient decile.

From the curves presented in Figure 2, the following conclusions can be drawn:

1. The nationwide Gini curve rose over 1964–68, but fell during 1968–

Table 8. Non-farm Family Income Distribution*

Quintile house-	Percentage share								
hold groups	1964	1966	1968	1970	1971	1972	1973	1974	1975
Q_1	7.4	7.9	7.7	8.9	9.0	9.1	8.9	9.1	9.6
Q_2	12.5	12.5	12.3	13.3	13.6	13.6	13.3	13.5	13.8
Q_3	16.7	16.1	16.4	17.2	17.4	17.2	17.0	17.0	17.4
Q_4	21.8	21.7	21.9	22.2	22.5	22.7	22.3	22.0	22.1
Q_5	40.7	41.7	41.7	38.4	37.6	37.4	38.6	38.4	37.2
Top fifth percen- tile (96–100%)	14.2	16.6	18.2	15.1	13.2	12.8	14.9	14.6	13.5
g. c. q.	.389	.384	.389	.340	.330	.328	.343	.336	.317
g.c d.	.365	.359	.366	.308	.308	.283	.319	.314	.296

* Data, same as Table 7.

Table 9. Farm Family Income Distribution*

Quintile house-	Percentage share								
hold groups	1964	1966	1968	1970	1971	1972	1973	1974	1975
Q_1	8.3	7.9	9.0	8.7	8.9	8.9	9.4	8.9	9.1
Q_2	12.8	12.3	13.2	13.7	13.0	13.4	13.7	13.8	13.9
Q_3	16.6	16.4	17.1	17.7	16.9	17.3	17.5	17.0	17.5
Q_4	22.3	22.6	22.6	22.5	22.5	22.4	22.9	22.1	22.2
Q_5	40.1	40.8	38.1	37.4	38.7	38.1	36.5	38.2	37.4
Top fifth percen- tile (96–100%)	15.5	15.4	13.8	13.7	13.2	14.3	12.6	14.0	13.7
g. c. q.	.366	.381	.338	.331	.345	.338	.316	.335	.324
g. c. d.	.342	.356	.316	.308	.320	.315	.294	.314	.303

g. c. d_1	1963	1965	1967	1969			
	.199	.255	.236	.198			
	1964	1966	1968	1970	1971	1972	1973
	.240	.256	.216	.164	.186	.140	.144

* Data for g.c.d_1 from (DAF, 1961–73). Other data, same as Tables 7 and 8.

75 excepting the brief reversal which occurred in 1972–73. This pattern in the national distribution curve closely parallels that of the non-farm curve, excepting trend differences in certain years. From this parallel movement we conclude that the trends in nationwide income inequality were largely determined by the non-farm family distribution and were little affected by that of farm households.[5] This is understandable considering that the non-agricultural sector has accounted for an over-whelmingly large share of Taiwan's national income. It is also worth

[5] Oshima has pointed out the same phenomenon regarding the U.S. and Japan (Oshima, 1975: 21).

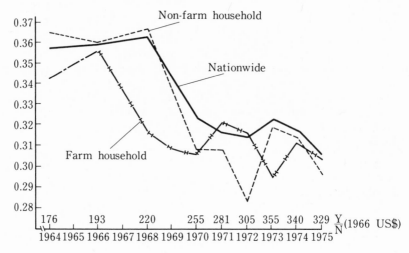

Figure 2. Gini coefficient curves, 1964–75*
  * Data from Table 7–9, g.c.d. entries.

noting that the national inequality index was decreasing in spite of the increase in the differential between the farm and non-farm households, particularly during 1968–73.

2. The Gini inequality index for non-farm families increased over 1964–68 while there was a trend towards greater equality after 1968, excepting only the retrogression of 1972–73. The post-1968, non-farm as well as the nationwide, trend toward equalization must have been influenced by movements in the factor distribution share. As mentioned earlier, after 1968 most non-agricultural sector enterprises came to rely on employed labor, and the distribution between capital and labor turned favorable for labor.

3. The inequality index for farm families increased over 1964–68 (or 1963–68 if we use the Gini ratio calculated from DAR data), whereas it decreased for most of the period thereafter. Comparing the farm pattern with the nationwide and non-farm patterns, we can see a broad similarity of trend. In both cases regression precedes equalization in the course of growth in income. However, the farm pattern is different in that it shows more fluctuations and trend reversals. In addition, after 1968–70 the pace of decrease or equalization seems to be slower compared to non-farm households. In this regard, we may observe in Figure 2 that the inequality index for the farm household was less than that for the non-farm household over 1964–70. Thereafter, the position

of the two was often reversed with the farm household having a higher Gini coefficient.

As can be seen in Figure 2, all three Gini curves indicate that, in 1968, the trend in the broad size distribution of Taiwanese family income changed from regressive to progressive. Unfortunately, the Gini series are available only for a short period, namely the five to six years prior to 1968, thus raising the question of the reliability of 1968 as a turning point. Nevertheless, a proxy measure can be found in the modern sector factor shares to give us more information concerning trends prior to 1968. First, we know that the modern sector, prior to 1968, already accounted for the overwhelming share of national income. Second, we also know from earlier evidence that the trend between capital and labor shares over 1953–68 was toward inequality. This factor share trend toward inequality reinforces our confidence in concluding that a similar trend is likely in the Gini curves for the years prior to 1964. We may therefore conclude that the Taiwanese pattern of income distribution exhibits most of the traits of the Kuznets curve, with 1968 as the turning point.[6]

An Inter-country Comparison of Size Distribution of Income

Let us now turn our attention to a brief comparative examination of Taiwan's size distribution of income. In his paper "Income Distribution at Different Levels of Development", Paukert has gone to great pains to assemble and analyze income distribution data for 56 countries at different stages of economic growth (Paukert, 1973). In his analysis he has divided developed and developing countries into six subcategories, taking the third quintile household to represent the middle group of each nation's income recipients. In Table 10 we have attempted to compare figures for Taiwan with Paukert's results. To facilitate the comparison, the classification of countries has been simplified and the fourth, instead of the third, quintile household has been chosen to represent the middle group.

The following comparative implications can be drawn from Table 10:

---

[6] "One might thus assume a long swing in the inequality characterizing the secular income structure: widening in the early phases of economic growth; becoming stabilized for a while; and then narrowing in the later phases" (Kuznets, 1955: 18) and (Kuznets, 1966: 217).

Table 10. An Inter-country Comparison of Size Distribution of Income*

Country	Number	GDP per capita (1965) (US $)	Quintile					Top fifth percentile (96–100 %)	$Q_1+Q_2+Q_3$	$\dfrac{Q_5}{Q_1}$	$\dfrac{Q_5}{Q_1+Q_2+Q_3}$	$\dfrac{Q_4}{Q_1}$	Gini ratio	Maximum equalization percentage[c]
			Q_1	Q_2	Q_3	Q_4	Q_5							
Developing[a]	43	101–1,000	5.3	8.7	12.5	19.0	54.6	28.7	26.4	10.49	2.06	3.63	0.467	35.6
Developed[a]	10	(1,001–2,000)	4.8	10.6	16.4	(22.2)	46.1	19.9	31.7	9.59	1.44	4.86	0.392	28.4
	13	1,001 & above				22.6								
Taiwan[b]	1	180–340	8.5	13.1	16.9	22.3	40.0	15.3	38.5	4.70	1.05	2.69	0.353	22.2

* Data adapted from (Paukert, 1973) and Table 7.
a Country group averages.
b Year of comparison: circa 1965.
c Maximum equalization percentage: the % of total personal income which has to be transfered between brackets in order to achieve equal distribution.

1. Taiwan's Gini ratio (0.353) is lower than that of developed countries (0.392) as well as that of developing nations (0.467).

2. The maximum equalization percentage for Taiwan is only 22.2 percent, a considerably smaller percentage than that for other countries.

3. The pattern derived from the general indicators examined in (1) and (2) above is emphatically supported by the patterns suggested by an analysis of particular groups. For example, the first (poorest), second, and third Taiwanese quintile households groups receive, respectively, 8.3 percent, 13.1 percent, and 16.8 percent of total personal income. Here each quintile share is larger than that received by the comparable quintile of income recipients in developing as well as developed countries.

4. The share received by the highest (richest) quintile is 40 percent, and that of the top 5 percent of Taiwanese families is 15.3 percent. Comparatively, these shares are lower than those received by the comparable brackets of families in other countries, either developing or developed.

5. The fourth quintile, or the middle group, of Taiwanese families receives 22 percent of total personal income. This share is larger than that received by the comparable bracket in developing nations, almost the same as that received in most developed countries, and somewhat smaller than that received in a few developed countries.

6. The share received by the lowest 60 percent of families in Taiwan (38.5 percent) is larger than that received by the comparable group in other countries, developed or developing.

7. The ratio ($Q5/Q1$) of the share of the richest quintile to that of the poorest quintile in Taiwan (4.7) is far lower than the comparable ratio for either developing (10.49) or developed (9.59) countries. Furthermore, the ratio ($Q5/Q1+Q2+Q3$) between the richest quintile and the bottom 60 percent (1.05) in Taiwan shows a narrower disparity as compared with developing (2.06) or developed (1.44) countries. This all suggests that the disparity between the richest and the poorest in Taiwan is comparatively small.

8. The ratio ($Q4/Q1$) of the share of the fourth quintile to that of the poorest quintile indicates the disparity between the middle and poorest group. Here too, we also find a smaller difference (*i.e.,* a more equal distribution) between these strata in Taiwan than other countries. In terms of per-capita income Taiwan has still a long way to go to reach the highest levels of developing countries. Yet, as far as the equality of size income distribution is concerned, Taiwan has already achieved a position more desirable than in most developed and all developing countries.

Summary

It has been maintained that size distribution of personal income showed no regressive tendency during the postwar period of rapid growth in Taiwan.[7] According to the findings of this paper, however, the trend in Taiwan's size income distribution was regressive prior to 1968 and did not begin to move toward equalization until that year.

The major elements which explain the changes in the trend of size distribution of family income can be broadly identified as follows: (1) changes in the capital-labor share; (2) shifts in the farm–non-farm relative income; and (3) variation in the degree of within-group income inequality (measured by the Gini index) for farm and non-farm families.

If we divide the period 1953–68 into five-year subperiods, the following changes can be identified with respect to factor share and between- and within-group income inequality:

(1) *Factor share.*   In 1958–63 the labor share decreased relative to its position in 1953–58, and it did not show any significant change in 1963–68 relative to 1958–63.

(2) *Between-group income inequality.*   As a result of the changes in the labor share mentioned above, the share of lower bracket non-farm families decreased prior to 1968. At the same time the Gini ratio for the urban sector rose. The post-1963 continuous lag in farmers' income increases also played a role in increasing differences in nationwide income distribution.

(3) *Within-group income inequality.*   Before 1966, the share of the lower income farm family groups declined the Gini ratio for within income inequality rose.

Before 1968, nationwide family income distribution tended to worsen. Between 1968 and 1975, however, the following movements have taken place: (1) Labor's share has risen relative to that of capital. (2) Consequently, the distribution of family income within the non-agricultural sector improved, and the Gini ratio decreased. (3) At the same time, the

---

[7] Fei has said, "In developing countries generally there first appears extreme inequality then a shift towards equality. But Taiwan is an exception. This is indeed a great pleasure and a miracle," (Fei, 1974: 200). Ranis also said, "Taiwan thus may constitute one of the few exceptions to the sober findings of Kuznets" (Rains, 1974: 285, 287). Shirly W.Y. Kuo, Vice Chairman, Economic Planning Council, Taiwan, concluded in a seminar paper, "that the income distribution in Taiwan improved during 1953–1964, and that improvement was faster in the period 1953–64 than in the period 1964–72" (Kuo, 1975: 93, 144, 151). In later work, however, the three economists referred to above have affirmed that a mild version of the Kuznets inverted U-shaped curve appears in Taiwan's income distribution with 1968 as a turning point.

within distribution for farm families became, in most years, more equal and the Gini ratio fell. (4) Finally, the income differential between farm and non-farm families, with the exception of a few years, continued to widen. However, its impact on the nationwide distribution was more than offset by the equalization effect of the other factors. It is as yet too early to tell whether the post-1968 trend toward equalization has continued into recent years.

With regard to international comparison, it seems that Taiwan, with a per-capita income level not yet high by developing country standards, has already achieved a more desirable income distribution position for the mass of people than in most developed and all developing countries for which we have information.

References

Bureau of Budget, Accounting and Statistics. Taipei City Government. *Report on the Survey of Family Income and Expenditure and Personal Income Distribution of Taipei City* (FIEPID), separate issues for 1971–75.

Chang, H. Y. "The Variations of Farmer's Income and Factors Affecting Them," *Economic Essays Vol. III*, The Graduate Institute of Economics, National Taiwan University, Taipei, December, 1972.

Chang, H. Y. "Farmer's Income and Rural Processing Industry of Farm Products," *Quarterly Journal of the Bank of Taiwan*, Vol. 24, No. 4, Taipei, December, 1973.

Council for International Economic Cooperation and Development (CIECD). *Capital Stock in Taiwan 1951–73*, mimeo.

CIECD. *Fixed Capital Stock of Industrial Sectors in Taiwan 1964*, mimeo.

Department of Agriculture and Forestry, Taiwan Provincial Government (TPG). *Report on Farm Record-Keeping Families in Taiwan* (FRKF), separate volumes for 1961–1975.

Department of Construction, TPG. *Report of Taiwan Labor Statistics*, issues for 1957–1973.

Department of Budget, Accounting and Statistics, TPG. *Report of the Survey of Family Income and Expenditure, Taiwan Province* (SFIE), separate issues for 1964, '66, '68, '70–74.

Director General of Budgets, Accounts and Statistics, Executive Yuan (DGBAS). *National Income of the Republic of China*. Taipei 1972, 1975.

DGBAS. *Taiwan Statistical Data Book* (TSDB), 1976.

DGBAS. *Provision for Capital Consumption in Primary Industries 1952–74*, mimeo.

Institute of Economics, Academica Sinica. *Seminar on the Present Economic Problems of Taiwan*, July, 1974.

Kravis, I. B. "Income Distribution, Functional Share," *International Encyclopedia of the Social Sciences*, Vol. 7. New York: Macmillan, 1968.

Kuo, S.W.Y. "Income Distribution by Size in Taiwan Area, Changes and Causes," in *Income Distribution, Employment, and Economic Development in Southeast and East Asia* (IDEED), Vol. i, July 1975.

Kuznets, S. "Economic Growth and Income Inequality," *American Economic Review*, Vol. XLV, March 1955.

Kuznets, S. "Distribution of Income by Size: Long-Term Trends," *Modern Economic Growth*. New Haven: Yale University Press, 1966.

Lewis, W. A. "Economic Development with Unlimited Supplies of Labor," Manchester School, May 1954. Reprinted in A. N. Agarwala and S. P. Singh (eds.), *The Economics of Underdevelopment*. New York: Galaxy, 1963.

Mizoguchi, T., *et al.* "Over Time Changes of the Size Distribution of Household Income in Korea," *The Developing Economies*, XIV-3, Tokyo, September 1976.

Ohkawa, K. *Analysis of the Japanese Economy—Growth and Structure*. Tokyo: Shunju Sha, 1969 (in Japanese).

Oshima, H. T. "Perspective in Income Distribution Research," *IDEED* 1975.

Paukert, F. "Income Distribution at Different Levels of Development," *International Labor Review*, Vol. 108, Nos. 2–3, August-September 1973.

Ranis, G. "Some Country Experience, Taiwan," in Chenergy H. B., *et al.*, *Redistribution with Growth*, London: Oxford University Press, 1974.

Over-time Changes in the Size Distribution of Household Income under Rapid Economic Growth: The Japanese Experience

Toshiyuki Mizoguchi, Noriyuki Takayama, and
Yasuhiro Terasaki

One of the most important policy problems faced by developing countries is the maintainance of economic growth while preserving the relative equity of income distribution.* In this respect, we will want to consider the Kuznets inverted-U hypothesis which maintains that there will be a regressive trend in the size distribution of income until some point in the development process, after which a progressive trend will appear. When plotted, the shape of the curve will resemble the letter U turned upside down. The knowledge that such a pattern exists might be very helpful in devising strategies for development countries. Unfortunately, the Kuznets hypothesis has been insufficiently tested, mainly because of the scarcity of data.

As Kuznets pointed out, it is very difficult to find appropriate long-term data. Several attempts, using various kinds of data, have been made to verify the Kuznets hypothesis. Some have tried to use historical data (Paukert, 1973), but most studies have depended on very special kinds of data such as tax statistics. Others have attempted to clarify the relation between income levels in U.S. dollars and degrees of inequality (Bacha, 1977). The difficulty with these approaches is that the degree of inequality varies with social factors and with the nature of the data.

We believe that the Japanese experience provides a good chance to test the Kuznets hypothesis, although we have data on the size distribution of income only for the post-world War II period. Judged by the magnitude of the change in the level of income, the quarter-century

* This paper was prepared as a report for the Income and Assets Distribution Research Project, Institute of Economic Research, Hitotsubashi University (IADR-PHU), and was financially supported by the Toyota Foundation.

233

of postwar Japanese development can be compared to a century of growth in most developed countries. Therefore, we can hope to get an idea of the long-term relation between economic development and changes in the inequality of the size distribution of household income. In this paper we shall, in Section II, investigate the over-time changes in size distribution of total household income in relation to the changes in inequality "between" and "within" selected household subgroups. In Section III, relying on more detailed data, we shall examine the causes of the changes in inequality for various subgroups.

Before proceeding, it is necessary to comment on the measures of inequality to be used in this paper. Among the various measures which have been used in income distribution studies, the most popular is the Gini concentration ratio or the Gini coefficient, which can be decomposed into additive factor components (Rao, 1969). Where $G =$ the Gini coefficient of total income, $G_i =$ the pseudo-Gini coefficient of the i-th income component (obtained from tables classified by total household income), and $w_i =$ the share of i-th income in total income, we have

$$G = \sum_i wi\bar{G}_i.$$

However, there are two deficiencies in the Gini coefficient. First, when the Lorenz curves being compared cross, the ordering pattern of this measure becomes arbitrary. In fact, it has been shown by Atkinson (Atkinson, 1970) that the Gini coefficient weighs the modal income classes more heavily than those at the margins. The other drawback of the Gini coefficient is its ineffective treatment of the between–within type of decomposition. When income distribution is calculated according to heterogeneous household groups, it is desirable to decompose the inequality measures into between and within components.[1]

Regarding the latter problem, we will want to look at the log variance decomposition. It is not necessarily admitted that the income distribution follows the log-normal distribution, but the log variances have been used to indicate the measures of inequality. In this case we can divide the total log variance into between and within components using the technique of variance analysis.

---

[1] The total Gini coefficient, G, can be decomposed into the between-group Gini, G_b, and the within-group Gini, $G_w(i)$, using the following formula:
$$G = G_b + \sum_i w_i \, G_w(i)$$
where $w_i = [g(Y_i)]^2 \, (\bar{Y}/Y_i)$
and $\bar{Y}$, Y_i, and $g(Y_i)$ are, respectively, the mean income of the total group, the measure of the i-th subgroup, and the population share of each group. Note that all Gs defined here are Gini coefficients, not pseudo-Gini coefficients.

Theil's measure, derived from information theory, is also a popular measure in the study of income distribution. One of the merits of this measure is that total inequality can be divided into the two components mentioned above. To some extent, Toyoda (1975) succeeded in generalizing the Theil measure. He gave us measures of the expected-utility type which are made up under a general weighing system with one parameter (a). When (a) equals unity, his measure is reduced to the well-known Theil measure (T), and when $a = 2$, his measure equals half the square of the coefficient of variation. Furthermore, when (a) is less than unity, his measure (B) corresponds to Atkinson's measure (A) in the following formula:

$$A = 1 - (1 - aB)^{1/a}, \; a \neq 0, \; a < 1$$
$$A = 1 - \exp(-B), \quad a = 1.$$

In this sense, B can be treated as Atkinson's variant when $a < 1$.

$$(a = 1 - E.)$$
$$B = (1/a) \, [1 - \sum(Y_j/\bar{Y})^a f(Y_j)] \qquad a \neq 0, \; a < 1$$
$$B = - \sum [\log(Y_j/\bar{Y})] f(Y_j), \qquad a = 0$$
$$B = \sum [(Y_j/\bar{Y}) \log(Y_j/\bar{Y})] f(Y_j) \qquad a = 1$$
$$B = (1/a) \, [\sum(Y_j/\bar{Y})^a f(Y_j) - 1] \qquad a < 1$$

where $Y_j, f(Y_j)$ and $\bar{Y}$ are, respectively, the income of the j-th class, its population share, and its mean income.

Corresponding to the form of decomposition of Theil's measure, we can decompose Toyoda's measure as follows:

$$B = B + \sum w_i \, B_w(i) \qquad\qquad w_i = g(Y_i) \, (Y(\bar{Y})^a$$

where $B_b, B_{w(i)}, Y_i, g(Y_i)$ are, respectively, the between-group inequality, the within-group inequality, the mean income of the i-th group, and the population share of that group. When (a) equals unity or zero, we have $w_i = 1$, and the total within-group inequality ($\sum w_i B_{w(i)}$) becomes just the weighted average of the within-group inequality. The smaller the value of (a), the heavier is the weight given to the lower income classes at the margin.

Total Household Income Distribution

This section aims to estimate the degrees of inequality for the size distribution of household income covering all types of household income in Japan. Such an attempt is important in showing the broad characteristics of Japanese income distribution and in understanding the behavior of occupational groups.

Needless to say, obtaining reliable data is the most important task in the study of income distribution. There have been published annually in Japan two kinds of reliable data on the size distribution of multi-member households: the Family Income and Expenditure Survey of the Bureau of Statistics, Office of the Prime Minister (hereafter FIES), and the Cost of Living Survey of Farm Households of the Ministry of Agriculture and Forestry (hereafter CLSF).[2] The sample size is medium —that is, about 10,000—and the reporting households are requested to make balance sheets for their income and expenditures. It is our impression that the non-sampling biases are more serious than the sampling biases in the income survey. In this sense, the two surveys have reliable figures on income in comparison with the figures of other kinds of surveys which depend on a simple questionnaire.

Restricting ourselves only to these data, however, we leave the following household groups unexamined: the nonagricultural entrepreneur multi-member household, the unemployed multi-member household, and the single-member household. According to the 1974 Employment Status Survey of the Bureau of Statistics, Office of the Prime Minister (hereafter ESS), the percentage of the number of households occupied by these groups is about 40; therefore, we cannot neglect these household groups in our study.

Since the early 1970s, some attempts at filling this vacuum in income distribution studies have been made. Wada (1975) estimated the size distribution for total households, relying mainly on the ESS,[3] which collects figures on the cash income of individuals. In the reports before 1968, the ESS estimated household cash income using questionnaires on household property and transfer income. Wada adjusted the figures for agricultural households by adding his estimates of income in kind. He also tried to revise the ESS property income figures, which he believed to have downward biases. Since we cannot get information on property income and transfer income from recent ESS surveys, we cannot really corroborate Wada's method. In addition, there remain some problems regarding the accuracy of ESS income figures. Because the main purpose of the survey is to provide information on employ-

---

[2] A brief explanation of these surveys was presented in (Mizoguchi, 1975).

[3] While Wada estimated the 1971 distribution, there was not much description of the method used to compensate for the lack of data on property and transfer income for that year. Therefore, we adopt in this section only his pre-1968 results.

ment structure, income has been treated as a matter of subsidiary interest. Further, the questionnaire used has been simplified in subsequent years. Additionally, it is somewhat inconvenient to use ESS data which are prepared every three years when most other Japanese data are published annually.

A second approach was proposed by the Research Group on Income Distribution Problems (hereafter RGIDP) organized by the EPA (RGIDP, 1976). They adopted the annual income data reported in the Family Saving Survey of the Bureau of Statistics, Office of the Prime Minister (hereafter FSS), in order to derive the size distribution of income for urban households. Since the samples for the FSS are taken from the sample households selected at the beginning of each year, the annual income information should be relatively reliable, even though gathered through a simple questionnaire.[4]

A third type of study was proposed by Mizoguchi (1975). While the FIES has income data only for employee households, it has expenditure data for other than employee non-agricultural households (let us call these households "Other Households"). Since we can get the annual saving ratios by income class for the Other Households from the FSS, we can derive the size distribution of disposable income by using the FIES and the FSS together.

Another approach would be to seek data which cover a range of household groups broader than the CLSF and the FIES and give more reliable income data than the ESS. Among various candidates, we should pay attention to the Survey of People's Living Conditions of the Ministry of Welfare (hereafter SPLC) and the Survey of Consumer Finances of the EPA (hereafter SCF). About 10,000 households are taken as the sample for the SPLC, which examines the income from July of the previous year to June of the survey year. Since the reports have been published, with some exceptions, annually, we can investigate the annual change in income distribution for all households. The interviewing has been done through the fixed districts used by the Office of Social Welfare Commissions, and it is said that, in comparison with other kinds of surveys, the refusal ratio is low for low-income classes.

The SCF has taken its sample households from the same population used for the FIES and the CLSF. Since the survey obtains income figures from a simple questionnaire, the SCF income data would be less reliable than that of the FIES. However, careful attention has been paid to income since the main object of this survey is to study con-

[4] The FIES asked the sample households their annual income for the preceding year. Because the samples have been rotated gradually, we cannot use the annual income in the study of income distribution.

sumption behavior. Thus, its income data are better in quality than the ESS's.

A comparison of estimates

Now let us compare various kinds of estimates obtained from different data. Because of data limitations, the comparison is restricted to the years after 1962. Since our purpose here is to follow the broad pattern of over-time change, let us adopt the most often used indicator, the Gini coefficient. All income data are presented in decile group breakdown using the packaged program developed in our project (Matsuda et al., 1976), and the coefficients obtained are shown in Table 1.

For the income distribution of all types of households, we have only two kinds of estimates. Although there are minor differences in the household coverage, it is not impossible to compare the two. Wada's calculations for the Gini coefficient are nearly constant from 1962 to 1968; our SPLC estimates show a decline. The difference between the pattern suggested by Wada and that used by us can be traced to the varying patterns of distribution for single-member households. The pattern of overtime change in distribution is similar in the two series with respect to multi-member households. For the multi-member households, we have four kinds of estimates. Differences in coverage are not so serious as to affect the estimates. Generally speaking, the overtime changes show very similar patterns. The coefficients rise until 1962, decline from 1963 to 1968, and increase thereafter.

The over-time income distribution pattern suggested by the four kinds of estimates for the non-agricultural multi-member household is also similar: there is a decreasing trend from 1960 to 1972 and an increasing trend afterwards. While the original draft of Wada's paper showed figures for only two years, 1956 and 1962, the result seems to be consistent with our estimates.

Regarding the period before 1961, we can get information on the size distribution of total households only through the ESS. According to Wada's calculations, the distribution changed regressively during this period. While we cannot check his results with other data, there are some figures which permit a partial examination of the reliability of the ESS data. The ESS suggests that the distribution within employee households showed a regressive trend from 1956 to 1959. This is consistent with the results from the FIES which are examined below. (See "Income Distribution of Employee Households"). Wada has calculated the Gini coefficients for agricultural households only for 1956 and 1962. The regressive trend he suggested there is supported by the results from

Table 1. Estimates of Gini Coefficients for Total Households Using Various Data Sources*

Data	Estimate by authors	1962	1963	1964	1965	1966	1967	1968	1969	1970	1971
					Total Households						
(1) ESS (CLSF)	Wada	0.3819	....	....	0.3766	....	....	0.3800	....	....	....
(2) SPLC	Mizoguchi	0.3759	0.3607	0.3528	0.3441	....	0.3523	0.3488	0.3539	0.3553	0.3521
				Multiple member households							
(3) ESS (CLSF)	Wada	0.340	....	....	0.337	....	....	0.324	....	....	....
(4) SPLC	Mizoguchi	0.3629	0.3461	0.3402	0.3276	....	0.3307	0.3257	0.3319	0.3284	0.3301
(5) FIES, CLSF & FSS	Mizoguchi	0.2744	0.2544	0.2440	0.2392	0.2373	0.2403	0.2191	0.2017	0.2197	0.2094
(6) SCF	Mizoguchi	....	....	0.2922	0.3050	0.3113	0.3004	0.2826	0.2732	0.2872	0.2661
				Urban multimember households							
(7) SPLC	Mizoguchi	0.3636	0.3464	0.3232	0.3232	....	0.3224	0.3184	0.3232	0.3140	0.3139
(8) FIES, CLSF & FSS	Mizoguchi	0.2745	0.2563	0.2380	0.2276	0.2284	0.2307	0.2104	0.2002	0.2043	0.2076
(9) FSS	RGID	0.2972	0.2968	0.2572	0.2988	0.2916	0.2864	0.2712	0.2652	0.2664	0.2756

a. While the SPLC is based on fiscal year income surveys from July-June, other surveys are based on calendar year income.
b. The SPLC was not taken in 1966; the ESS has been done once every three years.
c. The sources used by Wada and the RGIDP are shown in (Wada, 1975) and (RGIDP, 1976), respectively.
d. While (5) and (8) measure the distribution of household disposable income, all other income figures are for household pre-tax income.

the CLSF which are examined in Section III (see "Urban Rural Income Differences and Income Distribution of Agricultural Households").

Since these two household groups occupied a large portion of multi-member households in the 1950s, his estimates would be valid at least for these households.

However, we still must explain the difference in the level of inequality measures for the multi-member household as well as the non-agricultural multi-member household. For example, the results from the ESS and the SPLC range from 0.30 to 0.35; the estimates from the FIES, the FHES, and the FSS are generally lower. We can point out two reasons for these differences. The first is that the samples of the FIES are taken from households of relatively moderate income.

Although the FIES adopts the random sampling method, it is quite possible that the refusal ratio is high in low-income households due to the difficulty in keeping family account books. A similar situation could arise with the SCF or the FSS. In constrast with these surveys, the SPLC uses officers of the Social Welfare Commission as interviewers, and the refusal ratio is relatively low in low-income households. Since the ESS inquires mainly about the employment situation, the refusal ratio is said to be low in comparison with other surveys. The second reason

Table 2. Gini Coefficient for Household Subgroup*

Year	(1) Total H.H.	(1.1) Single-member H.H.	(1.2) Ordinary H.H.	(2.1)	(2.2)	(2.3)	(2.4)	(2.5)
				Subgroups of ordinary households				
				Regular employee H.H.	Daily employee H.H.	Agricultural H.H.	Non-agri-cultural self-employed H.H.	Unemployed H.H.
1962	0.3759	0.4215	0.3629	0.3244	0.2931	0.3192	0.3855	0.4275
1963	0.3607	0.4155	0.3461	.03116	0.2816	0.3023	0.3818	0.3699
1964	0.3528	0.3672	0.3402	0.3027	0.2598	0.3187	0.3950	0.3661
1965	0.3441	0.4131	0.3276	0.2988	0.2765	0.2917	0.3971	0.4057
1966	—	—	—	—	—	—	—	—
1967	0.3523	0.3541	0.3307	0.2961	0.2590	0.2949	0.4374	0.4131
1968	0.3488	0.4591	0.3257	0.2961	0.2973	0.2925	0.3977	0.3561
1969	0.3539	0.4046	0.3319	0.3043	0.2682	0.2844	0.4915	0.3903
1970	0.3553	0.3733	0.3284	0.2934	0.2530	0.2938	0.4467	0.4155
1971	0.3521	0.3987	0.3301	0.2986	0.2570	0.3081	0.4328	0.4012
1972	0.3570	0.4304	0.3388	0.3022	0.2586	0.3197	0.4215	0.3826
1973	0.3496	0.4760	0.3287	0.2936	0.3271	0.3126	0.4073	0.4210
1974	0.3443	0.3651	0.3268	0.2890	0.4683	0.3041	0.4505	0.4172

* Data from the SPLC.
a. H.H. = household.

concerns only the FIES. To avoid difficulties caused by FIES sample rotation, we have used here the average annual income calculated for household groups in the annual report of the FIES.

Since we believe that the nonsampling biases are small in the FIES and the CLSF, we must refer to these data to determine the pattern of over-time change in the Gini coefficients. However, regarding the absolute level of the Gini coefficients, the results from the SPLC are more realistic. Further, it is very fortunate for us that the pattern suggested by the SPLC is very similar to that of the FIES and the CLSF. Considering these circumstances, we can use the SPLC to investigate all types of household income distribution.

Decomposition of SPLC log variances

Various methods have been proposed for decomposing the inequality measures. However, let us use here the log variance of income. By using the technique of variance analysis, the total log variance in the data classified by occupational groups can be decomposed into weighted averages *within* variances and *between* variances. The results are shown in Table 3, where total variances for all households are first decomposed into those for single- and multi-member households. The variance for the multi-member household is again divided into five occupational groups. The pattern of over-time change is very similar to that of the Gini coefficients shown in Table 2. Therefore we can safely use the log variances, although we do not necessarily believe that the pattern of income distribution follows that of the log normal distribution.

First, let us examine the decomposition between the single- and the multi-member households. The within variances for the two groups change differently over time. The curve for the single-member household declines from the early to the late 1960s and rises afterwards. However, the opposite pattern is shown in most years by the multi-member household curve. Since about 80 percent of all households are multi-member, the overall within-variance pattern will closely resemble that of the multi-member household. In this context, it is very important to note that the between variance increases, especially after the mid-1960s. This could be explained if the relative income of single-member households had decreased remarkably after the mid-1960s. However, in fact the relative income of single-member employee households did not decline.

The single-member household includes the following four categories: (1) young employee households, (2) young unemployed households, (3) aged households, and (4) others. Although detailed analysis will be

Table 3. Decomposition of Log Variances for All Types of Household*

Year	(1) Total H.H. var.	(1.1) Var. between single and ordinary H.H.	(1.2) Weighted average of two H.H. groups	(1.2.1) within single H.H.	(1.2.2) Var. within ordinary H.H.	(2.1) Var. between five H.H. sub-groups	(2.2) Weighted average of within var. of sub-groups	(2.2.1) Regular employee H.H.	((2.2.2)) Daily employee H.H.	(2.2.3) Agricultural H.H.	(2.2.4) Non-agricultural self-employed H.H.	(2.2.5) Unemployed H.H.
							Weighted variances within subgroups					
1962	0.5227	0.0503	0.4724	0.5005	0.4702	0.0919	0.3783	0.3548	0.2800	0.3664	0.4681	0.5216
1963	0.5155	0.0640	0.4515	0.6018	0.4394	0.0847	0.3547	0.3313	0.2978	0.3335	0.4704	0.4284
1964	0.4604	0.0507	0.4103	0.5798	0.3963	0.0609	0.3354	0.2923	0.2539	0.3109	0.4793	0.5060
1965	0.4779	0.0627	0.4152	0.6527	0.3942	0.0538	0.3408	0.2898	0.2713	0.3317	0.4930	0.6174
1966	....	....	....	....	....	....	....	....	....	....	....	....
1967	0.4861	0.0845	0.4016	0.5159	0.3898	0.0623	0.3275	0.3019	0.2488	0.3311	0.6044	0.5588
1968	0.5026	0.0869	0.4157	0.5928	0.3940	0.0456	0.3484	0.2933	0.3759	0.3315	0.5321	0.4414
1969	0.5077	0.0830	0.4247	0.5658	0.4070	0.0460	0.3610	0.3076	0.2685	0.3130	0.7943	0.5521
1970	0.5019	0.1006	0.4013	0.4551	0.3930	0.0364	0.3560	0.2862	0.2248	0.3126	0.6749	0.5612
1971	0.4890	0.0921	0.3979	0.4273	0.3955	0.0272	0.3683	0.3005	0.2402	0.2490	0.6745	0.5330
1972	0.4962	0.0818	0.4144	0.5609	0.4021	0.0301	0.3720	0.3148	0.2534	0.3853	0.5741	0.5048
1973	0.4554	0.0533	0.4021	0.7334	0.3661	0.0161	0.3500	0.2751	0.3645	0.3503	0.5152	0.6232
1974	0.4515	0.0577	0.3938	0.4744	0.3855	0.0055	0.3800	0.2766	0.5629	0.3519	0.6495	0.6045

* Data from the SPLC.
a. H.H. = household: Var = variance.
b. Single households consist of (1) young employee households, (2) young unemployed households, (3) aged households, and (4) others.

presented below, we would like to point out here, without offering any numerical illustrations, that the most important factor underlying this increase is the rise in the number of households in category (2), which is largely composed of students living away from home.

Regarding the within variances for multi-member households, we can identify occupation and group differences in the over-time pattern of change. In the 1960s the pattern of change for employee households was progressive. While there was a regressive tendency in the early 1970s, we can safely say that the progressive changes in employee household income distribution played an important role in keeping the distribution of total households relatively equal in the process of rapid economic growth.[5] In spite of fluctuation, the trends in inequality measures for agricultural households have been relatively stable. This group is important in examining total household behavior in the 1950s because it represented a relatively large portion of households. Thereafter, we need not pay much attention to these households since their number as a proportion of total households declined sharply.

The distribution of the non-agricultural entrepreneur's income has changed regressively in both the 1960s and the 1970s. Further, the level of inequality measures is higher than that for either the employee or the agricultural household. Since this group represents about 20 percent of multi-member households, its pattern affects to some extent the pattern of total household income distribution. It is important to examine the regressive tendency itself using various sources of information. It is not surprising that high inequality values can be found for unemployed household income distribution because income in this sector is obtained from property income or transfer payments. But it is very interesting to note here that the inequality coefficients for the unemployed household were relatively stable in the 1960s.

The between variances regarding these five household subgroups decline significantly in this period. This decline can be seen in Figure 1, where we have presented the decreases in income differences between employee and agricultural households. The figures also indicate that income differences decreased during the 1960s between employee households and non-agricultural entrepreneur households, another reason for the decline of the between variances. In contrast to this trend the relative income of the unemployed household decreased, and this slowed down the speed of decline of the between variances.

---

[5] Since the number of daily worker households decreased sharply in the 1960s, we can use regular laborer households as representative of the employee households in our investigation.

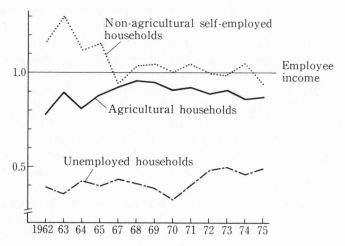

Figure 1. Over-time changes in relative income*

   * Data from the SPLC.

   a. Employee income = 1.0.

Detailed Studies of Income Distribution by Household Occupational Groups

In this section, let us examine in detail the causes of the over-time changes in income distribution inequality. For this purpose, we need information about the income components as well as income distribution for household subgroups. Unfortunately, the SPLC is not a good source, and we shall use other kinds of survey data (for a detailed explanation, see the notes to Table 4).

Income distribution of employee households

Table 4 shows the over-time changes in the Gini coefficient (G) and the Atkinson's measure (A: $\in$ = 5) of income distribution from FIES data for employee households. Both measures rose slightly in the latter half of the 1950s, decreased during the 1960s, and showed little change in the early 1970s. This tendency is consistent with that shown by the SPLC data for employee households, although the absolute levels of the inequality coefficients are higher in the SPLC than in the FIES. The degrees of income inequality computed for twelve-monthly (January to December) averages were significantly higher than those calculated from

Table 4. Employee Household Income Inequality*

From decile income group data of monthly income

	December included				December excluded			
	G	A (a = − 4)	B (a = 0)	B (a = 2)	G	A (a = − 4)	B (a = 0)	B (a = 2)
1953	0.2865	0.4876	0.1325	0.1410	0.2838	0.5034	0.1305	0.1376
1954	0.3145	0.5442	0.1615	0.1761	0.2908	0.5320	0.1382	0.1469
1955	0.3007	0.5240	0.1471	0.1580	0.2963	0.5363	0.14382	0.1542
1956	0.3134	0.5428	0.1616	0.1774	0.2899	0.5026	0.1384	0.1505
1957	0.3184	0.5623	0.1666	0.1822	0.2994	0.5211	0.1489	0.1643
1958	0.3212	0.5613	0.1711	0.1900	0.2991	0.5254	0.1479	0.1621
1959	0.3174	0.5752	0.1643	0.1759	0.2964	0.5249	0.1461	0.1605
1960	0.3217	0.5603	0.1702	0.1876	0.3015	0.5191	0.1516	0.1688
1961	0.3179	0.5657	0.1655	0.1797	0.2904	0.5288	0.1597	0.1793
1962	0.3081	0.5516	0.1555	0.1680	0.2963	0.5225	0.1465	0.1619
1963	0.3090	0.5325	0.1557	0.1687	0.2992	0.5115	0.1504	0.1688

From decile income group data of annual income reported

1963	0.2237	0.3213	0.0795	0.0828
1964	0.2134	0.2790	0.0725	0.0765
1965	0.2056	0.2655	0.0660	0.0696
1966	0.2110	0.2703	0.0708	0.0767
1967	0.2150	0.2818	0.0736	0.0776
1968	0.2008	0.2444	0.0641	0.0676
1969	0.1874	0.2338	0.0560	0.0582
1970	0.1859	0.2338	0.0546	0.0561
1971	0.1862	0.2309	0.0545	0.0561
1972	0.1872	0.2316	0.0555	0.0574
1973	0.1873	0.2286	0.0551	0.0570
1974	0.1974	0.2478	0.0603	0.0638
1975	0.1979	0.0306	0.0604	0.0643

* Data from the FIES

a. For multi-member employee households, the FIES is the most important data source, having some advantages over the SPLC. The income figures of the FIES are considered to be reliable since these are sums taken from the daily domestic account books in which income and expenditure entries are made and balanced. The FIES has published detailed figures on income, and, since 1963, household subgroup data have been included.

b. There are some difficulties in using the FIES for over-time comparisons, one of which concerns the revision made in mid-1962. The FIES has been taken monthly since 1971; at that time the survey covered only non-agricultural households in large cities with two or more family members. In 1962, the FIES was redesigned to cover such households in all the cities, towns, and villages of Japan. Since we use the enlarged coverage for the study of income distribution after 1963, we cannot compare directly with the pre-1962 FIES results.

c. There is also a discontinuity in the nature of the income distribution tables before and after 1963. One-sixth of the FIES sample is rotated successively so as to avoid data biases in the time-series comparison. This rotation system is efficient to prevent systematic biases, but makes it difficult to obtain annual income estimates from the accounts of each household. Because the seasonal variations of income are great in Japan, it is impossible to estimate the annual income by multiplying the monthly income by 12. Two devices have been proposed in the annual report of the FIES in order to construct annual tables. One proposal has been to use the relative position of monthly income. Since the tables present monthly income data, we can construct quintile or decile income groups for each month. Annual quintile or decile group data can be obtained by taking twelve-month average figures for each group. The other proposal, made in the 1962 revision, is to refer to the reported annual income inequality of the sample. After the revision, sample households have been asked to report a broad estimate of annual income for the previous year. Although the FIES does not adopt the reported amount as the income figure, it is used to construct annual income tables. Since we shall use the latter figures for the post-1963 period and the former figures for years prior to 1962, we cannot compare the absolute levels of the inequality measure before and after 1963.

the average income for "normal" months only (January to November). The differences are mainly due to the bonus payments which nearly all employees receive in December. This seems to imply that the bonus payment is one of the important factors in explaining the regressive trend of the 1950s, as has been suggested by Mizoguchi (Mizoguchi, 1975).

Based on the above findings, we should like to inquire in detail why the Kuznets inverted-U pattern of income disparity appeared during the postwar period of rapid growth, why the turning point was about 1960, and why bonus payments had the effect of widening income inequality. However, before presenting our detailed study it would be convenient to give a brief review of the views of various authors. Mizoguchi (1975) first suggested that the regressive trend in the 1950s was due to the concentration of income in the relatively high income classes and that this could be related to the *bonus toso* (bonus struggle) of the big trade unions which aimed at increasing bonus payments. He also suggested that the progressive tendency in the 1960s could be explained mainly by the scarcity of labor. Mouer (1973–74) pointed out that the population movements from rural to urban areas were an important factor underlying this progressive tendency. Other supporting evidence for Mizoguchi's labor scarcity hypothesis was given in an over-time comparison with the NFIE (Takayama and Yoshioka, 1976). Most of this work, however, should be regarded as tentative; here we hope to offer a rather strong hypothesis of our own.

Breaking down pre-tax income into its various components will shed much light on the various changes which took place, particularly with regard to the following components: (1) the regular employment income of household heads, (2) the extraordinary (*e.g.* bonus) or temporary employment income of household heads, (3) the employment income of other family members and the income of household heads from subsidiary jobs, and (4) other kinds of income. Table 5 shows a

Table 5. A Rao Decomposition of Employee Income Distribution*

		Gini coefficients					Income share (%)			
		(1)	(2)	(3)	(4)	Total	(1)	(2)	(3)	(4)
Monthly	1953									
income	1954	0.2326	0.4433	0.3900	0.2942	0.3139	55(41)	28(39)	13(16)	4(4)
decile	1955	0.2178	0.4249	0.3697	0.3274	0.3007	55(40)	29(41)	12(15)	4(5)
data	1956	0.2203	0.4490	0.3410	0.3326	0.3134	52(36)	33(49)	11(12)	4(4)
	1957	0.2216	0.4456	0.3694	0.2947	0.3184	50(35)	35(49)	11(12)	4(4)
	1958	0.2231	0.4505	0.3650	0.3119	0.3212	50(35)	35(49)	11(12)	4(4)
	1959	0.2214	0.4310	0.3645	0.3035	0.3174	48(34)	36(49)	12(13)	4(4)
	1960	0.2209	0.4384	0.3471	0.2988	0.3271	47(32)	39(53)	11(12)	3(3)
	1961	0.2151	0.4144	0.3920	0.3510	0.3179	46(31)	39(51)	11(14)	3(4)
	1962	0.1916	0.4014	0.4050	0.4254	0.3081	45(28)	39(50)	12(15)	4(6)
	1963	0.1938	0.4180	0.3497	0.4007	0.3090	45(28)	40(55)	11(12)	4(5)
Annual	1963*	0.1891	0.2937	0.3077	0.2291	0.2237	66(56)	17(22)	13(18)	5(5)
income	1964*	0.1785	0.2677	0.3265	0.2158	0.2134	66(56)	16(20)	12(19)	5(5)
decile	1965*	0.1696	0.2617	0.3164	0.2201	0.2056	66(55)	16(21)	13(20)	5(5)
data	1966*	0.1678	0.2807	0.3635	0.1453	0.2110	66(53)	17(22)	13(22)	4(7)
	1967*	0.1687	0.3047	0.3437	0.1598	0.2150	66(52)	18(25)	13(20)	4(3)
	1968*	0.1502	0.2646	0.3606	0.2187	0.2009	65(49)	18(24)	13(23)	4(4)
	1969*	0.1409	0.2243	0.3652	0.1791	0.1874	63(48)	20(25)	12(24)	4(4)
	1970*	0.1369	0.2270	0.3686	0.1526	0.1859	62(46)	21(26)	13(23)	4(3)
	1971*	0.1383	0.2216	0.3828	0.1328	0.1862	63(47)	21(25)	12(25)	4(3)
	1972*	0.1385	0.2384	0.3802	0.1350	0.1872	64(47)	21(26)	12(24)	4(3)
	1973*	0.1365	0.2172	0.3957	0.1750	0.1873	62(45)	22(25)	12(26)	4(4)
	1974*	0.1336	0.2867	0.3560	0.2577	0.1979	63(42)	21(31)	12(22)	4(5)
	1975*	0.1343	0.2854	0.3788	0.2470	0.1979	66(44)	20(28)	12(23)	4(5)

* Data from the FIES.
a. Figures for 1953–63 are calculated from annual income decile data; figures for 1963–75 are derived from monthly income data. Therefore, we cannot compare the Gini coefficients or the income share figures of pre- and post-1963.
b. Income share: (1) = regular employment income of household heads, (2) = extraordinary or temporary income of household heads, (3) = the employment income of other family members and the income of household heads from subsidiary jobs, (4) = other kinds of income.
c. The figures in parentheses under income share indicate the products of the income share x the pseudo-Gini coefficient.

Rao decomposition using these four income components. Regarding the period before 1963, it can be said that

(a) the degree of inequality for income categories (2) and (3) is larger than that of (1);

(b) the Gini coefficients of regular income seemed to show little change in the late 1950s while those of extraordinary income fluctuated from year to year;

(c) the share of the regular income of household heads was on the decrease: from 55 percent in 1955 to 45 percent in 1962. On the other hand, the share of extraordinary income increased: from 29 percent in 1955 to 39 percent in 1960.

(d) The inequality of extraordinary income distribution (as a percentage of total inequality) played the most dominant role in determining the income disparity for employee households. For example, its importance rose from 41 percent in 1955 to 53 percent in 1960. Meanwhile, regular income became less important, declining from 40 percent in 1958 to 28 percent in 1962.

This leads us to the conclusion that the slight increase in income inequality for employee households in the late 1950s mainly originated from the increased share of extraordinary income of household heads where the degree of inequality was largest. This has much to do with trade union activity and employer response during those years. The insistent requests for bigger bonuses made by the unions increased the share of this income category. The increases were made possible partly by employers' response preference for using bonus payments pointedly to reward their employees. The size of bonus payments differs according to the profits and the occupational status of employees, so the increase in bonus income relative to other types of income serves to boost income inequality.

For the post-1963 period, our findings are as follows:

(a) The degree of regular income inequality is generally lowest in this period. Differing from the pre-1962 data is the finding that the highest inequality can be found in the coefficient for the employee income of other family members.

(b) Gini coefficients for regular and extraordinary income show a decreasing trend in the 1960s, while those for employment income of other household members show an upward trend.

(c) In contrast to the drastic changes in income shares which occurred in the 1950s, the composition of employee household income was relatively stable in the 1960s, although there was a slight increase in the share of extraordinary income after 1969.

(d) The most important factor explaining the progressive trend in the distribution of the employee household income is the change in the inequality of regular income of household heads. But this effect has been canceled out to some extent by the regressive trend found in the income of other household members.

Now let us proceed to an examination of the effect of population movements on income inequality. Population movement from rural to urban areas has been significant and has resulted in changes in the by-city-size share of employee households. Figure 2 shows these changes using FIES sample distribution data which suggest that migration con-

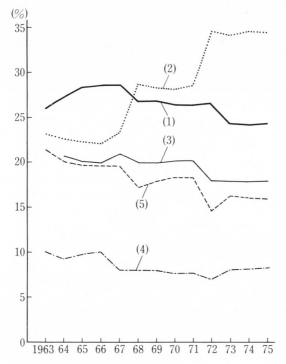

Figure 2. City size and number of households*

* Data from the FIES.
a. City size is defined as follows: (1) Major: population of 1,000,000 or more; (2) Medium: population of 150,000–1,000,000; (3) Small, Class A: population of 50,000 to 150,000); (4) Small, Class B: population of less than 50,000; (5) Towns and villages.

centrated on major cities until the mid-1960s; thereafter, the share of population in the medium size cities rose significantly. Because the mean incomes of small cities, towns, and villages was lower than that of the major and the medium-sized cities, the population movements described above have a progressive effect on income distribution. The question is whether the effect is so powerful as to account for the trend in inequality changes during the 1960s.

To answer this question we have calculated a measure of inequality for city size under the restriction that the population share in some years remains constant. Table 6 indicates that the 1963 population share fixed figures are higher than the "actual" figures, but the share fixed on 1968 population does not show a similar pattern. It would seem that in the mid-1960s population movements had some effect on income dis-

Table 6. Population Movement and Income Inequality*

	Actual	Population share fixed in	
		1963	1968
1963	0.0073	0.0073	——
1964	0.0068	0.0069	——
1965	0.0045	0.0046	——
1966	0.0053	0.0054	——
1967	0.0051	0.0052	——
1968	0.0019	0.0022	0.0019
1969	0.0015	0.0017	0.0015
1970	0.0012	0.0013	0.0012
1971	0.0010	0.0011	0.0010
1972	0.0007	0.0007	0.0007
1973	0.0009	0.0010	0.0010
1974	0.0006	0.0007	0.0006
1975	0.0002	0.0002	0.0002

* Data from the FIES.
a. B Measure with a = 1 for income disparity by city size.

tribution. However, in making a comparison between the actual and the population fixed figures, it is assumed that the mean income in each city group is independent of changes in the population share. But this is assumed only to simplify the calculation. As is shown in Figure 3,

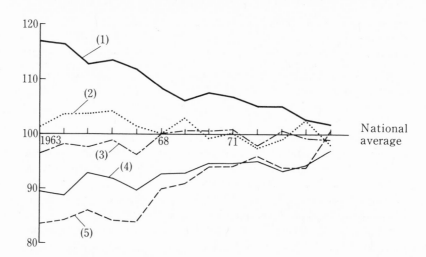

Figure 3. City size and relative level of employee household income *

* Data from the FIES.
a. Definition of city size - see Figure 2.
b. The Japanese national average is shown as 100.

the disparity in mean income by city size decreased during this period. First, the population movement to large cities decreased the relative income of large cities. Second, because of the scarcity of labor in the vicinity of large cities, many factories were dispersed into small cities and by the mid-1960s had spread into local areas. Taken together, the above phenomena might explain how population movements affected the tendency for income distribution to become more progressive. It might be added here that we could not find for Japan the tendency suggested by Theil (1967) for the United States.

Next we turn our attention to the decomposition of inequality measures by household subgroup. As was mentioned earlier, the inequality measures for regular income remained unchanged until the mid-1950s but decreased after 1958. This pattern can partially be explained by the behavior of trade unions, which, since the end of the 1950s, have tended to stress raises in the basic wage rather than concentrating on bonus demands. However, more fundamental is the scarcity of labor and related factors such as population movements. After the late 1950s, the scarcity of younger workers became pronounced, and the relative wage for young employees was pushed up. Although the Japanese wage system has been based upon seniority, the scarcity of young workers had the effect of decreasing wage differentials based on length of service.

In Figure 4 we have presented a synopsis of the behavior inequality calculations made from FIES household subgroup income class data for the following categories: (A) age of household head, (B) occupation of household, (C) family size, (D) city size, (E) industry of employment of household head, and (F) size of firm which employs household head. It should be emphasized that these are two-factor tables, with information given only for income and one of the above categories. Therefore, it is impossible to get the "pure" effect of these categories which are not independent. However, we can get the over-time effects of these changes on total income distribution. Figure 4 shows these over-time changes in between-group inequality for each of the above-mentioned categories; the changes can be summarized as follows:

(a) For categories (C), (D), and (E), the between-group inequality decreased in the 1960s.

(b) The inequality for (A) shows an unclear trend with relatively large fluctuations.

(c) The income gaps for (F) narrowed slightly until the mid-1960s, but widened thereafter.

The trends discussed under (a) above can be related to the scarcity of labor. Needless to say, this labor shortage has much to do with the rapid economic growth of this period. The rapidly increasing demand

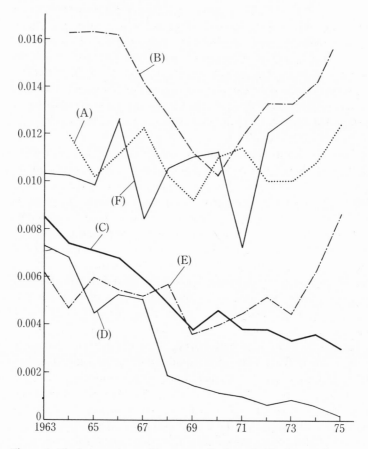

Figure 4. The between inequality measure for household subgroups*
* Data from the FIES.
a. (A) = age of household head; (B) = occupation of household head; (C) = family size; (D) = city size; (E) = industry of employment of household head; (F) = size of firm which employs household head.
b. B : a = 1.

for labor services caused an upward movement in wages as a whole, which brought about population movement from the rural to the urban sector, from declining to developing industries, and from occupations where labor was abundant to occupations where labor was scarce.[6] At the same time, firms have been relocating in small cities in order to seek

[6] In the period of rapid economic growth, the population share of non-office workers decreased while their income share increased (Takayama and Yoshioka, 1967).

workers. This urbanization process has been accompanied by the so-called nuclearization of families—*i.e.*, the independence of young families from their parents.[7]

The trend discussed under (b) above should be examined in light of the evidence computed from the National Survey of Family Income and Expenditures (NFIE) and shown in Table 7.

Table 7. The Toyoda Measure for Over-time Changes in Intra- and Inter-generation Inequality*

	Within age inequality					Between inequality	Total inequality
	20s and younger	30s	40s	50s	60s +		
1959	0.0412	0.0524	0.0903	0.1296	0.0984	0.0116	0.0900
1964	0.0218	0.0343	0.0579	0.0718	0.0902	0.0115	0.0607
1969	0.0523	0.0518	0.0589	0.0869	0.1253	0.0090	0.0721
1974	0.0277	0.0364	0.0406	0.0523	0.1028	0.0080	0.0506
	Percentage by Theil decomposition (%)						
1959	14	41	28	15	3	12.9	100
1964	12	42	28	15	4	19.0	100
1969	13	39	30	14	4	12.4	100
1974	12	37	32	15	5	15.8	100

* Data from the NFIE.
a. The percentages are defined as $w_i B_i / B$ and B_b / B.
b. B : a = 1.

There we can clearly see the decreasing trend in inter-generational inequality over the four periods (1959–64, 1964–69, 1969–74, and 1959–74) for which the NFIE are available. We should also consider the fact that economic prosperity has made it possible for students to spend a longer average length of time in school.

The trend discussed under (c) above shows that the impact of economic growth was not confined to the between-size inequality of firms. In general, the larger employee household income is, the bigger is the firm by which the household head is employed (Takayama and Yoshioka, 1976). Rapid economic growth makes it possible for big firms to develop relatively rapidly, but also enables some small firms to continue operating. The small firms seem to be supported by relatively low-quality, aged laborers. These trends, which have continued since the mid-1960s, serve to enlarge the income gap between firms of different sizes. The share of between inequality by firm size in total inequality

[7] The within inequality of the four-member household group is the lowest among the various family size groups. Generally, however, the larger the family size, the higher its within inequality.

is now at its highest levels. It amounted to nearly 25 percent in 1973 and reached over 30 percent in the same year if we calculate B (a = −4)—*i.e.*, if more weight is placed on low income classes at the margin. Next, we must touch upon the changes in income other than the regular income of household heads. From the beginning of the 1960s the distribution of the extraordinary income of household heads showed a trend similar to that of regular income. Moreover, the level of the extraordinary income had been determined by the level of regular income. At the same time, however, there were cyclical changes in the extraordinary income inequality. Regarding the employment income of other household members, we can identify a U-shape trend in income inequality, with the kink occurring in 1960. In the 1950s, wives or children of low-income households were forced to obtain additional income. The additional entry of these people into the labor force operated initially to decrease income inequality. But since 1960 the increasing demand for labor has attracted into the labor market even wives or daughters in relatively high-income households. This is verified by the increase in the average number of income earners in the high-income classes in the FIES data. Thus, the previous equalization effect of this income has been canceled out.

Although this regressive effect was overshadowed by other progressive factors, it is important to keep it in mind in light of changes which occurred in the 1970s. Overall inequality of income distribution ceased to decrease in the early 1970s and even showed a small increase by the middle of the decade. This movement could be explained as one of the effects of the stagflation which followed the oil crisis. However, we should not ignore the possible regressive effect produced by the employment income of other household members. However, a further examination of the changes in the income distribution of the stagflation period should be carried out in future when the Japanese economy returns to a steady growth path.

Urban-rural income differences and income distribution of agricultural households

We have pointed out two characteristics to be investigated regarding the income of agricultural households: (1) the relative equality in income distribution within agricultural households and (2) the decrease in urban-rural income differences. The basic factor underlying the equal distribution among agricultural households is the land reform instituted in the late 1940s by the Allied Occupation Forces. Under the reform, all tenants were able to posses their own farms after paying a small amount as purchase price. Since then, the typical Japanese farmer has been the owner of a small-scale farm whose average area is about one hectare. This relatively equal distribution of farmland resulted in income distribution equality. However, we cannot rely on the land reform to explain the trend of the past two decades. This trend can be explained by the sustained economic growth which was significant enough to alter the initial conditions set by the land reform.

This interaction between growth and initial conditions can be seen in the CLSF, which is composed of tables classified by "farm household income" defined either as pre-tax income minus transfer income or as farm household disposable income. The agricultural households defined in the CLSF are those who cultivated more than 0.3 hectares in Hokkaido and more than 0.1 hectares in other areas, or earned an equivalent agricultural income. This definition is somewhat different from that of the SPLC, which defines the agricultural household as one which cultivates more than 0.3 hectares.

In Figure 5 the average income of agricultural households is compared with that of the multi-member non-agricultural employee household obtained from the FIES. While there were some income differences between these household groups in the late 1950s, they decreased gradually. Since the late 1960s, agricultural household income has been higher than employee household income, although on a per-capita basis agricultural household income did not catch up with employee household income until the early 1970s. A similar trend can be seen in a comparison of consumption levels between farm and urban households.

Our problem here is to explain the process underlying the narrowing income differences. Readers should remember that the annual growth rate of nominal income of non-agricultural employee households was about 15 percent. In such a growing economy it is very difficult to decrease urban-rural income differences because the productivity of agriculture will rise slowly in comparison with that of modern industry. The usual process underlying decreasing income differences could be described as follows. With industrial development agricultural laborers move to the urban sector. The small-scale farming households tend to vanish, and relatively large-scale farming households remain. This process results in a decrease in the growth rate of wages in the urban sector and a rise in per-household agricultural income.

However, the Japanese pattern of change is somewhat different from the typical pattern described above. Although the number of full-time

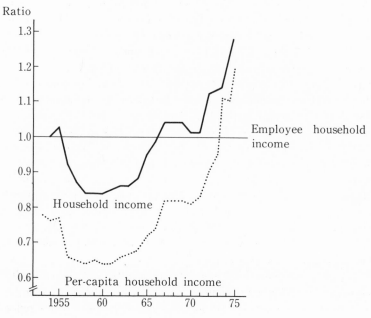

Figure 5. Ratio of agricultural household income to employee household income*
* Data from the FIES and the FHES.
a. Employee household income = 1.0

farmers decreased sharply, the number of agricultural households declined slowly in comparison. Further, the average size of per-household farmland did not change remarkably. This can be related to the law (*Nōchiho*) which prohibits farmland transactions between agricultural households. Although this was effective in preventing the revival of landlordism, it reduced the incentive to increase productivity in agriculture by enlarging the scale of production. The following two factors supported the economic existence of these households under conditions of rapid economic growth: (1) the increase in non-agricultural income of agricultural households and (2) the government rice price support. Agricultural households earn the following three types of income: (i) agricultural income, (ii) income from side businesses, including wages from non-agricultural employment, and (iii) property and transfer income. Figure 6 shows the decline of agricultural income as a percentage of total farm household income in the 1960s.

The CLSF's sample is a subsample of the Farm Household Economic Survey (FHES) with tables classified by size of cultivated land. Ac-

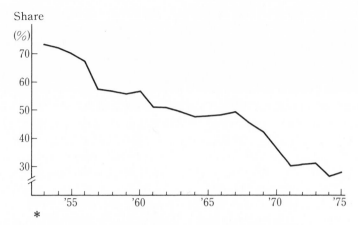

Figure 6. Share of agricultural income in household income*
* Data from the FHES.

cording to the FHES, until the late 1950s non-agricultural work occupied a relatively large portion of small-scale farm household work
hours, especially in households with farmland of 0.5 hectares or less.
From the early to the mid-1960s the share of non-agricultural income
increased in medium-sized farming households, and the tendency spread
to large-scale farming households in the late 1960s.

In view of this trend, it may be revealing to examine the ratio of
agricultural income of farming households to the average income of
urban employee households. In the mid-1950s, the urban wage was not
so high as to act as an incentive to reduce agricultural work in order
to get non-agricultural income. However, since the ratio was under 50
percent for the smallest-scale farming households, these households
were forced to seek non-agricultural employment. In the late 1950s,
young workers became scarce and wages in the non-agricultural sector
rose significantly. This gave job opportunities for non-agricultural work
to medium-sized farming households. In this process, nearly all the surplus labor of the agricultural households found jobs in non-agricultural
firms, and urban-rural income differences tended to decrease. After the
mid-1960s, the labor shortage became more acute, and many factories
located in local cities in order to seek employees. At the same time,
the use of labor-saving technology spread throughout Japanese agriculture. These changed circumstances resulted in nuclear family members, such as the household head or wife, in medium- or large-scale
farming households taking non-agricultural jobs. Agricultural produc-

tion has been maintained by aged family members, where present, or by the Sunday work of households heads. It is said that a relatively large agricultural income can be obtained from these activities if agricultural machines are used and if production is concentrated on rice.

While the increase in non-agricultural income is the major factor behind decreasing urban-rural income differences, as a subsidiary factor we should also mention the price support policies of the Japanese government. From the beginning of World War II, the government had intervened in the rice market in order to relieve the shortage of food and monopolized transactions in rice, wheat, and other cereals. After the mid-1950s, these controls were gradually loosened except for those on rice. This was not because the government was afraid of food shortages, but because controls were considered necessary in order to keep the price of rice at a relatively high and stable level in order to stimulate agricultural activities. Since the late 1950s, the rice price has been raised in accordance with the level of urban wages. This had the effect of postponing the shift of nuclear family labor in medium-scale farm families into non-agricultural employment.

In the late 1960s the supply exceeded the demand for rice, and the government was forced to cease its policy of successively raising the rice price. This reinforced the shift of labor from the agricultural to the non-agricultural sector. Non-agricultural income increased even in the relatively large-scale farm households. On the other hand, the government has given relatively large subsidies to farmers who engage in agricultural production other than rice. Since a substantial portion of large-scale farming households receive such subsidies, these agricultural household incomes tended to increase.

We will now turn our attention to the over-time change in the degree of inequality within agricultural households. According to Table 8, the degree was relatively constant in the 1950s. From the late 1950s to the mid-1960s, the degree of inequality declined; thereafter the trend was reversed, and a tendency to increase can be seen in the late 1960s. It is most interesting to observe that the progressive trend can be identified with the period when drastic changes were appearing in the composition of household income. Although the land reform induced relatively equal distribution of agricultural land, inequality of agricultural income remained. Since transactions in agricultural land were prohibited, the degree of inequality remained relatively unchanged throughout the 1950s, although there were some fluctuations caused by harvest conditions. The Gini coefficients calculated from the FHES tables classified by agricultural land size are not much different in this period from the Gini coefficients calculated from the income class data of the CLSF tables.

After the mid-1960s, the stable situation mentioned above began to change due to the increase in the demand for labor by the non-agricultural sector. The small-scale farming household had increased its non-agricultural income, and no doubt this tended to fill the income gap between the small-scale and large-scale farming households. This progressive tendency lasted until the mid-1960s, when most of the surplus labor in the agricultural household had been drawn into non-agricultural firms. Since the mid-1960s, the degree of inequality has shown an upward trend. With the spread of non-agricultural work to large-scale farming households, income differences by scale of agricultural production again appeared in the distribution of agricultural household income. Further, the government policy for increasing agricultural production other than rice benefited mainly large-scale farming households. A portion of these large-scale farming households endeavored to increase their non-rice agricultural production and obtained government subsidies. This may be one of the causes of the regressive tendency seen in Table 8.

This pattern is also supported by a Rao decomposition of Gini coefficients for agricultural household income where income can be decomposed into three major categories: (1) agricultural income, (2) non-agricultural income, and (3) transfer income. Transfer income includes the government subsidies allowed since 1966 for promoting agricultural production other than rice. When we investigate the overtime changes, a significant decline is found in the contribution of agricultural income. This originates mainly from the fall in the pseudo-Gini coefficients. Regarding the latter, we should note that the pseudo-Gini coefficients are calculated from income tables classified by household income. Before the mid-1950s, the distribution of agricultural income dominated that of household income. However, as the share of non-agricultural income increased, differences emerged between the patterns of distribution of agricultural and non-agricultural income. In such a situation, it is natural that the pseudo-Gini coefficients should tend to decline, even if agricultural income distribution remains stable. In fact, no downward trend can be found in the pseudo-Gini coefficients for agricultural income from the FHES tables classified by the size of agricultural land holdings. A simliar explanation could be applied to the changes in the pseudo-Gini coefficients for non-agricultural income. Looking at the post-1965 trend, we should note the role of transfer income. As mentioned before, government subsidies to large-scale farming

Table 8. Over-time Changes in Agricultural Household Income Inequality and a Rao Decompsosition of the Gini Coefficient for Agricultural Households*

| | Inequality measures for agricultural households | | | Rao decomposition | | | | | |
| | | | | Psuedo Gini coefficients | | | Percentages of inequalities explained by components of income (%) | | |
	Theil measure	Log variances	Gini coefficients	Agricultural income	Non-agricultural income	Transfer income	Agricultural income	Non-agricultural income	Transfer income
1953	(0.0992)	(0.1930)	(0.2436)						
1954	(0.0993)	(0.1910)	(0.2427)						
1955	0.994	0.1910	0.2427	0.2786	0.1823	0.1710	75.63	20.47	3.87
1956	0.0921	0.1936	0.2408	0.2505	0.2359	0.1698	66.20	29.15	4.65
1957	0.0979	0.1959	0.2476	0.2578	0.2749	0.0358	62.91	36.05	1.03
1958	(0.0962)	(0.1899)	(0.2444)						
1959	0.0932	0.1840	0.2421	0.2380	0.2871	0.0728	61.22	36.58	2.17
1960	0.0887	0.1807	0.2354	0.2395	0.2776	-0.0101	58.62	41.66	-0.30
1961	0.0928	0.1693	0.2409	0.2489	0.2663	0.0481	57.15	41.41	1.45
1962	0.0913	0.1895	0.2391	0.2323	0.3023	-0.0810	46.11	66.55	-2.69
1963	0.0853	0.1712	0.2316	0.2283	0.2961	-0.0877	44.27	59.06	-3.36
1964	0.0902	0.1768	0.2373	0.2179	0.3072	-0.0476	39.33	62.45	-1.79
1965	0.0831	0.1846	0.2286	0.2137	0.2908	-0.0551	40.19	61.51	-1.70
1966	0.0879	0.1796	0.2297	0.2012	0.2660	0.1645	37.14	56.54	6.29
1967	0.0844	0.1946	0.2344	0.2387	0.2409	0.1765	44.32	49.16	6.51
1968	0.0918	0.1796	0.2317	0.2294	0.2486	0.1523	41.91	52.07	6.03
1969	0.0919	0.1991	0.2310	0.2192	0.2678	0.1698	34.71	57.73	7.56
1970	0.0945	0.2054	0.2438	0.2162	0.2697	0.1993	28.34	61.47	10.19
1971	0.0951	0.2074	0.2469	0.2140	0.2964	0.1874	25.30	63.48	11.49
1972	0.0996	0.2730	0.2491	0.2105	0.2737	0.2196	23.04	64.92	12.02
1973	0.0932	0.1917	0.2414	0.2221	0.2495	0.2449	25.43	60.32	14.22
1974	0.1048	0.2260	0.2550	0.2103	0.2799	0.2409	34.19	55.72	10.09
1975	0.1021	0.2232	0.2523	0.2400	0.2586	0.2529	39.21	49.88	11.13

* Data from the CLSF.

households in the latter half of the 1960s had the effect of increasing inequality. We have also noted that non-agricultural work had spread to large-scale farming households by this time.

Income distribution of other groups of households

To complete our detailed examination we must investigate the distribution of household groups other than employee and agricultural households. Such groups include the multi-member non-farm self-employed household, the multi-member unemployed household, and the single-member household. Because of the paucity of reliable data, we can only hope to reach some preliminary conclusions by comparing results derived from various sources. Unfortunately, the multi-member unemployed household cannot be treated here due to lack of information.

Using SPLC data, we have already pointed out that in the 1960s there were regressive changes in income distribution for non-farm self-employed households. Wada (1975) also showed from ESS data that the Gini coefficients for these households rose remarkably. This trend was also pointed out by the Research Group on Income Distribution Problems (RGIDP, 1976), which reached the same conclusion relying on annual income data shown in the Family Saving Survey (FSS). These three data sources imply a regressive trend. In order to conclude that this is what has actually happened, we must present some supporting evidence.

The non-farm self-employed households include (1) merchants and artisans, (2) managers of unincorporated firms, and (3) professionals. Since we cannot get detailed information from the SPLC, we must look for other supplementary data. The NFIE gives income tables for these groups. When we calculate the B measures with a $= -4$, the results are 2.0207 for (1), 2.7997 for (2) and 10.2070 for (3). However, since the population share of (3) is low, we will focus our analysis on (1) and (2). Regarding the changes in income distribution for (1), the FIES can supply some information. As noted earlier, the FIES has asked sample households to report, relying on memory, their annual income in the previous 12 months. These replies must include some error, but they can be used to infer the broad trend in income distribution changes. According to the results shown in Figure 7, the over-time pattern of income distribution for group (1) was progressive.

Now we need information on the income distribution pattern of group (2). While we cannot find directly related information, the Unincorporated Enterprise Survey (UES) of the Bureau of Statistics, Office of the

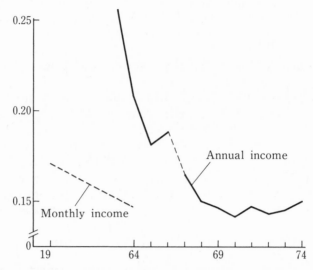

Figure 7. Over-time change in inequality between merchant and artisan households*
* Data for annual income from the FIES; data for monthly income from the NFIE.
a. B : a = 1.

Prime Minister, gives profit data for firms by size, in this case measured by the number of employees. According to Table 9, the population share of unincorporated enterprises with one or two employees grew during

Table 9. Income Disparities among Administrators of Unincorporated Firms*

Industries	Number of em-	Population share (%)				Relative income level (average = 100)			
	ployees	1959	1964	1969	1973	1959	1964	1969	1973
Manufacturing	≤2	31.9	37.5	38.4	47.9	41.9	40.3	44.7	52.0
	3	17.2	16.6	14.6	16.6	66.4	88.8	83.2	90.8
	4	13.1	13.4	13.8	9.9	74.8	86.2	94.8	100.3
	≥5	37.7	32.6	31.1	27.9	173.4	180.9	178.2	189.2
Wholesale and	1	26.2	26.5	23.7	29.5	38.4	34.7	34.0	33.9
retail	2	35.1	35.4	34.8	35.6	71.4	68.7	73.6	83.9
	3	18.0	16.8	18.1	16.2	126.4	109.6	110.1	121.6
	4	8.9	10.1	10.2	7.7	142.9	166.7	144.0	170.0
	≥5	12.5	11.1	13.2	11.0	258.5	276.4	237.3	252.6
Services	1		28.9	21.6	35.2		51.0	47.8	53.5
	2		30.5	34.6	31.4		80.9	86.8	94.4
	3		17.1	20.0	17.2		118.0	101.4	117.9
	4		9.9	11.8	8.0		127.2	134.4	157.4
	≥5		13.6	12.1	8.2		204.8	186.0	229.7

* Data from the UES.

the period of rapid growth. The rise in wages forced the unincorporated enterprise to manage with fewer employees. Nevertheless, the relative level of the profit income of large unincorporated enterprises with more than five employees increased during this period. Rapid economic growth provided the opportunity to expand business, the management was inclined toward expansion. When management attitudes in these unincorporated firm was more passive, these firms were forced to decrease the number of employees to counteract the rapid rise in wage payments. Therefore, economic growth has divided unincorporated firms into two groups, those of small-scale and those of relatively large-scale management. This separation might serve to widen the income disparity for group (2) households. In the early 1970s the Japanese economy was disturbed by factors such as the post-1972 galloping inflation and the 1974 oil crisis. It is likely that the inequality of income distribution increased as a result of the windfall profits acquired during this period by non-farm self-employed households. However, this conjecture cannot yet be supported by sufficiently reliable data.

For the income distribution of single-member households, we have less data than for any multi-member household group. To compensate for this lack of data, we, and others, have tried to piece together information on the various elements included in this group. For example, Wada has already made a brave attack on this problem using the ESS. His hypothesis is that a regressive tendency can be found in the income distribution for this group. In postwar Japan, many unmarried young sons or daughters have migrated from rural to urban areas to seek jobs and have formed separate household units. These young people present a a striking contrast with the aged unemployed single household or young students living away from home.

But is this contrast important, given the likelihood that the young and employed single member household will, sooner or later, become a standard household unit? Young students should be looked upon as members of the parent's household, as far as the family living unit in Japan is concerned. Furthermore, some salaried employees of big companies are assigned to work in local cities, but their families remain in Tokyo or Osaka where educational opportunities for the children are considered to be superior. Although these middle-aged employees are classified as single-member households, most of the salary is transferred to the family. Given the above complexities, it may be better to study the distribution of each subgroup rather than to attempt to analyze the total distribution of single households.

According to the 1969 NFIE, 84 percent of single-member households are employee households. The income disparity for this subgroup shows a progressive change: their Theil measures were 0.1040 in 1959, 0.0812 in 1964, 0.0768 in 1969, and 0.0593 in 1974. This trend is similar to that found in the multi-member employee household.

Our next concern is the aged, single-member household, employed or unemployed. Although it is difficult to find reliable data dealing exclusively with this subgroup, we can make indirect inferences using the SPLC. As mentioned earlier, the survey is said to cover the poor households, including this subgroup, relatively well. Since we can obtain income distribution data for single-member households, we can clarify the changes in income disparity by calculating the inequality measure, giving greater weight to the low-income classes in this calculation. According to the results shown in Table 10, the degree of inequality increased from the early 1960s and into the 1970s, with an interruption in the 1960s. This pattern might be partially explained by the rising share of the aged in single-member households. Although pensions and other social security payments are provided, almost all these people are retired and live separately from their children. Thus, only a very small portion can lead a life of comfort. It is most important for the Japanese government to develop policies to aid these households.

Table 10. Income Inequality of Single-member Households*

Year	Measure	Year	Measure	Year	Measure
1962	0.5882	1967	0.6273	1971	0.5969
1963	0.6839	1968	0.7279	1972	0.6833
1964	0.7122	1969	0.7156	1973	0.8074
1965	0.7474	1970	0.5876	1974	

* Data from the SPLC.
a. Atkinson measure: $\in = 5$.

Conclusion

Our study concludes that the inverted U-shape pattern can be seen in the Japanese size distribution of household income between 1953 and 1975. The turning point can be placed in the early 1960s when a scarcity of labor appeared in the Japanese economy.

During the 1950s, economic growth had a regressive effect on the size distribution of income because of the increase in the income gap between agricultural and non-agricultural households and the rise in inequality within employee households. The first phenomenon is similar to recent trends in most developing countries. The second phenomenon can be related to increasing differentials between firms according to size. The shift from a labor-surplus to a labor-scarce economy significantly altered the income inequality trend. For example, income differences within employee households declined. Declining inequalities between regions and between household groups by family size are important factors in explaining this progressive trend. Decreased regional inequalities can be related to the movement of factories to local cities, which was also effective in equalizing income distribution within agricultural households by providing non-agricultural job opportunities. While government policies supporting agriculture were effective in decreasing the income gap between the agricultural and the non-agricultural sector, these same policies have tended to increase the inequality within agricultural households. It is also rather problematic that the inequality within non-agricultural self-employed households has increased. This is very important because these groups include the service sector, whose productivity has risen less than that in the industrial sector. Hopefully, these facts will be taken into consideration in future policy formulation.

Based on our various findings, our impression is that the Japanese experience is not necessarily unique. For example, recent changes in income distribution in some Asian countries seem to be similar to Japanese trends (Oshima and Mizoguchi, 1978). We hope that our study can be of some contribution in discussing future changes in various Asian countries.

References

Atkinson, A. B. "On the Measurement of Inequality," *Journal of Economic Theory*, Vol. 2, No. 3, 1970.

Bacha, Edmar L. "Kuznets Curve and Beyond: Growth and Changes in Inequality," *5th World Congress of IEA*, 1977.

Bureau of Statistics, Office of the Prime Minister. *Annual Report of Family Income and Expenditure, 1951–1975.*

———. *Employment Status Survey, 1956, 1959, 1962, 1965, 1968, 1971 and 1974.*

———. *Family Saving Survey, 1969–1974.*

———. *National Survey of Family Income and Expenditure, 1959, 1964, 1969 and 1974.*

———. *Unincorporated Enterprise Survey, 1963–1975.*

Economic Planning Agency. *Survey of Consumer Finances, 1956–1975.*

Japan Economic Research Center and Council of Asian Manpower Studies. *Income Distribution, Employment and Economic Development in Southeast and East Asia,* 1975.

Matsuda, Y., Nojima, N., Sugiyama, A. and Terasaki, Y. "Size Distribution Analysis Packaged Program and Income Distribution Data Base," *IADRPHU Working Paper J-2,* 1976.

Ministry of Agriculture and Forestry. *Cost of Living Survey of Farm Households, 1955–1975.*

_____. *Farm Household Economic Survey, 1951–1975.*

_____. *Survey of Farmer's Tax Burden, 1951–1975.*

Ministry of Welfare. *Survey of People's Living Conditions, 1963–1974.*

Mizoguchi, T. "Size Distribution of Household Income in Japan," in (Japan Economic Research Center, 1975).

Mouer, Ross E. "Income Distribution in Japan: An Examination of the FIES Data" *Keio Economic Papers,* Vol. 10, No. 1 (1973) and Vol. 11, No. 1 (1974).

Oshima, Harry T., and Mizoguchi, T. (eds.) *Income Distribution by Sectors and Overtime in East and Southeast Asian Countries.* CAMS and IADRPHU, 1978.

Paukert, Flex. "Income Distribution at Different Levels of Development: A Survey of Evidence," *International Labour Review,* Vol. No. 2–3, 1973.

Rao, V. M. "Two Decomposition of Concentration Ratio," *Journal of Royal Statistical Association* S-A, Vol. 132, Part 3, 1969.

RGIDP. *Problems on Income and Assets Distribution.* EPA, 1976 (in Japanese).

Takayama, N. "Factors Governing the Inequality of Income and Financial Assets Distribution, *Keizai Kenkyu,* Vol. 27, No. 2, 1976 (in Japanese).

Takayama, N., and Yoshioka S. "Factors Determining the Size Distribution in Japan." *IADRPHU Working Paper J-4,* 1975.

Toyoda, T. "Inequality of Size Distribution of Income: Measures and Their Decomposition," *Kokumin Keizai Kenkyu,* November 1975 (in Japanese).

Wada, Richard O. "Impact of Economic Growth on the Size Distribution of Income: The Post-War Experience of Japan," in (Japan Economic Research Center, 1975).

The Formation of Income in the Household Sector in Thailand

Oey Astra Meesook

This study investigates the process of income formation in the household sector in Thailand.* The objective is to obtain a better understanding of how characteristics of individuals and of households affect total household income, the sum of the incomes of all household members.

Using regression analysis on detailed information at the level of the individual in the context of his household, the paper examines in turn the factors which affect the labor force participation decision of household members, the probability of being unpaid family workers, the probability of having different types of income, and, finally, income itself. Both personal and household characteristics are considered here; both types are expected to have their impact in the determination of labor force participation and income. In particular, it seems important to explicitly incorporate unpaid family workers in the analysis of household incomes in Thailand. This paper investigates the role of the unpaid family workers and secondary income earners who contribute to raising total household income by supplementing the income of the household head.

The Model for Income Formation

Let there be N individuals in a household, and let each household

* The research reported in this paper was carried out between October 1975 and September 1976, while the author was a Research Fellow at the National Bureau of Economic Research. The National Economic and Social Development Board and the National Statistical Office of Thailand were very helpful in providing the data used here. Excellent research assistance by Kris Chinn is gratefully acknowledged.

member be indexed by i, $i = 1,2,\ldots,N$. Then, if Y_i is the income of household member i, and Y_T is total household income, we have

$$Y_T = \sum_i Y_i. \qquad (1)$$

The income of household member i, Y_i, is a function of his labor force participation, P_i, and his characteristics, *e.g.* age, sex, and level of education, summarized by X_i:

$$Y_i = Y_i(P_i, X_i). \qquad i = 1,2,\ldots,N \qquad (2)$$

The labor force participation of an individual is a function both of X_i, his personal characteristics, and of various household characteristics, Z_i:

$$P_i = P_i(X_i, Z_i) \qquad i = 1,2,\ldots,N \qquad (3)$$

An example of a household characteristic is the presence or absence of young children in the household which may be expected to affect the labor force participation decisions of the adult members.

Equations (2) and (3) together show that a household member's income is a function of both his personal characteristics and those of the household as a whole. One problem which needs to be considered is the fact that many household members who participate in the labor force do so as unpaid family workers. They do not receive any cash remuneration for their work, but since total household income can be expected to be higher when they work than when they do not, this should be taken into account in the income-generating equations.

Source of Data

Without detailed data at the individual level, classified by household, it would be impossible to carry out the analysis described above. This study makes use of the original data tapes of the 1968–69 Socioeconomic Survey conducted by the National Statistical Office of Thailand.[1] Thus the information presented here is in addition to that given in the official published report of the Survey, which necessarily deals only with aggregates.

---

[1] Official tabulations of this survey appear in (National Statistical Office, 1973). Details concerning the sampling procedure and the type of information collected are given on pages 25–28.

The Socioeconomic Survey was a multi-purpose survey designed to give a representative picture of the whole country. The basic sampling unit is the household, but information was also collected for each household member.[2] Thus we have details concerning personal characteristics of individuals, while at the same time these individuals are grouped into households.[3] Accordingly, it is possible to combine household information with data on individuals belonging to the household as well as to combine information on certain individuals (for example, the household head or the spouse) with data on the household.

For each individual in the sample we know age, sex, marital status, level of educational attainment, major and minor occupations, relationship to the household head, and money income from different sources for both the month and the year preceding the survey date. This gives us considerably more scope and flexibility than if we only had data on the household head.

For all household members we have some information in common: the region and location of residence; the ownership by the household of certain consumer durables such as radios, refrigerators, automobiles, ploughs, and fishing nets; consumption expenditures both in cash and in kind for over 200 items of consumption goods and services; and changes in assets and liabilities for the month preceding the survey. The consumption information was only collected for the household as a whole with no attempt made to break it down for individual members.

Additional information concerning the entire household can of course be derived from that pertaining to its members: household size; the number of household members in given age groups; the number of income-earning members and unpaid family workers; and total household income which can be broken down by source into wages and salaries, net profit from self-employment, and so on. Moreover, by summing all consumption classified as home-produced or obtained free, we get an estimate of own consumption which can be added to household money income to obtain total income.

The major advantage of having data in a disaggregated form is that it is possible to aggregate it in any way that one wishes. One is not bound by the way in which the data have been aggregated previously.

---

[2] The definition of a household in the Socioeconomc Survey is given as a private household consisting of a person or a group of related persons who live, eat, and consume other living essentials together; but some persons may keep their finances separately.

[3] Tabulations of the National Statistical Office always use the household as the unit of reference. No information is ever given concerning individuals.

Labor Force Participation

Whether or not a person participates in the labor force depends on both supply and demand considerations—that is, on the opportunity open to him for work and also on his own willingness or need to work.[4]

Two different types of factors are important in determining the supply of work opportunities facing an individual. The first involves those factors which affect the supply of jobs in the whole economy. At times of rapid growth, an economy would naturally be in a position to absorb more workers. In times of recession and stagnation, the job market shrinks. Thus the participation of any single individual in the labor force is affected in a general way by the overall economic situation. Within the economy itself it is possible to find different conditions relating to employment opportunities. For example, the urban sector may be buoyant while the rural sector stagnates. In general, therefore, the work opportunities facing each potential entrant into the labor market are influenced by the economic environment in which he finds himself.

The second type of factor affecting supply opportunities is specific to each individual. Employers demand labor of different kinds to different degrees. There are many personal characteristics which differentiate individuals—for example, age, sex, and level of educational attainment. To the extent that such characteristics affect the desirability of an individual in the eyes of his prospective employer, they have an effect on his labor force participation through the supply of job opportunities which faces him.

In terms of demand considerations, factors which influence the decision of individuals to seek employment can be classified as specific to the person himself or to the household as a whole.[5] Personal attributes of an individual, such as age, sex, and level of educational attainment, affect his desire to work as well as his opportunity to work. In addi-

---

[4] Individuals are considered to be in the labor force if they report one or more occupations, regardless of whether they report any income. The Socioeconomic Survey classified the following people as not having an occupation: (1) people under 11 years of age; (2) people looking for work; (3) housewives or persons who work around the house; (4) students; (5) people unable to work because of old age; (6) people unable to work because of physical or mental disability or because of chronic illness; (7) people who are voluntarily idle; and (8) people receiving subsidies.

A very serious shortcoming of the data is the fact that there is no information recorded on either the number of hours worked in a week or the number of weeks worked in a year. This has to be borne in mind in interpreting the results.

[5] This problem has been extensively examined for the U.S. and elsewhere. See, for example, (Bowen and Finegan, 1969).

tion, household characteristics also influence the demand for work by individuals. In this connection, we must first make the distinction between heads of household and other household members. For definitional reasons, the labor force participation rate of household heads in the 1968–69 Survey is 100 percent since the head of the household was defined as "a person who was generally recognized as head by other members of the household. Usually he was responsible for the welfare of other members."[6] In terms of a cross-sectional analysis, therefore, it is necessary to separate out household heads. The designation of head has already been made even though the choice of a new household head may be influenced by the personal characteristics of individuals, their relationships with each other in the household, and their labor force status at the time this choice has to be made. As they all participate in the labor force, heads of household are thus a distinct group compared with individuals age 15 and older who are not heads of household and whose average labor force participation rate is 74 percent.

Among non-heads the following household characteristics are expected to influence labor force participation:

(i) Number of adults (persons between 15 and 64 years of age). This in effect represents the available supply of potential workers.

(ii) Presence of children. The presence of children, especially young children, requires that there be one or more adults at home to take care of them. However, the presence of very young children may be mitigated by that of older children who are able to help in taking care of them. The presence of children is likely to affect the participation of females more than that of males since females have traditionally assumed the responsibility of child-rearing. As an alternative, one could use the number, instead of the presence, of young children.

(iii) Income of household head. Since the household head always works, we may consider the labor force participation decision of the household as taking place in two stages. The household head has the responsibility of taking care of the other members. If the head dies or is no longer able to work, then some other member has to take over as head and will assume this responsibility. The labor force participation decision of other members depends, therefore, on how adequately the household head is able to provide for his household members. The less

---

[6] In the Thai section of the Survey the second sentence of the definition reads: "Usually he is a person with an occupation or income and is responsible for providing living essentials for, and looking after the welfare of, other household members."

adequate the head's income, the more incentive for other household members to work and earn additional income. A measure of the adequacy of the head's income must of course take into account the size and composition of the household. In this study we use the income of the head divided by the household size as the measure of the material well-being of the household in the absence of other workers besides the head. In this formulation of the labor force participation decision, the participation of the household head and that of other household members are considered separately, and the outcome of the first decision in terms of income influences the second. Such a formulation seems less ambiguous than the "other family income" of Bowen and Finegan (1969: 132–145).

(iv) Convenience of work. Finally, we should not overlook the question of the ease with which household members may participate in the labor force. This is especially important for decisions to work part-time, such as in the case of women with young children. There are certain work arrangements which do not force individuals to make a clear-cut choice between work and staying at home since the two are not completely separated. In such cases, working does not mean giving up child-rearing and other household-related activities altogether, nor does it involve time and costs in getting to the place of work. The work is in or near the home, the "employer" is flexible about working hours, and the individual can switch between work and the home many times during the course of the day if necessary. There are many instances in which this kind of work is available to household members. Typically, the enterprise involved belongs to the household itself; thus, the household head and the employer are one and the same person. The family farm is an example of such an enterprise, in which household members "pitch in" with work and are able to combine this with taking care of the home. The phenomenon is not restricted to the rural sector by any means. Many city households own and operate a shop or a restaurant and have living quarters upstairs or at the back. Helping to run the family store or wait at tables in the family restaurant is quite compatible with looking after the home and clearly involves considerably less effort and cost than seeking outside employment. The prevalence of the family farm and family enterprise, as indicated by the large number of unpaid family workers in the labor force, means that, at least for these households, many of their members do not, or cannot, consider wage employment as an alternative. However, that part of the labor force which operates in the monetized sector of the economy does respond to money wages. For them the analysis should include their expected wage rate as a determinant of labor force participation, but this has not been done here.

In the estimation of the labor force participation equations, only household members who are not heads are included. Individuals are classified by both their personal and their household characteristics, as shown in the following scheme:

Classification	Category
A. Personal characteristics	
1. Age	10–14
	15–19
	20–29
	30–39
	40–49
	50–59
	60 and over
2. Education*	none
	1–9 years
	10 years or more

* Unfortunately, while the Survey paid more attention to higher levels of schooling, it failed to differentiate among the first nine years of education. Since most people have no education or only a few years of schooling, it did not seem worthwhile to keep the breakdown for the group with ten years or more education.

3. Sex	male
	female
B. Household characteristics	
1. Sex of individual; presence of children:	Category 1. Female individual with at least one child under 7. Category 2. Female individual with no children under 7 or male individual with or without children under 7.
2. Number of adults (15–64)	1
	2
	3
	4 or more
3. Income of household head per household member**	< 1,000 baht per year
	> 1,000 but < 2,000 baht per year
	> 2,000 baht per year

** *Money* income was used here although total income, the sum of money and non-money income, is preferable conceptually. However, there is a problem in isolating that part of non-money income which is produced by the household head since non-money income is reported for the household as a whole and this already includes the contributions of other household members.

4. (Potential) existence of a family enterprise*** The household head has income from self-employment; the household head has no income from self-employment

*** This classification is considered to be an extremely crude proxy for whether or not a household has a family farm or enterprise. The household head having income from self-employment is a necessary but not sufficient condition for a family enterprise. Thus we include too many households in the family-enterprise category. The definition is expected to be less defective in the agricultural sector.

5. Sector of household head   agriculture; non-agriculture
6. Area of residence   urban; rural

The joint classification of individuals by these characteristics yields 2,849 non-empty cells, and for each of these the labor force participation rate is the proportion of all individuals who report one or more occupations.[7] The non-empty cells are used as observations in the regression equations. The dependent variable is the cell labor force participation rate. The independent variables are dummy variables corresponding to the category in each classification which defines the cells. The regressions are weighted by the size of the underlying population. Separate regression estimates were obtained for males and females, and each of these was separated into urban and rural areas.[8] The results are shown in Table 1.[9]

The personal and household characteristics included in the regression equation all have their effects on the labor force participation rates of household members when all other characteristics are held constant. The youngest age group, consisting of 10–14-year-olds, has the lowest rate of participation. The rate rises with age, reaches a peak among those in their thirties, and then declines steadily thereafter.

The relationship between education and labor force participation is not straightforward. The participation rate is higher for individuals with

[7] There are potentially 6,048 cells, but some are empty, and others would not be expected to have any observations in any case, for example those which would involve people 10–14 years of age with 10 or more years of schooling.

[8] The term urban area is used interchangeably with municipal area as officially defined. There are three types of municipalities:

Type of municipality	Minimum population size	Minimum population density (per square kilometer)
City (nakorn)	50,000	3,000
Town (muang)	10,000	3,000
Small town (tambol)	no specific criteria	

Correspondingly, a rural area refers to a nonmunicipal area and consists of sanitary districts and villages.

[9] The estimated equations suffer from the fact that the assumption of a homoscedastic error term is not satisfied.

Table 1. Determinants of Labor Force Participation Rates: Thailand, 1968–69*
(dependent variable: labor force participation rate)

Independent variable	Urban areas				Rural areas			
	Males		Females		Males		Females	
	Estimated coefficient	t-statistic	Estimated coefficient	t-statistic	Estimated coefficient	t-statistic	Estimated coefficient	t-statistic
Constant	.9329	21.22	.7746	21.20	.8734	18.68	.7896	29.46
Age: 10–14	−.9354	−38.51	−.5438	−26.59	−.6743	−23.07	−.5559	−32.60
15–19	−.6040	−24.67	−.2880	−13.22	−.1905	−6.30	−.0972	−5.24
20–29	−.1363	−5.38	−.0665	−3.19	−.0291	−.95	−.0352	−2.07
40–49	−.0265	−.75	−.0529	−2.17	−.0078	−.15	−.0400	−1.97
50–59	−.1367	−3.44	−.1864	−6.43	−.2234	−3.47	−.0998	−3.96
60+	−.4897	−13.62	−.4210	−13.67	−.5817	−11.90	−.4525	−17.02
Education: 1–9 years	.1318	4.53	.0361	1.85	.1368	3.82	.0694	4.16
10 years or more	−.0040	−.13	.0091	.34	−.0821	−1.50	−.2251	−4.89
Children: With children under 7			−.0621	−4.96			−.0582	−5.16
Number of adults: 1	.1542	4.61	.0889	2.16	.1467	3.40	.0616	1.79
2	.0023	.11	−.0898	−4.75	−.0346	−1.63	−.0174	−1.21
4 or more	−.0011	−.07	−.0067	−.42	.0004	.02	.0363	2.79
Income of household head per member:								
< 1,000 baht/year	.0629	3.83	.0564	3.12	.0564	3.40	.0455	3.67
≥ 2,000 baht/year	−.0198	−1.43	−.0280	−1.93	−.0192	−.85	−.0292	−1.76
Family enterprise: Household head is self-employed	.0294	2.46	.0794	6.39	−.0336	−2.09	.0476	3.81
Sector: Non-agricultural	−.1253	−5.60	−.1790	−8.21	−.1784	−10.50	−.1672	−12.73
R^2	.8867		.5992		.8219		.7024	
Number of observations	477		898		474		1,000	

* The data used are from (National Statistical Office, 1973).

one to nine years of schooling than for either those with no schooling at all or for those with more than nine years. Thus, for the majority of people who typically have no more than four years of formal education, it is the case that some schooling is associated with higher participation. At higher levels of schooling, however the participation rate falls off sharply, being comparable to that of the uneducated group in urban areas; participation rate figures for rural areas are even lower. This differs markedly from results obtained for the U.S. in which there is a clear positive relationship between schooling and the labor force participation rate for both males and females (Bowen and Finegan, 1969: 53–57, 114–27).

As far as household characteristics are concerned, the presence of children under 7 (the typical school-entering age), lowers by 6 percentage points the probability that a woman will be in the labor force, in both urban and rural areas. It is somewhat surprising that this effect is not weaker in the rural areas where the compatibility between farm and home work might be expected to show children to be a relatively mild deterrent to labor force participation.

To test the hypothesis that household members respond to the level of adequacy of the head's income in providing for the household's material needs, dummy variables are entered in the regression which classify households into three groups corresponding to different levels of the head's income per household member.[10] We will take as the base group the household whose per-member annual income falls in the $>1,000$ but $<2,000$ baht range. The worst-off group will consist of households with a per-member income of less than 1,000 baht per year; the best-off group will consist of households whose per-member income is 2,000 baht per year or greater.

The probability that a worst-off household member will work is significantly higher than that of a base group member: 6 percentage points for both males and females in urban areas, 6 points for males in rural areas, and 5 points for females in rural areas. On the other hand, the probability that a best-off household member will work is lower than that of a base-group household member: 2 percentage points for males and 3 points for females. Thus, economic necessity is an important factor affecting the level of labor force participation of household members.

Information is not available on whether the household operates a family enterprise or not. We expect labor force participation to be

---

[10] We assume here that the household head is the only family member in the labor force.

encouraged where there is one. However, a reasonable proxy for a family enterprise is when the household head is self-employed, since then he can potentially run an enterprise in which his household members can work. The group of households in which the head is self-employed overstates the number of family enterprises to the extent that not all self-employed household heads operate family enterprises, but understates it to the extent that a family enterprise may be run by a non-head member of the household. If in most cases family enterprises are run by household heads, then this proxy variable would overstate the number of enterprises. The finding that the probability of participating in the labor force is increased in most cases would therefore give the bottom limit of the encouraging effect of family enterprises.

In urban areas this encouraging effect is shown by a 3 percentage point increase in male participation and an 8 point increase in female participation. It is surprising that the effect is smaller in rural areas and, moreover, that male participation is lower when the head is self-employed. The probable explanation is that in the equation for rural areas there is colinearity between the family enterprise and sector variables since, for most of the agricultural households, the head is self-employed. The dummy variable for non-agriculture already includes the effect of the heads not being self-employed, and therefore the magnitudes of the family-enterprise coefficients are not comparable between the urban and rural equations.

For both urban and rural areas, and for both males and females, labor force participation is higher for agricultural households, defined according to the economic sector of the household head. The effect is very large, amounting to 13 percentage points in the case of urban males, 18 points for urban females and rural males, and 17 points for rural females, although part of the effect in the rural equation may be due to family enterprises.

Table 2 gives the labor force participation rates for males and females with no education and in households with no children, with three adults, with the income of head per household member $\geq 1,000$ but $< 2,000$ baht per year, and with the head not self-employed. The table attempts to compare participation rates by sex and location of residence. Thus, we take the more common sector in each case: non-agriculture in urban areas and agriculture in rural areas. Characteristics other than sex and location of residence are, however, held constant.

Within a given area of residence, male participation rates are higher than those for females with the exception of those under 20 in both areas and those 50 and older in rural areas. Thus, more females than

Table 2. Labor Force Participation Rates for People with No Education in Households with No Children, Three Adults, and Head Income per Member 1,000–2,000 Baht per Year and with Head Not Self-employed*

Age	Urban (non-agriculture)		Rural (agriculture)	
	Male	Female	Male	Female
10–14	a	.0518	.1991	.2337
15–19	.2036	.3076	.6829	.6924
20–29	.6713	.5291	.8443	.7544
30–39	.8076	.5956	.8734	.7896
40–49	.7811	.5427	.8656	.7496
50–59	.6709	.4092	.6500	.6898
60+	.3179	.1746	.2917	.3371

* Calculated from Table 1.
ᵃ Predicted value is negative.

males participate in the labor force in the school-attending ages as well as in the older age groups in rural areas. In urban areas, for those over 20 years of age male participation exceeds that for females by increasing amounts with age: by 14 percentage points in the 20–29 age group, by a peak of 26 points in the 50–59 age group, and by 14 points in the 60 and older group. In rural areas, male participation exceeds female only in the 20–49 age range, with the differential being much narrower than in urban areas, on the order of 8–12 percentage points.

For both males and females, and for all age groups with the exception of males 50 and older, rural participation rates are higher than urban rates. On the whole, the urban-rural differences in participation rates are greater for women than for men.

Household-related variables as well as personal characteristics are thus seen to be important in explaining the labor force participation behavior of household members in Thailand.

Choice of Economic Sector of Household Members

Among household members who enter the labor force, not all, by any means, do so in the same economic sector as the household head. Quite a number shift sectors, and we should see if any pattern can be discerned. Table 3 gives the proportion of household members who participate in the labor force in the same economic sector as the household head. Only two economic sectors are considered, agriculture and non-agriculture. The figures are broken down by sex and by area of residence.

Table 3. Probability of a Household Member in the Labor Force Being in the Same Sector as the Household Head*

| | | Household head's sector | |
		Agriculture	Non-agriculture
Urban			
Males:	Agriculture	.4878	.0259
	Non-agriculture	.5122	.9741
Females:	Agriculture	.6857	.0189
	Non-agriculture	.3143	.9811
Rural			
Males:	Agriculture	.8595	.4101
	Non-agriculture	.1405	.5899
Females:	Agriculture	.9257	.3953
	Non-agriculture	.0743	.6047

* The data used are from (National Statistical Office, 1973).

The probability of being in the same sector as the household head varies by sex and area of residence, as well as by the household head's sector. A few conclusions can be drawn. First, in the urban areas it is more likely for household members to be in the head's sector if this is non-agriculture rather than agriculture, and the opposite is true in rural areas. Thus in urban areas we find that 97 percent of male and 98 percent of female members with heads in non-agriculture also work in this sector. For those whose household heads are in agriculture, only 49 percent of male and 69 percent of female members work in agriculture. In rural areas 86 percent of male and 93 percent of female members work in agriculture if their heads do so. By comparison, in non-agriculture 59 percent of males and 60 percent of females work in the same sector as the household head. The probability of a switch from agriculture to non-agriculture is much higher in urban than rural areas, while a switch from non-agriculture to agriculture is more likely in rural than urban areas. In fact, the probability of a household member's being found in agriculture when his head is in non-agriculture is extremely low. Third, men are much more likely to switch out of agriculture than women. The probability of a male household member's being in the non-agricultural sector, given that the household head is in agriculture, is 51 percent as compared with 31 percent for females in urban areas and 14 percent as compared with 7 percent for females in rural areas. Thus, male household members appear to be able to move out of the agricultural sector more easily than female members.

It would be problematic, however, to interpret these probabilities as transition probabilities between sectors for household members, given the economic sector of the household head. Such an interpretation would lead one to expect higher probabilities of moving out of agriculture among the young and among the better educated. But, except for rural males, this is not the case. Statistically speaking, the hypothesis that the probability of being in the same sector as the household head does not vary by the age and education level of the individual cannot be rejected for rural females or for the urban population. The explanation for this is that what we observe is only that part of the transition matrix involving sectoral transfers within either urban or rural areas. However, by far the most important part of the complete matrix involves rural-to-urban migration as the mechanism through which individuals move out of the agricultural sector. Taking a cross-sectional view of households such as we are doing here completely misses out on the migratory dimension: individuals who have migrated are not shown with their parents' economic sector. The individuals who can be expected to be most mobile in terms of geographical relocation, the young and better-educated who have already made their move, are not represented in our table of probabilities as movers. We only capture such individuals who change economic sectors without migrating.

Unpaid Family Workers

Individuals working in family enterprises may or may not be paid in cash for their efforts. Presumably this depends on the practice of the household in question. Certainly the level of economic well-being of all household members is directly linked to how many of them work. In the family enterprise situation, individuals do not necessarily take into consideration the wage rate facing them if they were to offer their labor services in the market. Because of various considerations, including domestic obligations, many individuals may not even consider the possibility of outside employment and will contribute to the family farm or enterprise while receiving no direct payment in return.

Table 4 gives the distributions of paid and unpaid workers by various classifications as well as the proportion of unpaid workers in each group. Unpaid family workers are defined as those individuals who report an occupation, and hence are considered to be in the labor force, but do not report any income. Of all those reporting themselves as working, as many as 46 percent are unpaid workers. This is a very high proportion which certainly highlights the significance of the family farm or enterprise in the production system. Presumably individuals are only prepared to work without being paid if the fruits of their work directly benefit themselves and their immediate families.

Table 4. Characteristics of Paid and Unpaid Workers: Thailand, 1968–69*

Classification	Distribution of paid workers	Distribution of unpaid workers	% unpaid in this group
Age: 10–14	1.09	15.25	92.32
15–19	7.61	25.71	74.39
20–29	18.73	25.09	53.53
30–39	24.94	15.29	34.52
40–49	21.16	9.66	28.18
50–59	14.33	5.89	26.13
60+	12.14	3.12	18.11
Education: None	19.80	14.34	38.38
1–9 years	75.14	84.71	49.23
10 years or more	5.06	.95	13.95
Sex: Male	69.56	31.41	29.97
Female	30.44	68.59	65.96
Sector of head: Agriculture	59.43	91.59	57.00
Non-agriculture	40.57	8.41	15.13
Location: Urban	13.35	3.57	18.68
Rural	86.65	96.43	48.91
Same sector as head who is self-employed	67.07	82.00	51.26
Not in same sector as head or head is not self-employed	32.93	18.00	31.97
TOTAL	100.00	100.00	46.24

* The data used from (National Statistical Office, 1973).

The characteristics of paid and unpaid workers are quite different. Whereas 15 percent of unpaid workers are under 15 years of age, only 1 percent of paid workers are; 26 percent of unpaid workers are between 15 and 19, compared with only 8 percent of paid workers. Unpaid workers are a great deal more heavily represented in the younger age groups; the proportion of unpaid workers declines steadily with age, from 92 percent and 74 percent in the 10–14 and 15–19 age groups, respectively, to 18 percent in the over-60 group. In terms of the level of educational attainment, the proportion of unpaid workers is highest among those with some education and is in fact lower in the uneducated group. This is not really surprising and simply reflects the impact of governmental policy making primary education compulsory for all children. Thus, the younger generation has more years of schooling on the average, while it is mostly older people who have no education at all.

Women workers represent over two-thirds of the unpaid work force. This compares with their share of only 30 percent in the paid group. Whereas 28 percent of all male workers are unpaid, 66 percent of female workers fall in this category. As would be expected, unpaid workers are to be found in greater proportions in rural areas, in the agricultural sector. Fully 57 percent of agricultural workers are unpaid, compared with only 15 percent of non-agricultural workers.

Thus, the unpaid worker, more than the economically active population as a whole, could be characterized as the young worker with little schooling, the female worker, and the agricultural worker in rural areas. We need now to show the effect of each of these factors individually while controlling for the effects of all the other factors.

Given that an individual works, we are interested in the probability that he or she will be an unpaid family worker. Accordingly, individuals who are household members, not heads, are classified by their age, level of educational attainment, sex, sector of the household head, urban/rural location, and whether or not they work in the same sector as their household head, where the head is self-employed. Within each cell classified by the above characteristics, the proportion of unpaid family workers is calculated. These cells are used as observations in the regression equation, with the proportion unpaid as the dependent variable. The regressions were run separately for males and females and for urban and rural areas. The results are presented in Table 5, the base group in each case consisting of individuals 30–39 years of age with no education where the household head has his major occupation in agriculture and the individual is not employed in the same sector as the head, or where the individual is employed in the same sector as the head but the head is not self-employed. If the individual is employed in the same sector as the head and the head is self-employed, he is treated in a separate category from the base group.

The chances of being an unpaid worker are highest for young workers, especially those under 20. In urban areas a male worker under 15 has a 44 percentage-point greater chance of being unpaid than a male worker in his thirties; the corresponding figure for the rural area male worker is 36 percentage points. In urban areas a female worker under 15 has a 14 percentage-point greater chance of being unpaid than a female worker in her thirties; the corresponding figure for the rural area female worker is 18 percentage points. The proportion of unpaid workers is lowest for those between 20 and 50 years of age, but increases for older workers. Women workers in urban areas are 10 percentage points more likely than male workers to be working unpaid. In rural areas women workers are 8 percentage points more likely than male workers to be working unpaid. Having more education significantly reduces the chances that an individual will be an unpaid worker. Generally, urban households have a lower proportion of unpaid family

Table 5. Probability of Being an Unpaid Family Worker: Thailand, 1968–69*
(dependent variable: proportion of unpaid family workers in total)

Independent variable:	Urban areas						Rural areas					
	Males		Females		Total		Males		Females		Total	
	Estimated coefficient	t-statistic	Estimated coefficient	t-statistic	Estimated coefficient	t-statistic	Estimated coefficient	t-statistic	Estimated coefficient	t-statistic	Estimated coefficient	t-statistic
Constant	.3148	3.86	.4012	7.16	.3350	6.52	.5196	4.26	.5897	9.78	.4966	8.80
Age: 10–14	.4352	4.78	.1447	2.30	.2209	4.04	.3616	4.62	.1796	2.92	.2456	5.34
15–19	.1826	3.94	.1119	2.76	.1341	4.14	.2040	2.82	.0292	.60	.0884	2.28
20–29	.1036	2.51	−.0221	−.62	.0237	.82	.0254	.35	.0243	.53	.0077	.20
40–49	−.0052	−.09	.0126	.31	.0099	.27	−.0953	−.76	.0106	.19	−.0027	−.06
50–59	−.0242	−.34	.0976	1.81	−.0591	1.29	−.0871	−.44	−.0586	.85	.0421	.68
60+	.0774	1.00	.0241	.31	.0404	.69	.0572	.28	.1130	1.20	.0996	1.20
Education: 1–9 years	−.0455	−.72	−.0375	−.98	−.0505	−1.48	−.1545	−1.36	−.0029	−.06	−.0347	−.82
≥ 10 years	−.0603	−.88	−.1419	−2.73	−.1102	−2.64	−.2839	−1.62	−.2029	−1.20	−.2120	−1.85
Sector of head: Non-agricultural	−.2556	−5.69	−.2616	−7.09	−.2725	−9.00	−.0950	−1.62	−.1794	−3.89	−.1536	−4.26
Same sector as head: Head is self-employed	.2492	8.67	.4296	16.91	.3632	17.83	.3122	7.63	.2476	6.97	.2781	10.35
Sex: Female					.0962	4.49					.0831	3.10
R²	.6350		.8006		.7146		.5854		.4921		.5125	
Number of observations	105		117		222		119		123		242	

* The data used are from (National Statistical Office, 1973).

workers. The proportion of unpaid workers is lower for households in which the head's major occupation is outside of agriculture: in urban households by 26 percentage points for both males and females; in rural households by 10 percentage points for males and 18 points for females. As would be expected, the probability of being an unpaid worker is considerably increased for those who work in the same sector as the household head where the head is self-employed: by 25 percentage points for male urban workers and 43 points for female urban workers; by 31 points for rural male workers and 25 points for rural female workers.

It is important to estimate the proportion of those in the labor force who are unpaid family workers, because otherwise the incomes of those actually receiving income would be underestimated. The underestimation would not be uniform since, as we have seen, certain population groups have a higher probability of being unpaid than others. Moreover, the contribution of unpaid family workers shows up elsewhere as part of the household head's income and as own consumption.

Income

Total household income consists of money income and non-money income which includes own consumption. Household money income is simply the sum of the money incomes of all household members who receive income. Money income is reported in the Socioeconomic Survey, 1968–69, for both the month and the year preceding the survey. In this study, income for the year preceding the survey is used. For each individual in the sample, the amount of money income received is reported separately for each of the following seven categories:
    (i) wages, salaries, overtime, bonuses, and commissions;
    (ii) net profit from self-employment;
    (iii) interest and dividends;
    (iv) pensions and annuities;
    (v) income from rents;
    (vii) other income.
    In this study we combine rent income with interest and dividends, and subsidies and other income with pensions and annuities. Thus we have four categories of income:
    (i) wage income: wages, salaries, overtime, bonuses, and commissions;
    (ii) self-employment income: net profit from self-employment;

(iii) rent and interest income: interest, dividends, income from
                                 rents;

(iv) transfer income: pensions, annuities, subsidies, other income.

With respect to non-money income, the Socioeconomic Survey
reports the cash expenditures made by the household on over 200
items of goods and services for the month preceding the survey. At
the same time, information on the quantities of various goods which
were home-produced or received free and consumed by the household
was also obtained. Such consumption items were valued at retail prices
prevailing in the area and recorded in the survey. By summing these
values, we obtain the total value of goods home-produced or received
free. Adjusted to an annual basis, this is defined as the household's
non-money income.

Table 6 gives the proportions of the income-receiving population
having each of the four types of income and the corresponding average
incomes. The tabulations are given by sex and area of residence. Each
row sums to more than 100 percent, reflecting the fact that some people
have income from more than one source. It is evident, however, that the
majority of individuals have either wage or self-employment income,
that very few have any rent or interest income, and that a little over 10
percent receive transfer incomes. A smaller proportion of women than
of men receive wage income. In urban areas, a larger proportion of
women than men receive income from self-employment and transfer
income; a slightly larger proportion of women have rent and interest
income. Average wage and self-employment incomes are much lower
for women than for men. In addition, for a given sex and area of residence, wage income is lower than self-employment income. Average
rent and interest and transfer incomes are somewhat difficult to interpret since they include those for whom these are not necessarily the
major sources of income.

Because of the problem of unpaid family workers, it is useful to
consider three different groups of individuals in estimating the income-
generating equations: unpaid family workers, ordinary paid workers,
and workers whose incomes include the contributions of unpaid family
workers. In estimating income, non-money income is allocated to the
self-employment income of the household head, so long as he already
has some money self-employment income. If he does not, the non-
money income is added to the head's total income but is not used in the
equation for self-employment income. The reason for this is that if we
automatically add non-money income to the self-employment income
of the head, this will greatly increase the number of self-employed

Table 6. Income-receiving Working Population, Types of Income, and Average Annual Income*

| Area of residence | Income-receiving working population and type of income (%) | | | | Average annual income for income-receiving working population (baht) | | | | |
| | Type of income | | | | Type of income | | | | |
	Wage	Self-employment	Rent & Interest	Transfer	Wage	Self-employment	Rent & Interest	Transfer	Total
Rural:									
Males	40.45	66.95	2.36	12.23	4,463.07	8,262.61	4,951.73	2,459.97	8,224.78
Females	33.81	60.59	2.66	11.69	2,338.38	4,365.16	2,817.40	2,752.50	4,025.45
Total	38.52	65.11	2.45	12.07	3,922.84	7,211.82	4,280.40	2,542.03	7,008.19
Provincial urban:									
Males	55.74	44.54	3.78	11.01	10,827.35	25,260.99	14,437.70	6,913.00	19,088.94
Females	42.56	52.95	3.91	13.17	7,157.09	8,622.85	6,827.23	5,490.58	8,741.29
Total	50.58	47.83	3.83	11.86	9,618.15	18,049.72	11,397.86	6,294.38	15,037.41
Bangkok-Thonburi:									
Males	71.55	27.20	2.73	8.89	14,865.92	22,509.12	14,826.20	12,787.72	18,766.09
Females	61.71	34.55	2.89	9.00	8,490.36	12,542.58	21,192.37	9,029.38	11,146.00
Total	67.67	30.10	2.79	8.93	12,573.52	17,998.86	17,423.09	11,294.84	15,761.66

* The data used are from (National Statistical Office, 1973).

persons when in fact many of these have only some small non-money income. The estimates for self-employment income would, thereby, be thrown off.

The observations used in the regressions include household heads and other household members reporting money income. Unpaid family workers are not entered as observations, but the total number of unpaid family workers in a household is obtained, and a series of dummy variables is created corresponding to 1, 2, 3, and 4 or more unpaid family workers such that they can be non-zero for the household head only. Thus, all four dummy variables for unpaid family workers will be zero for individuals who are not heads of household as well as for heads of households containing no unpaid family workers. For heads of households in which there are unpaid workers, the dummy variable corresponding to their number takes the value one. The family-worker variables are included to explain the head's income irrespective of whether he has non-money income.

Two sets of regression estimates were obtained separately for agriculture and non-agriculture:

A. Probability of having income. In the first set of equations, the probability that an individual will have each of the four categories of income defined above is estimated given age, level of education, sex, sector, and area of residence. For this the sample consists of the working population reporting income. The results are reported in Tables 7 to 10.

B. Income. Income equations are estimated for each of the four income categories as well as for total income given age, level of education, sex, sector, and area of residence of the individual. Again, the sample consists of the working population reporting income. The contributions of unpaid family workers are taken to accrue to the household head, either in money terms or as own consumption, and are estimated in the family-worker coefficients which are applicable to household heads only. The regressions are reported in Tables 7 to 10 for the four categories of income and in Table 11 for total income.

Since most of the individuals with income have either wage or self-employment income, we find corresponding trends in the regression equations estimating the probabilities of having these two types of incomes. Thus the probability of having wage income tends to decline with age, while that of having self-employment income increases. The tendency, therefore, is for individuals to start out as wage earners but later switch to self-employment. In non-agriculture a higher level of schooling is associated with a higher probability of having wage income

Table 7. Regression Estimates of the Probability of Receiving Wage Income and Annual Wage Income*

Dependent variable:	Probability of receiving wage income				Annual wage income (baht)			
	Agriculture		Non-agriculture		Agriculture		Non-agriculture	
Independent variable	Estimated coefficient	t-statistic	Estimated coefficient	t-statistic	Estimated coefficient	t-statistic	Estimated coefficient	t-statistic
Constant	.4362	23.25	.5287	38.63	2485.94	10.81	3810.67	10.11
Age: 10–14	.2848	4.70	.3814	12.25	−1079.15	−1.99	−4915.18	−7.97
15–19	.4032	15.13	.2254	16.85	−784.01	−3.22	−4355.52	−14.74
20–29	.1283	6.83	.0926	9.12	−338.88	−1.70	−2072.07	−8.87
40–49	−.0889	−5.40	.0309	2.80	452.16	2.22	1526.47	5.86
50–59	−.1913	−10.59	−.1467	−10.22	288.38	1.11	3728.19	9.43
60+	−.2714	−13.51	−.3309	−21.26	439.54	1.29	−26.34	−.05
Education: 1–9 years	−.0683	−4.42	.0545	4.66	5.08	.02	3099.34	9.08
≥ 10 years	−.0002	−.00	.3215	20.51	6419.56	7.96	10194.05	26.04
Sex: Female	−.0993	−7.32	−.1902	−24.48	−965.54	−5.47	−2522.12	−12.76
Area: Urban	−0.334	−.67	.0373	4.68	3520.01	4.87	4120.18	21.97
Number of observations	5,964		15,587		1,910		9,636	
R²	.1187		.1640		.3977		.5003	

* The data used are from (National Statistical Office, 1973).

Table 8. Regression Estimates of the Probability of Receiving Self-employment Income and Annual Self-employment Income*

Dependent variable:	Probability of receiving self-employment income				Annual self-employment income (baht)			
	Agriculture		Non-agriculture		Agriculture		Non-agriculture	
Independent variable	Estimated coefficient	t-statistic	Estimated coefficient	t-statistic	Estimated coefficient	t-statistic	Estimated coefficient	t-statistic
Constant	.7149	39.79	.5555	38.99	4500.02	10.72	5606.06	4.30
Age: 10–14	–.4600	–7.92	–.4164	–12.84	–1876.05	–.97	–6813.06	–1.35
15–19	–.4531	–17.76	–.2816	–20.21	–2503.45	–3.11	–4227.65	–2.62
20–29	–.1129	–6.28	–.1409	–13.32	–1775.25	–4.48	–4234.28	–3.99
40–49	.0491	3.11	–.0309	–2.69	1311.57	3.94	–872.96	–.81
50–59	.1056	6.10	.0454	3.04	79.76	.22	4886.98	3.70
60	.0811	4.22	–.1226	–7.56	140.46	.35	–3195.77	–2.05
Education: 1–9 years	.0552	3.74	–.0311	–2.56	755.03	2.50	3636.59	3.45
≥ 10 years	.0672	1.01	–.3089	–18.93	9009.52	6.67	26677.18	12.96
Sex: Female	–.0464	–3.57	.1137	14.06	–1558.66	–5.07	–4829.79	–5.94
Area: Urban	–.0042	–.09	–.0697	–8.40	5997.73	6.08	9090.76	10.77
Unpaid family workers: 1					1672.04	5.26	7734.07	6.90
2					2787.60	7.47	8185.88	5.02
3					4613.96	11.05	8611.61	3.46
≥4					6132.94	14.56	12122.93	4.72
Number of observations	5,964		15,587		4,338		5,473	
R^2	.1012		.0935		.5056		.2034	

* The data used are from (National Statistical Office, 1973).

Table 9. Regression Estimates of the Probability of Receiving Rent and Interest Income and Annual Rent and Interest Income*

Dependent variable:	Probability of receiving rent and interest income				Annual rent and interest income (baht)			
	Agriculture		Non-agriculture		Agriculture		Non-agriculture	
Independent variable	Estimated coefficient	t-statistic	Estimated coefficient	t-statistic	Estimated coefficient	t-statistic	Estimated coefficient	t-statistic
Constant	.0377	6.15	−.0207	−3.93	2414.66	2.23	1223.36	.37
Age: 10–14	−.0234	−1.18	−.0181	−1.51	{		{	
15–19	−.0188	−2.16	−.0264	−5.13	{ 82.67	−.07	{ −156.35	−.04
20–29	−.0069	−1.18	−.0229	−5.87	{		{	
40–49	−.0148	−2.75	.0133	3.15	−576.01	−.46	2878.46	1.09
50–59	−.0131	−2.22	.0592	10.71	1010.30	.81	7183.92	2.73
60⁺	.0104	1.59	.1319	22.01	−704.28	−.64	5351.14	2.15
Education: 1–9 years	−.0156	−3.09	.0452	10.06	{ 678.67	.73	{ 3293.36	1.29
≥ 10 years	.0553	2.44	.0676	11.21	{		{	
Sex: Female	.0021	.47	.0123	4.12	−1350.58	−1.58	−2317.78	−1.25
Area: Urban	−.0294	1.79	−.0061	−2.00	3465.42	1.69	7752.04	4.24
Number of observations	5,964		15,587		129		600	
R²	.0100		.0478		.3089		.1855	

* The data used are from (National Statistical Office, 1973).

Table 10. Regression Estimates of the Probability of Receiving Transfer Income and Annual Transfer Income*

Dependent variable:	Probability of receiving transfer income				Annual transfer income (baht)			
	Agriculture		Non-agriculture		Agriculture		Non-agriculture	
Independent variable	Estimated coefficient	t-statistic	Estimated coefficient	t-statistic	Estimated coefficient	t-statistic	Estimated coefficient	t-statistic
Constant	.0704	4.89	.0841	9.62	405.19	.37	−1341.48	−1.80
Age: 10–14	.0225	.48	−.0904	−4.55	(−338.39	−.30	−1924.62	−2.77
15–19	−.0961	−4.70	−.0566	−6.62				
20–29	−.0338	−2.34	−.0477	−7.35	(			
40–49	.0118	.94	.0042	.59	1342.74	1.44	570.15	.85
50–59	.0703	5.07	.0432	4.71	624.49	.67	2148.52	2.82
60+	.0890	5.78	.2926	29.44	2270.92	2.20	4210.84	6.41
Education: 1–9 years	.0509	4.29	−.0103	−1.38	1115.28	1.31	3210.10	5.45
≥ 10 years	.0420	.79	.0584	5.84	12521.54	3.31	8327.40	10.42
Sex: Female	.0094	.90	.0293	5.91	553.66	.72	826.68	1.81
Area: Urban	−.0574	−1.49	−.0042	−.83	436.65	.13	4359.23	9.35
Number of observations	5,964		15,587		791		1,826	
R²	.0176		.0940		.0855		.2851	

* The data used are from (National Statistical Office, 1973).

Table 11. Regression Estimates of Annual Total Income*

| Dependent variable: | Annual total income (baht) | | | |
| | Agriculture | | Non-agriculture | |
Independent variable	Estimated coefficient	t-statistic	Estimated coefficient	t-statistic
Constant	5831.31	17.71	6512.67	10.68
Age: 10–14	—4129.19	—3.88	—7919.02	—5.71
15–29	—3867.70	—8.27	—7281.49	—12.22
20–29	—2310.70	—7.00	—5043.95	—11.14
40–49	2473.76	8.56	1449.95	2.95
50–59	2134.40	6.73	6836.43	10.69
60+	1684.74	4.78	650.08	.94
Education: 1–9 years	1154.09	4.26	4365.59	8.39
≤ 10 years	11216.72	9.19	14643.54	20.97
Sex: Female	—3023.01	—12.69	—4607.94	—13.31
Area: Urban	4613.54	5.23	5767.30	16.25
Number of observations	5,964		15,587	
R^2	.4644		.2510	

* The data used are from (National Statistical Office, 1973).

and a lower level of schooling with being self-employed, but this is not true in the agricultural sector. In non-agriculture, women are less likely to be wage earners when compared with men of otherwise similar characteristics and are correspondingly more likely to be self-employed. However, in the agricultural sector, women are 10 percentage points less likely than men to be wage earners and 5 points less likely to be self-employed. Outside agriculture, urban workers are more likely than rural workers to earn wages and less likely to be self-employed.

The results of trying to predict the probability of having rent and interest or transfer income are not good, reflecting the failure of personal characteristics of individuals to explain such variations. However, we can say that older people outside the agricultural sector are more likely to have rent and interest income and that increasing age is associated with a greater likelihood of having transfer income. Women in non-agriculture have a somewhat higher probability than men of having these two types of income.

In general terms, the results of the income equations are as expected. For each type of income, holding other characteristics constant, increasing age is associated with higher income, except for a falling off of wages and self-employment income for those 60 and older in the non-agricultural sector. More education and higher incomes go together. Women make less than men in terms of wage and self-employment income, given otherwise similar characteristics. Incomes are higher in urban areas.

As was the case with the probability equations, personal characteristics such as those included in the regression do not explain successfully rent and interest and transfer incomes. And indeed we would not expect them to. Average transfer income is in fact higher for those with more schooling, reflecting the fact that employment opportunities which are available to the better educated have better pension benefits.

The results in Table 8 show that the contribution of unpaid family workers to household income is definitely positive. Among household heads with similar personal characteristics working in the same sector and area (rural or urban), those with unpaid family workers have a higher total income (*i.e.*, money income plus the value of own consumption) than those working alone. The total contribution to household income of unpaid family workers increases with the number of such workers. The regression equations give us an imputation of unpaid labor: one unpaid family worker in the agricultural sector contributes an additional 1,672 baht to household income over what the head earns; two, three, and four or more workers contribute, respectively, another 2,788 baht, 4,614 baht, and 6,133 baht. Depending on the total number of family workers, the average addition to household income by a worker is thus 1,672 baht, 1,116 baht, 1,826 baht, or 1,519 baht over the contribution of the head.

Income and the Household

Tables 12 and 13 present some of the results in a different way. Table 12 gives the composition of the household by the income of the household head per member and sector of the head, enumerating the numbers of children, unpaid family workers, and secondary earners. Unpaid family workers are household members who work for the household enterprise without any remuneration, while secondary earners are household members besides the household head who earn additional money income. Thus, for all households the average number of members is 5.77, of whom 2.58 are children under 15. On average there are 1.08 unpaid family workers and .53 secondary workers who earn supplementary money income.

When the information is tabulated by the annual money income of the household head per household member, we find, not surprisingly, that the average household size is inversely related to this income: it is

Table 12. Composition of Household Members by Head Income per Member and Sector*

Sector	Annual money income of household head per household member (baht)									
	0–499	500–999	1,000–1,499	1,500–1,999	2,000–2,499	2,500–2,999	3,000–3,999	4,000–4,999	5,000 or more	All classes
Agriculture:										
Number of household members	7.14	6.58	5.89	5.47	4.86	4.59	4.55	4.66	4.85	5.94
Number of children	3.39	3.30	2.56	2.28	1.87	1.52	1.46	1.38	1.83	2.66
Number of unpaid family workers	.83	1.30	1.51	1.56	1.58	1.62	1.61	2.06	1.49	1.41
Number of secondary earners	1.13	.55	.41	.31	.21	.20	.19	.14	.19	.46
% of children	47.48	50.15	43.46	41.68	38.48	33.12	32.09	29.61	37.73	44.78
% of unpaid family workers	11.62	19.76	25.64	28.52	32.51	35.29	35.38	44.21	30.72	23.74
% of secondary earners	15.83	8.36	6.96	5.67	4.32	4.36	4.18	3.00	3.92	7.74
Non-agriculture:										
Number of household members	6.26	6.46	5.81	5.67	5.34	5.33	4.79	4.47	4.06	5.39
Number of children	2.53	3.28	2.82	2.75	2.33	2.41	1.95	1.61	1.34	2.41
Number of unpaid family workers	.08	.36	.41	.39	.26	.45	.48	.43	.33	.37
Number of secondary earners	1.72	.93	.69	.58	.61	.49	.48	.40	.41	.66
% of children	40.42	50.77	48.54	48.50	43.63	45.22	40.71	36.03	33.00	44.71
% of unpaid family workers	1.28	5.57	7.06	6.88	4.87	8.44	10.02	9.62	8.13	6.86
% of secondary earners	27.48	14.40	11.88	10.23	11.42	9.19	10.02	8.95	10.10	12.24
Total:										
Number of household members	6.95	6.56	5.87	5.53	5.07	4.95	4.67	4.55	4.23	5.77
Number of children	3.20	3.29	2.62	2.43	2.07	1.96	1.70	1.52	1.45	2.58
Number of unpaid family workers	.66	1.13	1.25	1.18	1.00	1.04	1.05	1.06	.58	1.08
Number of secondary earners	1.25	.62	.48	.40	.39	.35	.33	.30	.37	.53
% of children	46.04	50.15	44.63	43.94	40.83	39.60	36.40	33.41	34.38	44.71
% of unpaid family workers	9.50	17.23	21.29	21.34	19.72	21.01	22.48	23.30	13.71	18.72
% of secondary earners	17.99	9.45	8.18	7.23	7.69	7.07	7.07	6.59	8.75	9.19

* The data used are from (National Statistical Office, 1973).

Table 13. Composition of Per-member Household Income by Head Income per Member and Sector*

Sector	Annual money income of household head per household member (baht)									
	0–499	500–999	1,000–1,499	1,500–1,999	2,000–2,499	2,500–2,999	3,000–3,999	4,000–4,999	5,000 or more	All classes
Agriculture:										
% of households	8.74	32.33	26.90	13.26	6.49	3.45	5.20	1.76	1.86	100.00
Money income of head	341.93	757.19	1213.63	1700.78	2242.42	2707.36	3422.30	4320.62	8566.67	1355.47
Own consumption	179.46	395.22	489.22	513.84	558.41	551.65	612.48	604.69	769.14	442.20
Supplementary money income	527.13	191.13	200.69	215.62	157.54	120.16	174.42	70.44	182.28	225.76
Total income	1048.52	1343.54	1903.54	2430.24	2958.37	3379.17	4209.20	4995.75	9518.09	2023.43
% money income of head	32.61	56.36	63.76	69.98	75.80	80.12	81.31	86.49	90.00	66.99
% own consumption	17.12	29.42	25.70	21.14	18.88	16.33	14.55	12.10	8.08	21.85
% supplementary money income	50.27	14.23	10.54	8.87	5.33	3.56	4.14	1.41	1.92	11.16
Non-agriculture:										
% of households	5.04	15.19	17.92	13.32	10.77	7.03	10.62	5.90	14.22	100.00
Money income of head	246.71	759.80	1242.46	1731.59	2234.05	2719.78	3387.53	4405.92	10050.40	2672.82
Own consumption	105.23	210.09	212.63	230.95	234.53	313.37	306.63	302.45	422.09	253.45
Supplementary money income	1582.99	719.40	678.59	711.91	675.53	1357.49	740.24	747.91	997.61	833.74
Total income	1934.93	1689.29	2133.68	2674.45	3144.11	4390.64	4434.40	5456.28	11470.10	3760.01
% money income of head	12.75	44.98	58.23	64.75	71.06	61.94	76.39	80.75	87.62	71.09
% own consumption	5.44	12.44	9.97	8.64	7.46	7.14	6.91	5.54	3.68	6.74
% supplementary money income	81.81	42.59	31.80	26.62	21.49	30.92	16.69	13.71	8.70	22.17
Total:										
% of households	7.54	26.78	24.00	13.28	7.88	4.61	6.95	3.10	5.86	100.00
Money income of head	323.37	757.66	1220.52	1711.03	2238.52	2713.95	3404.68	4372.26	9684.15	1754.12
Own consumption	165.00	361.74	423.12	419.75	407.47	425.18	457.49	421.71	507.75	385.08
Supplementary money income	732.87	286.67	314.89	380.70	398.95	776.91	461.15	480.59	796.35	409.75
Total income	1221.24	1406.07	1958.53	2511.48	3044.94	3916.04	4323.32	5274.56	10988.25	2548.95
% money income of head	26.48	53.88	62.32	68.13	73.52	69.30	78.75	82.89	88.13	68.82
% own consumption	13.51	25.73	21.60	16.71	13.38	10.86	10.58	8.00	4.62	15.11
% supplementary money income	60.01	20.39	16.08	15.16	13.10	19.84	10.67	9.11	7.25	16.08

* The data used are from (National Statistical Office, 1973).

6.95 persons for households where the head's income per person is under 500 baht per year and decreases to 4.23 persons for those where the head's income per person is 5,000 baht or more per year. The average number of children per household also decreases with the level of the head's income per person. This is to be expected; what is more interesting is that the proportion of children out of all household members goes down, from nearly one-half for the under-1,000-baht class to one-third for households in the top two classes where the income of the household head per household member is 4,000 baht or more per year. On the whole, the proportion of unpaid family workers goes up while that of secondary earners goes down with the level of the head's income per person. In the bottom class, in which there are on average 6.95 household members, .66 persons, or 9.50 percent, are unpaid family workers and 1.25 persons, or 17.99 percent, are secondary earners. In the 4,000–4,999 baht class 1.06 persons, or 23.30 percent, are unpaid family workers and .30 persons, or 6.59 percent, are secondary earners. The highest income class tends to behave somewhat differently from the general pattern.

The results are similar when we consider the agricultural and non-agricultural sectors separately. In agriculture a household on average has 5.94 members, of whom 2.66, or 44.78 percent, are children; 1.41, or 23.74 percent, are unpaid family workers; and .46, or 7.74 percent, are secondary earners. Non-agricultural households are smaller on average, with 5.39 members, of whom 2.41 are children, .37 are unpaid family workers, and .66 are secondary earners. It is not surprising to find that a smaller proportion of household members are unpaid family workers and a larger proportion are secondary earners than in agricultural households.

In addition to the division of household members into those who do and do not contribute to total household income, we look at their actual contributions in Table 13. For all households the average household income per member is 2,549 baht per year, of which 1,754 baht, 68.82 percent of the total money income, is contributed by the household head. Own consumption amounts to 385 baht, or 15.11 percent, and supplementary money income of secondary workers is 410 baht, or 16.08 percent of total household income. In the agricultural sector the household head's money income is 66.99 percent, while in non-agriculture it is 71.09 percent of the total. Own consumption is more important in agriculture, making up 21.85 percent of the total, compared with only 6.74 percent in non-agriculture; supplementary money income is 11.16 percent in agriculture and 22.17 percent in non-agriculture. The head's money income plus the household's own consumption represent the combined contributions of the household head and the unpaid family workers.

Looking at the breakdown by income class of the head's money income per household member, we see that there are some definite trends, whether we consider the two sectors separately or together. The proportion of the household head's contribution to the total increases with the income class: from 26.48 percent for the under-500-baht class to as much as 88.13 percent in the 5,000-baht-or-more class. Income of secondary earners moves in the opposite direction: from 60.01 percent in the bottom class to 7.25 percent in the top class. Except for the bottom income class, the proportion of own consumption in the total declines with the level of the head's income per household member. For both sectors taken together, this is 25.73 percent for the 500–999 baht class and declines to 4.62 percent for the top income class.

Thus, it is clear that the importance of additional workers, both unpaid family workers and secondary earners of money income, lies not simply in the extent of their contribution to total household income but in the equalizing effect that they have on the distribution of income; secondary earners contribute more as a proportion of the total in those households in which the primary earners provide less adequately for their household members as measured by their income per household member.

Conclusion

This study uses data from the Socioeconomic Survey, 1968–69, for Thailand to analyze the process of income formation in the household sector. It examines the labor force participation of household members and the incomes earned by them. Both personal and household characteristics have a significant influence on labor force participation and income. Unpaid family workers and secondary earners of money income contribute significantly to total household income. Moreover, their contribution tends to reduce the degree of inequality in the distribution of income to the extent that it forms a larger proportion of the total for poorer households, as indicated by a lower income of the household head per household member.

The prevalence of family farms and enterprises in Thailand and the significance of household characteristics in determining the level of household income suggests that more attention should be directed at the household sector as a way of achieving a better understanding of the problem of income distribution in Thailand.

Since personal and household characteristics turn out to be important in determining the labor force participation behavior and income of individuals, a study of this nature will raise questions concerning the role of these characteristics in shaping the distribution of income as development proceeds. Changes in their distribution, in addition to this direct impact, can alter the structure and composition of the labor force and hence the income distribution.

Consider demographic changes which can be expected to accompany economic development, such as lower fertility and mortality rates and later marriages. These can affect the distribution of income in the short run, directly by changing the size and composition of households and indirectly to the extent that they lead to changes in the size and composition of the labor force and hence in income. For example, fewer children as a result of a fall in fertility may raise the participation rate of women. On the other hand, the resulting higher level of income of the household head per household member may deter entry into the labor force by household members. In the longer run, changes in the distribution of income have their impact through the generation of individuals directly affected by the original demographic changes.

Changes taking place over time can have both a direct and an indirect effect on the distribution of income. Thus, policies designed to alter the distribution of educational attainment affect the distribution of income directly to the extent that the level of schooling is related to the level of income. But, as we have seen, the level of schooling is an important factor in determining whether or not an individual will be in the labor force as well as whether he will work as a paid or unpaid worker. Moreover, changes in the composition of the educational distribution of the labor force will alter the relative rates of remuneration between different education classes and thus affect the distribution of income in this way as well.

The labor force participation of household members has been shown to be influenced by household characteristics such as the adequacy of the head's income in providing for the material requirements of the household, the presence or absence of a family enterprise, and, in the case of women, the presence of children in the household. Changes in these factors, such as the diminishing importance of the family farm or enterprise, will have their effect on the distribution of income.

One of the phenomena accompanying economic growth is rural-to-urban migration and the movement of the labor force out of the agricultural sector. The labor force participation rates of individuals have been found to vary significantly between rural and urban areas and to depend on whether or not they belong to agricultural households.

Their incomes also differ greatly between locations and sectors, and income distribution is correspondingly affected. In these cases the situation is complicated by the fact that the effect of any given change is not necessarily unambiguous. A movement of the labor force out of the agricultural sector can be expected to reduce participation, even though those who move may receive higher incomes. Of course, both the participation rates and the income differentials themselves are subject to change as well, and therefore the problem is compounded.

Individual and household characteristics affect not only labor force participation and income but also savings and consumption. As these characteristics change, the size of savings and the pattern of consumption will also change, thereby affecting income on the production side by changing the relative demands for different factors of production.

This study attempts to understand the process of income formation in the household sector in Thailand. It concludes that household and personal characteristics of individuals are important in explaining the different aspects of household income. But it is also evident that there is still a great deal more to learn before we can hope to grasp the thorny problem of income distribution.

References

Bowen, W. G., and Finegan, T. A. *The Economics of Labor Force Participation.* Princeton, N. J.: Princeton University Press, 1969.

Draper, N. R., and Smith, H. *Applied Regression Analysis.* New York: John Wiley & Sons, Inc., 1966.

National Statistical Office, Office of the Prime Minister. *Report, Socio-Economic Survey, B. E. 2511–2512.* Bangkok, 1973.

Additional Remarks

On Households

Kazushi Ohkawa

Households: Accounting Aspects

One of the common threads that runs through many of the papers in this volume is the emergence of the household as a central unit in the compilation of national accounts statistics, particularly for the developing countries.

In Part I, a number of chapters deal with the household sector. Choudhury presents interesting ideas for modifying the SNA to incorporate more information that will enrich our empirical knowledge of this sector. Hayami *et al.* present the results of their pilot survey of rural households mostly engaged in farming. Their interpretation of various interdependent rural household activities demonstrates the possibility of useful and effective extension of such field work in applying the conventional system of accounts. In the full but compact presentation of financial flows for India by Divatia one can identify the extremely important role played by the household sector: its net saving (*i.e.,* net of its own investment) is the major domestic source of financing investment in the modern private and public sectors. India's experience, reinforced by a similar pattern found in the historical experience of Japan, would strongly urge us to investigate savings performance in countries of this region.

Viewed from the standpoint of clarifying the Asian characteristics of development, the household is, I believe, the most important sector. It basically composes the core of the Asian socioeconomic and cultural structure inherited from traditional society. Since the commencement of "modern economic growth" in most of the countries of this region, this sector has continued to perform its basic activities over the past quarter century. If one shares the view that, at least during the initial phase of development, the performance of the traditional sector and its components are extremely important in shaping the pattern and mechanism of modernization, we have to know much more about the activities of households.

The application and modified extension of national accounts to this sector, however, requires a great effort. To the first Asian Regional Conference of IARIW Professor H.T. Oshima presented a pioneering paper, "National Accounts for the Analysis of Asian Growth", proposing such a conceptual framework of accounts. At the second conference, in addition to the conceptual follow-up, we devoted a great deal of discussion to the difficulty of improving the statistical reliability of estimates, in particular for this sector. In the conventional national accounts the household is actually a mixed sector: genuine households and unincorporated enterprises of both the farm and non-farm sectors. This is often called the "unorganized" or "informal" sector in development analysis—giving, I am afraid, the erroneous impression that the organized, modern sector plays the major role and that traditional activity is minor or subordinate. This view can only be valid for fully developed countries. In the case of Japan, for example, self-employment was the dominant pattern of labor employment until 1960, when the number of hired employees finally exceeded that of the self-employed (*i.e.*, proprietors and family workers). Almost a century was needed to arrive at this stage of development in Japan. In spite of the many technical difficulties faced by the accounting components in making estimates, we must attach particular importance to achieving a breakthrough on this front.

The long and wide experience of the advanced countries no doubt can present useful lessons for the developing countries in this field. However, there are problems which cannot be solved drawing solely on the historical experience of advanced countries because some of their problems are new or of different significance. In order to come to grips with these challenges, we really need to make a particularly strong effort to improve the conventional system by widening the scope of its concepts, by devising estimates useful for development planning, and by creating new systems if necessary and possible.

Households: Social Aspects

The papers in Parts II and III of this volume cover too wide a field to be comprehensively treated here. Part II treats "social development" and presents a number of contributions towards solving both conceptual and statistical problems. In view of the pioneering nature of this work, even preliminary efforts should be appreciated. In recent years, increasing attention has been devoted to the problem of the relationship between growth and equity. This concern has arisen from reflections on past development performance: the benefits of output growth could not be shared by the mass of people, so the social aspects of development were ignored and the problems unsolved. Without dwelling upon the validity of the notion of "trade-offs", itself a controversial issue, one can share the view that the performance of the household sector is again the core of the problem since the major issue in what we call "social development" must pertain to the people's way of life or any change in that way of life. The traditional way of life has changed during the process of modernization. The changes resulting from modernization, unfavorable or favorable, can and should be grasped systematically at the household level in terms of the various occupational and regional distribution effects.

Thus, in a broad sense, income distribution is one of the most important aspects of social development. In Part III we can see a number of useful results of the efforts made, mostly at the household level, toward measurement and interpretation. Except for the paper which deals with income formation and labor participation in the Thai household sector, the papers in Part III discuss the distribution problem as part of the process of rapid industrialization, describing the experiences of the region's relatively more developed countries. The selection of countries for description was not made according to the design of the Conference program. Although we do have at present a number of studies on income distribution for developing countries in this region, the number of country studies is still limited with regard to reliable data for over-time change. The cases of Hong Kong, Japan, Singapore, and Taiwan, despite some dissimilarities and data deficiencies, reveal a significant common phenomenon: a recent tendency toward equalization in income distribution following an earlier worsening trend. Because of this seemingly common phenomenon, the inverse U-shape curve, à la Kuznets, is one of the central points of discussion for this region's experience. For other countries, however, much more effort will be needed to clarify the trend.

The interpretation presented in these papers attracts special attention. The rise in the major sources of lower-class income (i.e., real wage rates and the earnings of unskilled workers as well as the income of farm-households, including income from non-farm jobs) seems to be the major explanation of the recent tendency toward equalization. Although reliable information is still insufficient, the real wages of rural and urban unskilled workers in most Asian developing countries appear to have remained almost unchanged or even slightly declined in the postwar period (ADB, 1977). These two findings, taken together, suggest that a structural change in the labor demand-supply situation, from surplus to limited supply, appears to be most relevant to the reversal in the income distribution trend from disequalization to equalization. Certainly, this is one of the most important issues for further scrutiny with particular relevance to analyzing the previously mentioned problem of "trade-offs".

In this regard, I would like to make two remarks, the first of which concerns the time dimension of development. The period covered by these papers is relatively short: even for Japan, only the postwar period is treated; for other countries, an even shorter period. Therefore, the inverse U-shaped curve can be suggested only with reservations as a tentative finding. Furthermore, in the light of Japan's experience, treatment of income distribution trends cannot be divorced from the effects of relatively long-lasting growth rate swings.

My second remark concerns the sectoral nature of various kinds of household income, preferably in relation to the production activities classified as traditional and modern. As mentioned earlier, the people's traditional way of life has changed through the process of economic modernization, and the problem of income distribution can realistically be clarified in this context in addition to that of macro-sectoral measurement of the conventional type. This involves the problem of linking the "size" and "share" distribution approaches in the proposed context.

Reference

Asian Development Bank. *Rural Asia: Challenge and Opportunity*, The Second Asian Agricultural Survey, Part I, 1977.

Problems in the Use of National Accounts for Planning

Harry T. Oshima

There appears to be an underlying dissatisfaction with national accounts planning. The core of this dissatisfaction seems to lie in the changing needs of development planning as strategy has shifted from a capital-intensive, urban-based strategy to a labor-intensive, rural-based strategy; data collection from the labor-intensive units of production has also caused great difficulties. The two problems are closely related and need to be discussed further if adequate solutions are to be found. They are complex problems because the collection of information from the labor-intensive units of production is not an easy task. The problems of planning and data collection are far more complex than problems in the capital-intensive strategy of the 1950s and 1960s.

First and foremost is the problem of compiling reliable data from the small units of production, peasants, fishermen, shop-owners, storekeepers, craftsmen, and so on. As Ohkawa emphasized, these small units are responsible for the overwhelming bulk of production, consumption, and investment in most of the Southeast and South Asian countries. Most of these producers do not (and some cannot) keep records of their production and must be interviewed frequently even though they are scattered throughout the country, some in places difficult to reach. Their conditions of work are different from those of the large producers. Irregularity and intermittency of work are the norm, partly because of pronounced seasonality and partly because production is "hand to mouth", with these tiny shops and factories operating only when sales or orders are received by the owners. Hence, production is not regularly scheduled by the year or even by the month, but by the week and by the day, and the labor force in these units must change jobs frequently during the year, giving rise to the problem of multi-jobs and multi-occupations. Thus, the surveys must be frequent, not just once or twice a year.

The regional heterogeneities in the conditions of production, living, and culture are much more extensive than in the more developed countries where the process of development (via the means of transport and communication, education, organized labor, and commodity markets) has homogenized conditions of production and consumption. Only large sample surveys can adequately cover the various sections of the country if the needs of regional planning are to be met.

Under these conditions, people are in and out of the labor force (especially the unpaid family workers). There is often no sharp demarcation between work and non-work; within work often no clear-cut measurement is available for the amount of work performed during the day (since most of the workers do not possess clocks or watches). For each day of work, the quality and intensity of work and production may vary, depending on the season of the year. Evenness in work intensity throughout the year probably came with modern productive methods, especially the factory system.

Even under the most favorable conditions (*i.e.*, where data are collected from well-educated people in stable businesses accustomed to record-keeping), income and output data may be suspect since the owners may be under-reporting profits to circumvent income and sales taxes, and over-reporting wages and other costs. Few countries in Asia have good administration of tax laws, so businesses tend to report falsely. No wonder, then, that planners in many of the Asian countries show dissatisfaction with the national accounting data. But the first step in the solution of the problem is for the planners to demand more funding for their statistical organizations. If the experience of Japan in the 1950s and 1960s is at all relevant, it is that the budget for data collection must be doubled and trebled. Otherwise, there cannot be more frequent and large-size sample surveys of households and enterprises. Nor can the frame of these surveys be kept up to date with only one population census in a decade.

With more money, statistical offices can make more imaginative and innovative attempts at data collection, as the experience of the Philippines has shown. Starting with 1975, the Philippines has taken its first mid-decade census (truncated), followed up with a large sample survey (about 7 percent of the total population) of household economic activities. This survey, integrated with the mid-decade census, will not only furnish each of the 72 provinces with demographic, social, and employment information, but will also indicate for each district of a province the level and distribution of household incomes, the varieties of industries and occupations from which the incomes are earned, days of work and operation, the capital resources used by each type of industry, and so on. Combining these data with data from the economic censuses for establishments, it should be possible to estimate the income originating in each province and the distribution of household income. And, incorporating the smaller household expenditure survey, it should be possible to roughly estimate regional personal consumption expenditures.[1] Experiments are under way with conducting the household economic activities survey quarterly but on a smaller sample basis for over-time analysis by region. With a larger budget, the Philippines has been able to hold quarterly sample surveys of the labor force and to make various attempts to get at employment beyond the fixed reference week. Indonesia has also conducted for the first time a mid-decade census and has plans for quarterly surveys of various types.

Development planners must take into account more and more social aspects, and these call for surveys on health and nutrition, housing needs, education and skills, slum and poverty groups, and so on. In order to develop labor intensively, knowledge of social conditions is essential because the low productivity of unskilled workers is partly the result of inadequate social conditions. Regional planning is necessary in a labor-intensive strategy. This implies the need to establish data-collecting units in the regions and even in the provinces.

One issue which has been raised is the need for the national accounting units to undertake analysis of the data, going beyond mere quantitative descriptions. In part the need to go beyond the national accounts and get at the micro data may be due to the inability of the national accounting statistics to answer many questions which are different from those emerging from capital-intensive planning. It may be too much to expect national accounting units to furnish the kind of analysis that planning groups need if the planners themselves cannot get the answers from the national accounting data. The national ac-

---

[1] Expenditure data obtained by interview methods are likely to be of limited value. Most surveys are conducted once a year; food expenditures are obtained for the reference week only and multiplied by 52 weeks. Because of seasonality of food production and of work, the kinds and quantity of food consumed are likely to vary throughout the year, but it is too expensive to hold monthly surveys of consumption. Probably some form of record-keeping must be introduced. If illiteracy is the problem, picture books showing pictures of various types of foods and other expenditure items might be used since numeracy can be assumed to be extensive. Similarly, with the quarterly surveys of employment and incomes, recall problems are great. Picture books showing various types of occupations for each day of the month might be tried, and work amounts could be measured for each day by the quarter of the day, which people without timepieces can estimate by the approximate position of the sun. It is better to have approximate data than bad or no data.

counting data are inadequate for labor-intensive planning, having originated in the West and being based on Kuznets's framework and on the Keynesian model of business cycle analysis for industrialized economies.[2] For developing economies, it is now customary to look at developmental problems in terms of rural and urban development. Problems of rural development and urban planning have now come to the fore from an analytical point of view. Under the former, issues of agricultural and fishery productivity, off-farm employment, rural public works (roads, irrigation, and electrification), cooperatives, credit, extension, health, education, and so on are discussed. These issues are different from those of urban development such as housing, pollution, traffic, slums, squatters, crime, and so on. If this is so, planners may have to re-orient their procedures starting with the separation of problems between rural and urban areas and moving away from sector-oriented thinking. Data collection then must start with an urban and rural demarcation (perhaps without discarding the ISIC sectorizing which will now be presented under rural and urban sectors), and be done for provinces, regions, and for the nation as a whole.[3]

For rural and urban problems, the kind of information needed by planners may go not only beyond national accounts, but also beyond quantitative information. When Japan began to prepare for the establishment of a comprehensive system of social welfare, its planners were faced with questions which forced them to resort to qualitative surveys (satisfaction, attitudinal, and perception). Through these surveys, they learned what old people wanted in the form of social security schemes, what families wanted in the form of health schemes, and so on. Similarly, to promote rural development successful planners in each region (i.e., in the cities, towns, and villages of each province) of a country will have to know specifically in what ways to generate employment and improve productivity. Planners and officials too often do not know enough about the problems affecting the lower-income families in the villages, since they are usually brought up in higher-income families in the big cities. It will be useful to devise surveys in which these lower-income families are questioned about specific projects (roads, irrigation, electrification, cooperatives, housing, schools, clinics, community halls, etc.) and policies which might improve their ability to earn incomes in their villages. Labor-intensive strategies of development, unlike capital-intensive ones, involve many small projects employing large numbers of low-income earners; in these cases various types of

[2] This argument is developed in (Oshima, 1960: 7–11).
[3] ISIC = International Standard, Industrial Classification of All Economic Activity.

qualitative surveys are needed to supplement the quantitative information.[4]

But better and new sources of data are costly and will require that planners include in the plans themselves provisions for sufficient funds to rapidly improve the statistical system; present levels of funding may well need to double over the next four to five years. In responding to the urgent problems arising from the population and labor force explosion, food supply and consumption, low productivity and low incomes, limited farm lands and urban congestion, the contribution of better and more extensive data is likely to be enormous in the coming years. Good planning can avert tragic and costly mistakes and save many lives and vast sums of money for the nations of Asia where population densities are already the highest in the world.

The existing statistical systems in most countries of South and Southeast Asia have not reached the minimal threshold beyond which they begin to yield cumulative increases in benefits for planning and other uses. Good planning for labor-intensive strategies cannot be conducted with only one or two employment and income surveys whose sample size is 10,000 or less. Such surveys do not yield data which will permit the planner to comprehend the pattern of low levels of employment and productivity throughout the seasons of the year for the provinces and regions of the nation. Without information of this sort good plans for labor-intensive development are difficult to construct or to implement.

Statistical systems are like systems of mass communication (such as telephones) and mass transportation (such as railroads). They are subject to "indivisibilities" and "lumpiness", so that a certain threshold must be reached before they begin to work satisfactorily. The expressions of dissatisfaction with the national accounts and other statistical constructs are perhaps the result of the fact that the existing statistical systems have not yet come up to the threshold size in most of the nations of Southeast and South Asia.[5]

Like so many public projects, the costs are easy to estimate but the benefits, especially the indirect and long-term ones, are almost impos-

[4] It is now widely surmised that the efficient working of organizations (cooperatives, associations, clubs, etc.) and other institutions is essential for the success of labor-intensive projects and programs. If so, it may be worthwhile to conduct sample surveys of organizations to find out how they are operating, including questions relating to finances, membership, frequency of meetings, elections, participation, and activities. In addition, these institutional surveys can serve as a check on the efficiency with which governments (both national and local) operate: to what extent credit is extended; to what extent which farmers receive extension, health, educational, irrigation, and other services.

[5] A minimal threshold can be tentatively identified as that existing in either South Korea or Taiwan.

sible to quantify, even roughly. Thus, political leaders tend to underestimate the value of statistics for governmental purposes. As is also the case for so many public projects, benefits "spilling over" to the private sector are elusive and barely noticeable. National income statistics can be used by private businesses for their own planning, implementation, and evaluation; in addition, statistics can facilitate the education and training not only of students at all levels of education, but also of the public via the mass media, promoting high levels of understanding on public issues and lower levels of friction in public debate. As such, statistical constructs should be regarded as part of a system of social and physical infrastructure and as vital as transportation, communication, education, or health. Unfortunately, there are no pressure groups to push for larger expenditures for statistics as there often are for other infrastructure investments. Hence the underdevelopment of statistical systems may well become a chronic situation throughout the developing countries.[6] Planning agencies themselves must push hard for a much more extensive system of data if they are to carry out their responsibilities adequately.

Reference

Oshima, H. T. "National Accounts for the Analysis of Asian Growth," in International Association for Research in Income and Wealth, *Asian Studies in Income and Wealth*. Bombay, 1965.

[6] In developed countries like the U.S. it is the pressure of economic groups (businesses, labor unions, farmers' and other professional associations) that accounts for the extensive system of statistics; the U.S. government itself has no comprehensive planning needs for such a system.

Index

313